D1452427

# HURON

# HURON

## THE SEASONS OF A GREAT LAKE

Napier Shelton

 WAYNE STATE UNIVERSITY PRESS    DETROIT

## GREAT LAKES BOOKS

*A complete listing of the books in this series
can be found at the back of this volume.*

Philip P. Mason, Editor
*Department of History, Wayne State University*

Dr. Charles K. Hyde, Associate Editor
*Department of History, Wayne State University*

**Library of Congress Cataloging-in-Publication Data**

Shelton, Napier.
  Huron : the seasons of a Great Lake / Napier Shelton.
    p.   cm. — (Great Lakes books)
  Includes bibliographical references.
  ISBN 0-8143-2834-2   (alk. paper)
  1. Limnology—Huron, Lake (Mich. and Ont.) 2. Natural history—Huron, Lake
(Mich. and Ont.)   I. Title.   II. Series.
  GB1227.G85S48   1999
  508.774—dc21                                                    98-35662

To my parents,
Frederick D. Shelton
and
Charline McCanse Shelton,
who encouraged my interest
in the natural world,
and to
Warren J. Worth and
Elizabeth L. Worth,
master and mistress of the cottage
at Port Sanilac

# CONTENTS

# PREFACE

In 1967 my wife's parents bought a cottage on the sandy shore of Lake Huron at Port Sanilac, in the Thumb of southeastern Michigan. For part of almost every summer since then, we have made a pilgrimage to the cottage, taking our children when they were small, and occasionally meeting them there after they were grown and married. Our visits, in total, spanned the period from early May to early September.

Every year I felt sad when we had to leave, because I wanted to see the full progression of seasons on Lake Huron. In 1995, having retired from the National Park Service, I got my wish. I arrived early in January and left late in December, with only a couple of interruptions during the year. This book, a natural history and a look at use and management of the lake, is largely a record of my experience and observations during that year, but it has been broadened and deepened by interviews and research in the literature. The summer sections benefit from the experience of many years, including a slow trip around the lake in June 1996.

I was interested not only in the lake and its creatures and plants, but also in the people who had a close association with it: commercial fishermen, scientists, artists, birdwatchers, cottagers like us, and others. By sharing their knowledge and experience, they became a part of the story and helped me immeasurably in writing this book.

Many people contributed in some way. I would especially like to thank the following: George and Irene Purvis, Forrest Williams, Denny

Root, and Rob Taylor, commercial fishermen who gave interviews and allowed me to go out on their boats; Milford Purdy, Russ Herrick, Jimmy Prescau, Leonard Dutcher, Murray Hore, Mike Meeker, Robert (Bert) Herbert, Bryan Perks, Marshall Nadjiwon, and Rusty Raney, commercial fishermen who granted me interviews; Myles and Marilyn Willard, Doreen Bailey, Terry and Judith Land, Christopher Bell, Martin Parker, the late Dennis Rupert, Tom Heatley, Monica Essenmacher, Ron Weeks, and Bob Grefe, birders and naturalists who shared their special knowledge during trips afield; Gary and Mary Curtis, Charles (Chuck) Bowen (who took me on the research trip to Six Fathom Bank), and Roger Bergstedt, of the U.S. Geological Survey Great Lakes Science Center; Mark Ebener, Chippewa/Ottawa Treaty Fishery Management Authority; Rod McDonald, Sea Lamprey Control Centre; James Baker, Michael Hanson, Doug Reeves, Charles Bauer, and Arnie Carr, Michigan Department of Natural Resources; Stephen Gile, Ontario Ministry of Natural Resources; Judith Jones and Joe Johnson, botanists; the retired ship captains Morgan Howell and Patrick Owens; Dr. Fred Ludwig; Lt. Fred Sommer and crew of the *Neah Bay;* the Cleveland office of the U.S. Coast Guard; Dennis Schommer, Joe Bulone, Harry Greening, Bill Lyons, Dick Schaffner, Cecil Tubbs, Harold Schlicting, Jack Falls, Raymond Denison, Paul Messing, Paul Slivka, Garry Biniecki, all friends and acquaintances in Port Sanilac and vicinity who helped in various ways; Robert Whittam, Wye Marsh Wildlife Centre; Peggy Murphy, Killbear Provincial Park; and, for miscellaneous assistance, Tom Muer, Peter Ohrnberger, Daniel Miller, Chris Parent, William Grigg, Mark Wiercinski, Stephen Crawford, and Rob Simpson.

I am also indebted to several reviewers of the manuscript. Myles and Marilyn Willard read it all. Gary Curtis, Roger Bergstedt, Mark Ebener, Stephen Gile, Stan Munroe, James Baker, Mike Hanson, George Purvis, Milford Purdy, Forrest Williams, Doreen Bailey, Judith Land, Judith Jones, Joe Johnson, Harold Schlicting, Morgan Howell, and Patrick Owens reviewed chapters pertaining to their areas of expertise. Any errors, of course, remain mine.

The excellent maps and drawings are the work of Taina Litwak of Gaithersburg, Maryland. Several photographs, as credited, were taken by Myles Willard. The rest are mine.

Many hands are involved in the publishing process, but I must extend particular thanks to Arthur Evans, director of the Wayne State University Press, for his interest and for so carefully apprising me of developments at each step preceding production of the book.

Almost no one with a family writes a book without their support, or at least acquiescence. I thank my children for their interest in the project and especially my wife, Elizabeth, for doing without me for most of a year and acknowledging the writer's need for solitude.

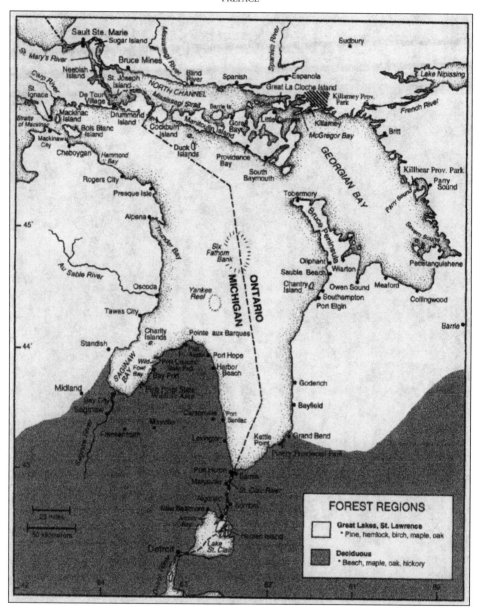

Lake Huron area. The forest regions shown here generalize a more complex mixture of tree species. White pine, aspen, and paper birch, for example, occur commonly in the northern part of the deciduous region. White spruce, balsam fir, and aspen are increasingly important components northward in the Great Lakes, St. Lawrence region. (Credit: Taina Litwak)

12

# PROLOGUE
## WHAT LIES BEYOND THE SUMMER?

I have seen the summer at our beach on Lake Huron. Many summers.

I know how the light falls on the lake, how the bands of blue, purple, grey come and go. I have watched the winds and waves change, the calm and storms.

I know when the sandpipers will come, running and probing a few days in the sand, on their way to southern shores. The gulls will cruise up and down the beach all day, and at night will cluster by the harbor. I see the fishing boats far out, trolling back and forth, and in my mind's eye the salmon swirl deep down in the cold dark water, striking terror in their prey and feeling terror when they take the hook.

In the fog, a ship's horn will sound, pause long, sound again. Lying in bed, I will hear it for an hour, fading way up at Harbor Beach. Ships go up, ships go down, carrying the commerce of the lakes.

In summer, the harbor is full. Sailboats and yachts say the pleasure season is here. Owners recline in their deck chairs, sipping drinks. The townspeople smile—the boats mean money. I will have to wait in line at Platt's Drug Store to buy whisky.

It is our pleasure season too. The children dig in the sand, splash in the water. The brave swim out to the Whale Rock, upon whose smoothness one can sit when the lake is low. In our cottage on the shore we listen to Tennessee Ernie Ford bellowing out hymns. Grandmother Worth forever digs in her garden or plants another maple. Grandfather

Worth barks orders, turns the news up too loud. But he is a decent fellow, we know.

The cottage is a good time, a place of happy dreams. The pains of life seem to cease there, easing away with the summer warmth.

But I wonder what lies beyond the summer. How does the light fall on November waves—waves that have sunk a hundred ships? When will the sea ducks come down, skimming the water in long, heavy lines? What is it like to ride the season's last ship down the lake? How does the ice come and go, and how does it sound, piling up on the shore? When ice fills the harbor, do the townspeople still smile? What do the old men say, drinking their morning coffee down at Mary's Diner? What will our lives be like, in the autumn and winter of life? What resurrection will we see in the spring?

I think I will stay and find out.

# CHAPTER 1

# THE COTTAGE

And I did—stay through all the seasons. I arrived at the cottage on January 9, under a cloudless blue sky. Five inches of snow covered the ground and rounded the edges of the wall around our sunken garden patio. Beyond the snow-covered garden the white cottage stretched down toward the lake. There, clear water lapped gently against a low bank of ice along the shore. The Whale Rock rose darkly a foot above the surface while nearby three ducks were diving. It was a cold but peaceful scene. I felt welcomed.

It did seem a little strange, though, to be here at this season. Always before, it had been a summer retreat. Nearly every year since 1967, when my in-laws, Mama and Papa Worth, bought the cottage at Port Sanilac, we had come for at least a week or two, and sometimes for most of a summer. In the early days, Elizabeth and I played on the sandy beach with our children and splashed around in the cold water. Sometimes we swam out to the Whale Rock, so named by our children because it looked to them like the back of a whale. An adventurous destination for the children, it has always been for me an announcement of the current lake level: How much of the Whale Rock can you see this year? Inside the cottage, we played simple games and listened to music. Eleanor, our oldest, leaked tears when *La Boheme*'s Mimi died.

In the beginning, the cottage was just a small box. Beyond the narrow deck, bouncing bet and goldenrod sprouted up in the sand, which

15

The cottage at my arrival, January 9.

stretched down to the beach between framing willow and poplar trees. One year, spotted sandpipers nested on the sand just a few feet from the deck. You could stand at the rail and watch their comings and goings. Then we extended the lake end of the cottage, making a big, step-down living room with large windows all around so you could see the ships passing and the ever-changing moods of the lake. When her parents deeded the cottage to Elizabeth, she decided we needed a second story over the living room to house a spacious bedroom. Reached by a spiral staircase, this became our sanctuary from the extended-family commotion below. Here, too, big windows and a deck gave broad views of the lake.

Harry Greening was the builder of this eyrie. Crew-cut, solid, slow but careful, sixty-year-old Harry had rented out his cropland and turned full time to construction. Later, when Elizabeth decided the other end of the cottage was too confining, Harry extended "Papa's parlor" and the main downstairs bedroom westward. Harry was always the one we called on when we needed help for building or repairs, and he always responded.

16

My wife, as you can see, likes to change her environment, reshaping it to her image. So it was that the sunken garden patio came into being. Eighty-four-year-old Gene Knight dug the hole with his backhoe and seventy-three-year-old Glenn Willett did the stone and cement work, creating a beautiful, circular, multi-colored wall, inside which we could sip evening drinks, and beyond which Mama Worth could tend her flowers.

This was the home in which I began my solitary life that bright January day. It wasn't exactly a remote place in the wilderness—not even a Thoreau cabin a few miles from Concord. Sometimes I could hear a car on the highway 300 yards away, and other cottages nestled close alongshore, running north for miles and south half a mile to the village and beyond. But there was no one in any of the nearby cottages, and it *felt* remote. Walden Pond, after all, had a railroad and wagon road going by it.

My first concern was keeping warm while preventing the expensive electric baseboard heating from coming on. Harry had provided two things toward this end: a styrofoam wall just beyond the kitchen, so only the one-story west half of the cottage would have to be heated, and two cords of firewood. I lit some kindling—easily split, straight-grained ash—in our new one and a half cubic foot Lopi wood stove, and then began feeding in the maple, ash, and cherry logs. It was seven degrees outside that first night but warm inside. Next morning the stove, located in Papa's parlor, was still radiating a little warmth from the coals and the temperature in the bedroom and kitchen was in the upper fifties, above the fifty-degree mark at which the baseboard would kick in. So the system was working. When the weather turned mild a couple of days later, the temperature in the parlor soared into the low eighties. I had to turn on the ceiling fan to move some of the heat kitchenward.

The wood stove, like the hearth in so many dwellings through human history, became the center of my existence. I ate, read, wrote, and, I admit with some guilt, watched television in front of it, enjoying the sight of dancing flames and glowing logs through the stove's glass window. The only problem with living in this three-room space was that I couldn't see the lake. For that I had to go outside and walk around to the deck. But that enhanced the attraction of the lake and the first morning look to see what the day on the lake offered.

My wife had kept asking, "Won't you be lonely?" But after the first night or two the strangeness wore off and the quiet seemed natural. Besides, I had animal neighbors. I quickly put up the bird feeder and loaded it with black oil sunflower seeds. On the ground below I spread millet. In no time I had a regular clientele of four or five chickadees, six to eight juncos, eight to ten mourning doves, four tree sparrows, a dozen or so house finches, several goldfinches, a pair of cardinals, and a very cute little red-breasted nuthatch. The chickadees and nuthatch would land on the feeder, grab a sunflower seed, and fly into the row of arborvitaes behind. A red squirrel, apparently headquartering in the conifers next door to our north, soon grew bold enough to climb on the feeder and nibble sunflowers, hoggishly, for many long minutes at a time. As light dimmed in late afternoon, two rabbits would emerge from the arborvitaes to feed on the millet.

Other animals that I never saw left their tracks in the snow. During a warm spell a skunk had walked from our deck to the cottage on our south side. Another night, soon after I came home from an outing, a fox left its dainty, linear trail past the side door. On the beach, two deer had wandered.

It wasn't long before I discovered I had an animal neighbor *inside* the cottage. The first evidence was a chewed roll of toilet paper, then toilet paper unrolled to the floor, as if some little creature had been running on it like a treadmill. One morning, a picture on the wall was askew; something must have jumped on it. Things became more definite when, two nights in a row, I heard gnawing inside the bedroom wall.

I was then faced with a great moral question: to trap or not to trap. Perhaps this mouse would do something serious, like gnaw through an electrical wire, but probably it wouldn't. Maybe it was a native deer mouse, much more welcome in my mind than an alien house mouse, which really belonged in central Eurasia. As the days passed and no further evidence appeared, I let the matter slide. A mouse, after all, wants a warm, safe place as much as I do.

Later, browsing through a historical document, I came upon the words of Oliver Hazard Perry, hunting in the Thumb of Michigan in 1853: "I am so overrun with deer mice that I can hardly live in the woods. They ate the strings of my tent, my shoes, pork, hard bread, gloves, leather strings, bags, etc., and commenced last night working in my hair and planting their cold noses on the scalp of my head. I have tried one experiment in trapping them but it did not succeed. I must devise some way of killing them, or leave the woods." Reading this, I decided my one mouse was no problem.

Each of the first days I was eager to get out along the shore, walking north to Gene Knight's place or south to the harbor. And each day the lake presented a different scene. Under a strong northerly wind, angry grey-brown waves full of bottom sediment crashed up against the shore ice, throwing spray that froze and built the ice higher. Then we had days of fog with light wind, the occasional cry of an unseen gull piercing the mist. Slush ice or floes, sometimes flotillas of round pancake ice with its raised edges, came and went.

Usually I saw a few ducks near shore—buffleheads, goldeneyes, and common mergansers—diving for fish or other animal life. The males of all these species were resplendently black and white—fitting colors for the dark water and white ice. One day nine little buffleheads swam in a tight group among the floes, the males courting the females with up and down head bobbing, bill dipping, and wing flapping, almost in unison. The brown females, however, continued diving as if unimpressed. Perhaps in January the need to pair up was not yet strong, or perhaps the nonchalance was part of the mating game.

So the winter lake and I got acquainted. Some days, as a chill wind whipped over grey waves, it was menacing. Other days, when the sun appeared, it made my heart leap with its blue water and shining ice. I looked forward to the days and months ahead, exploring its varied shores and waters, looking for the larger story beyond the glimpses gained at our cottage.

# CHAPTER 2

# PORT SANILAC

O n my first walk down to the harbor, everything was socked in with fog. Dimly I could see the shapes of the empty cottages and the bare poplars around them. Wind the day before had swept most of the snow off the beach, but human footprints and the tracks of two skiers were still visible. Small steps of ice led down to the slush-filled water. At Liens Creek, which has built a small point, I crossed on ice. That day the harbor, within its breakwalls, looked frozen solid.

When I had errands, I drove. The village was busier than I expected. The last census said Port Sanilac had 700 permanent residents, and I think I saw most of them in one place or another. Down at the main intersection—with its blinking light—Raymond's Hardware ("Established 1850—Oldest Hardware Store in Michigan") and Platt's drugstore ("Est. 1865—Oldest drugstore in Michigan") always seemed to have customers. Mary's Diner, the Stone Lodge, the Bellaire, Leo's By the Lake Cafe—all were open, serving meals at some time of day. Foley's Grocery kept its usual long hours. The bakery opened at six o'clock every morning, and always somebody was there, getting coffee before the day's work. The party store dispensed food, drink, and gasoline to a constant stream of customers, and Hometown Video's "Open" sign seemed always to be in the window. Only the places dependent on summer tourists, like the Peir Pressure miniature golf and hamburger joint, were closed. (I keep wondering what a "peir" is.)

Port Sanilac harbor, iced in.

Most of my fellow villagers looked landward in their winter life, as did the town's organized events. A music program, with local singers and musicians, warmed the hearts of a small audience (mostly friends and relatives of the performers) one zero February night. Many, like me, went to see how the Carsonville-Port Sanilac High School basketball team was faring (poorly). The VFW offered venison stew one Sunday.

And then there was the rabbit bowhunt, sponsored by the Blue Water Inn. (This is one of three bars in town. Port Sanilac has four churches, so I guess you could say sanctity slightly outweighs sin here.) I entered the dark, low-ceilinged precincts of this establishment in the evening to see how the hunt had gone. As I nursed a beer at the long bar, watching pool players in the next room, the hunters straggled in, helped themselves from the chili pot, and ordered up pitchers of beer. One pair actually brought in a rabbit, still feebly kicking. They laughed. The others simply reported their results to the organizer. Teams of two, with or without dogs, had been out on various farms in an all-day snowstorm. Altogether, seventy arrows had been shot and thirteen rabbits killed. Of the eighteen teams, Rod Reid and Bill Harrison won with three rabbits taken. Not bad, I thought, with fast-moving targets in flying snow.

The Super Bowl—that January object of anticipation for most of male and some of female America—was another sort of community event. At the Blue Water Inn, cheers for the San Francisco Forty-niners and hugely underdog San Diego Chargers soon died away as another Super Bowl rout became apparent. Many drifted to the pool tables. Down at the Stone Lodge, where I went for the third quarter, conviviality reigned around a U-shaped bar in a brightly-lit, high-ceilinged room. Many ignored the game, but the guys down one side of the bar had made bets on the score. Cheers still rose when San Francisco crossed the goal line yet again.

In spite of the ice and cold onshore winds, some people looked lakeward. At the Port Sanilac Marina, sailboats and power boats sat ashore on their cradles. But inside the marina store, Bill Lyons said that the marina only closes for two and a half weeks around Christmas and New Year. "Things will start to pick up with the boat show in Cobo Hall [Detroit] in February. Even now [January], people are coming up to work on their boats."

Outside on the harbor ice, lanky Mike Hanson, the Department of Natural Resources conservation officer for Sanilac County, hunched over one of his round fishing holes. "Don't walk near those docks," he cautioned. "You'd be sure to go through." An inveterate fisherman, Mike had already caught thirty brown trout and steelheads here this winter. As I watched the yellow bobbers in his fishing holes move around, propelled by the minnows on the hooks below, one suddenly dipped. Mike yanked on the short rod but missed. "A twelve-pound brown," he said, "about thirty-two inches. I saw it." Earlier in the day, he had missed a ten-pounder. He could tell the weight by the pull on the line.

A few days later, during a long spell of mild, wet weather, Rick, the town barber, was complaining. "I'm going crazy because I don't like to go out in sloppy weather, and there's not enough ice for ice-fishing on Saginaw or Anchor Bay." Apparently, he also didn't trust the ice in the harbor. "I broke through the ice there twice when I was a boy. Once it was knee-deep and once waist-deep. It wasn't life threatening but it wasn't pleasant either."

Garry Biniecki was in his dive shop one weekend in February, working on diving gear. His regular job is running the drugs division of the Sanilac County sheriff's office, but his first love is diving. Explaining this, he said, "I guess it was the yearning to know what's down there, the attraction of the unknown, the opportunity to blaze new trails." He and some associates had discovered four sunken boats off Sanilac County since 1986, and were instrumental in getting the state to establish the 163-square-mile Sanilac Shores Underwater Preserve. He was teaching scuba diving that winter and looked forward to more shipwreck exploration when the ice went out of the harbor, which usually happens in mid-April. But you can't keep a good diver up. Two days before Christmas, he and some friends had gone diving through the ice on Higgins Lake in northern Michigan.

Port Sanilac surely has more artists per capita than most American towns. I visited one of them on a pleasant Sunday afternoon, down on Lake Street by the shore. Joe Bulone and his wife moved here in 1985, after he retired from the design department of General Motors. That freed him to devote himself full-time to painting, which before he could do only in his spare time. The walls of his garage studio were lined with finely detailed paintings of local scenes. Prominent among these was the white tower of the Port Sanilac Lighthouse, which has stood on the shore just up the street from Joe's house since 1886. "About a third of my paintings are seascapes," he said. "I love to paint sunrises over the lake, and some of them are spectacular." Joe had already done four or five paintings this winter, one of them a lake sunrise. He likes fishing, too. "Up 'til five or six years ago you could catch a lot of perch right off the jetty in front of my house. But then something happened. Maybe the [introduced] salmon got them."

The earliest settlers of Port Sanilac, which was then called Bark Shanty Point, had a long, isolated winter. The only transportation was by water, and ice prevented this until early spring. All through the winter, settlers brought in deer and elk hides, furs, hemlock bark (for tanning), split pine shingles, cedar posts and barrels, and pail and tub staves made of ash. They traded these at one of the four general stores, including Uri Raymond's (now Raymond's Hardware), for salt pork, flour, tea, axes, gunpowder, clothing, and other necessities of frontier life. The bark, shingles, and posts were piled on the beach for spring shipment to Detroit or Toledo.

Bark Shanty Point was given its name by sailors passing by. They could see a bark-covered shanty that had been built by men who had come here around 1835 to collect tanbark from hemlock trees. They lived in this shanty on the beach. A settlement was established in the summer of 1850 when the Thomson and Oldfield families and Uri Raymond arrived, Raymond from Sanilac Mills just a few miles to the south, and the others from Cincinnati. Thomson and Oldfield set up a saw mill to make lumber from the giant white pines that towered over the other forest trees here as they did in much of Michigan.

The whole Thumb area—the part of southeastern Michigan that bulges out like the thumb of a mitten—was forest in the mid-1800s. Chippewa Indians from the Saginaw River valley came here to hunt and tap the sugar maples. A few settlers hacked out farms on eighty- or 160-acre homesteads. Until 1871 lumber was the chief product shipped out of the shore towns, but in that year a devastating fire swept across southern Michigan, destroying much of the remaining forest and opening the land for farming. Another big fire in 1881 removed more forest. Ever since those years, the Thumb has been farm country, growing corn, wheat, beans, and sugar beets, the acreage gradually expanding with settlement and drainage of swamps. A specialty from about 1890 to 1920 was red raspberries, and the people of Sanilac County became known as "Berry Pickers."

Changes in transportation dictated the fortunes of many shore towns like Port Sanilac (so renamed in 1857). In the third quarter of the nineteenth century, boats ruled. Although a shore road was built in the 1860s, it was little more than ruts in the sand and was no competition for water travel. Oldfield's dock, built in 1857 on log cribs, projected some 500 feet into the lake and received the numerous freight and passenger boats that stopped here. Thomson's 400-foot dock, built on pilings in 1864, also served this purpose until January 1875, when ice pushed by a severe northeaster tore it up. By 1875, Port Sanilac had three blacksmiths, one boatbuilder, two carpenters, a cabinetmaker, a druggist, at least eight fishermen, two hotel operators, a lawyer, three doctors, a painter, and a dozen or more dealers and manufacturers of various kinds.

But the railroad was coming, and not to Port Sanilac. By 1880, progressing inland up the Thumb, it had reached Carsonville, eight miles to the west. Trains had the advantage of running all year, and so, in 1914, the last stop of the steamer *Hazel* ended lake shipping from Port Sanilac, except for the boatloads of salt fish that went out for a few more years. The population of the town, which had once reached 600 or 700, was now half that.

Things began to pick up again in the 1920s, when more and more travelers drove automobiles along the now graded and graveled shore road. People began building the weekend and summer cottages that now fringe much of the Michigan shoreline, and tourists came to enjoy the lake. In 1951 the U.S. Army Corps of Engineers built the first Harbor of Refuge on the Great Lakes at Port Sanilac, where no natural harbor existed. The two concrete breakwaters provided shelter for a growing number of sail and power boats that stopped or headquartered at the new marina. Sport fishermen came for the abundant perch, and later, salmon and trout stocking by the state offered an exciting alternative when the perch declined. The discovery of shipwrecks offshore has brought divers, sparking plans for a maritime museum built in the shape of the *Regina,* a freighter that went down near Port Sanilac during the terrible storm in November 1913. Once again the town's population has reached 700, its future tied to the pull of the lake.

The lives of Dennis Schommer and his family span much of Port Sanilac's history and like the town itself have often been dependent on the lake. During the sweeping fire of 1881, Dennis's great-grandmother fled with her children from their farm west of Port Sanilac into the water of Lake Huron, along with many other people and even wild animals. Fortunately for them, the fire stopped in the open farmland before it reached the town.

Dennis's father was a fisherman. This is a strongly seasonal occupation, "so those fishermen always had some other little business going on the side," Dennis said. "My father would buy old cedar poles, cut them into fireplace lengths, and split these up for kindling in little bundles. It made a nice little bit of income in the winter."

When he wasn't going to school, Dennis went fishing with his father and Leonard Dutcher. Leonard Dutcher's father also fished with them. "Sometimes he would come in the morning with a hangover, two days' growth of beard, not saying anything. But he could always take us right to the nets. When it was foggy, Mrs. Papeneau would come down to the shore and bang on an angle [iron] to tell us where the shore was. Sometimes we'd stop the engine and listen for the sound of tires on the gravel road, or take soundings with a lead weight to see if it was getting shallower.

"But I wasn't a very dedicated fisherman. I was always looking at the sky or something." Dennis was in his heart an artist, a true vocation that he has pursued through all the up and down years, doing whatever else he has had to do to make a living. He tried working in a factory, hated that, and went to work at his father's gas station at the highway junction in town. Commercial fishing had ceased at Port Sanilac in the early 1960s because of the lamprey invasion of the Great Lakes that decimated whitefish and lake trout. Later, the sportfishing for perch became bad, too. "One fellow got so mad he threw his tackle box and two rods in the harbor. When he got to the gas station he put a match to his fishing license and swore he'd never fish again."

Dennis and Patti Schommer.

One day Dennis heard from a friend in the Department of Natural Resources that they planned to start planting salmon here. So Dennis hitched his fate to that prospect and opened a log sport shop beside M-25 on the edge of town. But salmon planting didn't start until five years later and it took the salmon another year after that to grow enough to provide sport. "Those were rough years," he said. "The first winter my wife and I ate a lot of bluegills."

Eventually, the big fish and the fishermen came, and the sport shop paid off. Dennis expanded into making and selling his own lures. But the hours were long. "In the summer we worked seven days a week, 5 A.M. to 8 P.M. I got tired of it. One day two of my long-time customers asked me if I wanted to sell the shop. I said sure."

Today, Dennis and his wife Patti, also an artist, do interior decorating and own some storage sheds. Dennis's paintings are sold in three galleries around the country and at local shows. Over the years, I've watched his style change. Early on, his paintings of hunting and fishing scenes resembled Winslow Homer's. On my latest visits to his studio he has shown me vivid paintings of storm scenes over the lake that suggest Ryder or Charles Burchfield. "I'm always experimenting," he says.

Now in his late fifties, Dennis is no longer dependent on the lake for his living, but it continues to inspire him.

CHAPTER **3**

# Up North

In late January, as flurries lingered after a big snowstorm, I headed north for a few days. Above Standish, the farm fields disappeared and the forest took over. Increasingly, pines and balsam fir mixed in with the maples, birch, and aspen, puffs of snow still clinging to the dark branches of the conifers. The ice puzzled me. It was gone from Tawas Bay, where I had seen it a couple of weeks earlier, but it covered Thunder Bay, just fifty miles to the north. I needed to learn more about the ways of ice.

At the mouth of the Au Sable River, two men in orange coveralls fished from the jetty in a bone-chilling wind. Mallards settled on somebody's lawn by the river, where corn had been spread for the ducks. At every stop were signs of winter's hold on the land. Cheboygan: the Coast Guard icebreaker *Mackinaw* lay at her dock, with engines running. Mackinac Bridge: ice covered the south side of the straits but the north side was open. St. Ignace: nine degrees, snow blowing; the sign at Shepler's boat dock, from which runs are made to Mackinac Island, read "Closed. Reason— Freezen. Open—Hopen April 30." St. Ignace was preparing for a 100-mile sled dog race in the adjacent national forest. The roar of snowmobiles was heard in the land. Crossing the Upper Peninsula to Sault Ste. Marie, I drove through miles of spruce, fir, cedar, and tamarack. I felt then that I was truly in the north.

At the Soo, my first order of business was to look for the gyrfalcon that had been reported hanging around the Edison power plant. For years this has been a traditional wintering spot for this largest of falcons. Gyrfalcons breed in the Arctic and in North America normally winter no farther south than the northern edge of the United States. Fast and powerful, they prey mostly on waterfowl and other large birds, which the St. Marys River area offers them. Like peregrines, they are favorites of falconers, including Arab sheiks, as well as of birders.

This species had eluded me throughout fifty years of birdwatching. One showed up at Kettle Point, at the south end of Lake Huron, one winter while I was studying at the University of Michigan, but exams kept me from chasing it. Years later, I drove to Blackwater National Wildlife Refuge in Maryland to look for a reported gyrfalcon, but the marshes and water showed me only ducks. In the winter of 1993–94, one was discovered in a broad farm valley north of my home in Washington, D.C.; naturally, by the time I heard about it, this one too had gone. However, when Myles Willard, a birdwatching friend in Mayville, Michigan, called me soon after I arrived at the cottage to tell me about a gyrfalcon at the Shiawassee National Wildlife Refuge near Saginaw, I thought my quest might be over. The next day, with Bob Grefe, a refuge volunteer, we drove the Shiawassee roads to the place where Ron Weeks, a birder from Midland, had watched the bird perched on a gravel pile eating a mouse. Around the diked fields we saw bald eagles and rough-legged hawks in the bare trees and flocks of Canada geese flying about, but no sign of the gyrfalcon. Skunked again!

In spite of this dismal history, my anticipation was high when I pulled in beside the Edison power plant at the Soo. A cold, damp wind blew down the St. Marys River, this fast part of it still open, as I trained my spotting scope on the window ledges of the long, massive brick building sitting astride the end of a power canal. I had been told that the bird roosted at night on a window ledge facing the river. As it was 4:00 P.M. and growing dim under cloudy skies, I thought it might be bedtime. But none of the several dozen ledges appeared to have a falcon shape perched on it. Then I looked up and saw a dark object on a platform atop the building. At last! There it was!

I watched the gyrfalcon for nearly an hour and a half, noting all its markings and hoping it would launch out in pursuit of prey. It was dark, with streaks and barring underneath and a long tapered tail. I could see the yellow around its eyes, on its beak and its feet, and an indistinct mustache streak. The color was dark brown or dark gray, indicating it probably came from the western or central Arctic, as the northeastern Arctic birds tend to be white. The gyrfalcon sat for some time with its back to me, just looking around. Then it shifted sideways and began to preen, getting its feathers in order and fluffing out its chest. Meanwhile, three common mergansers and two goldeneyes appeared in the river below, and several pigeons and a starling flew along the side of the building. The gyrfalcon watched all these but did nothing. At 5:23, it lifted off its perch and circled down onto a window ledge, with its back facing out. The gyrfalcon's day was over.

Next morning I arrived at 8:05. The gyrfalcon was sitting in the same exact spot up on the platform, looking around. Three mallards flew over, mergansers and goldeneyes dove in the river, pigeons and starlings flew about at the end of the building. The gyrfalcon did nothing. Twenty-seven ravens flew high across the river in small groups, croaking as they headed southward. At 8:40 the gyrfalcon launched itself off the platform and out of sight, perhaps to hunt pigeons in the city or ducks on the river. But not for my benefit. It had its own agenda.

Crossing the bridge to Canada, you get a grand view of the canals, locks, and river. On the American side, the parallel canal and lock systems occupy about half of the river. Then you arch over the shallow rapids—which once spanned the entire river—next some wooded islands, and last the boat and power canals on the Canadian side. On the shore the St. Mary's Paper Company plant and the huge complex of the Lake Superior Power Company pour white smoke into the sky.

From the bridge I thought I had seen trails on the islands so I investigated. The area turned out to be a national park, administered by Environment Canada. A museum exhibit tells the story of canal and lock construction on this side, and trails loop around St. Marys Island, where young forest growth is obliterating the debris of canal construction and the military encampments of two world wars. Crunching through the snow beside a stream, I saw beaver cuttings and a flock of quacking mallards.

Whitefish Island, across that stream, was occupied by Indians who fished in the rapids here for 2,000 years. Walter Havighurst wrote that in the early summer and fall, when whitefish came in great numbers, "two men in a canoe could obtain five thousand pounds in half a day—big, rich whitefish weighing six to fifteen pounds—with a scoop net on a pole." The river here is also the home of trout, perch, and other sport fish. Fishermen of all ethnic groups are still drawn to these rapids.

As I walked the island trails, I was thankful for the bit of natural river that remained and for the preservation of the islands, but they were dominated by the engineering works of man—the canals, the locks, and the bridge overhead, with its rumbling traffic. A microcosm of the state of nature in so much of our world today, I reflected sadly.

St. Marys River rapids and the international bridge, Sault Ste. Marie.

At the power canal by the Lake Superior Power Company, mergansers and goldeneyes dove and drifted backwards in the swift current, then flew upstream to begin again. The mouth of the adjacent boat canal, however, was jammed with ice. The floes coming downriver were crackling and grinding as they hit the head of the ice jam. Sitting on the canal wall, two heavily bundled men fished in holes between the floes. "I caught eight whitefish Monday, six yesterday, but nothing today," one said in a strong French-Canadian accent. Next to them, a white-haired gentleman aimed a giant camera lens, mounted on a tripod, at the ice floes. "You want to see an oldsquaw?" he asked. Looking through the lens, I saw the marvelous black and white pattern and long thin tail of a male oldsquaw, sitting still and perfectly camouflaged less than fifty yards away among the floes. I had heard about this particular bird and was looking for it, but never would have seen it if it hadn't been pointed out to me. This sea duck probably had nested on the Arctic tundra like the rest of its species, and had chosen to remain on the Great Lakes for the winter, as some do, while most head for the east or west coast.

East of the Soo in Ontario, Highway 17 plays peekaboo with channels of the St. Marys River and then the North Channel of Lake Huron. I had glimpses of open water where the current was strong and of ice where the current slowed or the shore was embayed. Farmland near the Soo soon gave way to forest. Aspen, birch, white spruce, and fir formed the central theme of this forest, with maples on the gentle uplands and many white pines on the low, rocky hills that soon appeared. Swift rivers were open but the inland lakes were locked in ice. Aside from occasional human activity, the black shapes of ravens passing overhead were the only signs of sentient life. Small towns broke the vast forest scene: Bruce Mines—population 600; Thessalon—900; Blind River, with a fishing boat in the river mouth, 3,900; Spanish—1,100; and Espanola, with its big paper mill spewing clouds of white smoke, 5,500.

As I reached Great La Cloche Island, heading south to Manitoulin Island, the landscape changed dramatically. From the granite and quartzite of the North Shore, the road had entered the great arc of limestone that extends all the way from Niagara Falls, up the Bruce Peninsula, through the islands in northern Lake Huron, and around the north and west shores of Lake Michigan. From the rugged, humpy hills of Huron's North Shore I had passed onto the gentle terrain of Manitoulin, where low flat-topped hills stretched along the horizon.

Manitoulin Island, some eighty miles long, is the largest freshwater island in the world. It can be thought of as a giant slab of limestone sloping gently southward, with cliffs along its north side and low shores on the south, where it angles beneath the water of Lake Huron proper. Deeply indented shores, particularly along the North Channel, and numerous large and small interior lakes make it look on the map—as writers have frequently noted—like a long, well-nibbled piece of Swiss cheese. This mixture of land and water gives Manitoulin many different habitats for animal life, and the limestone base adds to the richness of plant life, whose vascular species (flowering plants, ferns, etc.) add up to more than 1,100. Numerous pastures for livestock and occasional patches of cropland alternate with forest, which becomes extensive at the west end of the island where the Donahue company has a large holding. The mosaic of field and forest produces an abundance of deer. Black bears, which catch suckers in certain streams in the spring, hide in the heavier forest. Occasionally someone sees a moose or wolf.

Gore Bay, a small north side town at the head of a bay enclosed by high headlands, became my headquarters for the next couple of days. Ice covered the bay and extended out as far as I could see into the North Channel. Three boys practiced hockey on a snow-cleared patch at the marina. Sailboats and a float plane sat on the shore. Most of the sailboats had "Gore Bay" lettered on their sterns, but I noted one "Toronto" and a "Miami."

The town, which is the governmental seat of Manitoulin District, is close to Port Sanilac in size. The highway sign said 900, but the waitress at the Twin Bluffs Bar and Grill said they really had 800 in winter—"about 100 people are snowbirds—they go south in winter." However, Gore Bay seemed a little more upscale than Port Sanilac. Tables at the Twin Bluffs, the only restaurant serving dinner, had cloth napkins, candles, and real flowers. The Provincial liquor store offered wines from Germany, France, Hungary, Chile, Italy, and Australia, as well as Ontario. An "international" health food store has been here since the 1950s. I wondered if Canadians are more worldly or sophisticated than Michiganders, or was this just a more affluent town. The winter populace I ran across, however, didn't seem much different from the folks in my own home port, down in the Thumb.

Instead of basketball, Gore Bay—like most Canadian towns—went in for ice hockey, and curling. One night I watched Gore Bay's bantam hockey team (thirteen- and fourteen-year-olds) take on Wikwemikong (known as "Wiky"), a town in the large Indian reserve at the east end of the island. I watched from the side behind a chest-high wooden barrier, mindful of the flying puck and flying bodies that often banged into it. The skill level was impressive, and there were no fights. When I left, after two periods, they were tied at 2–2. The next night I watched ladies' curling teams at the Gore Bay Curling Club. The ladies, of all ages, seemed to be having a high old time as the sweepers swept in front of the stone as it slid, slowly turning, toward the target circle.

My deeper acquaintance with Manitoulin began with Terry Land. Late one afternoon I met him at his law office to do a little birding while the light still held. Terry donned a heavy coat over his suit and tie and we drove out to Janet Head, at the mouth of the bay. From here, ice appeared to cover the whole North Channel, with only a few patches of open water. A handful of mergansers and a few wandering herring gulls were the only signs of life. Like the fisherman who only caught fish yesterday or the day before, Terry told me about all the wonderful birds he had seen here earlier in the winter, before the freeze-up—like the Iceland gull—and the golden eagle a woman had discovered eating a rabbit.

We turned to personal history. Terry had come to Gore Bay seventeen years earlier to practice law with a law school friend who lived here. Terry's wife is a teacher, like many other people in town who teach at the Gore Bay grade school or elsewhere on the island. The fact that some who teach in other towns live here suggests there is some special attraction to this little settlement. Besides the physical beauty of its surroundings, Terry likes it as a "friendly, safe place to raise children. I can't see why anyone would prefer Little Current," he said, "except it's an hour closer to any place off the island."

Terry had taken up birdwatching only three or four years previously. His father was a birder, and Terry thought this might make a good hobby. Like many late converts, he pursues his new interest with a passion. He birds all day Saturday if he can, on Tuesday during drives to the firm's branch office in Mindemoya, and during lunch hours. So far he had spotted forty-two species that January—two behind his birding mentor Doreen Bailey, with whom he had a fierce competition.

The next day I met Doreen. Like Terry, she was stout, sharp-minded, and totally addicted to birdwatching. She had taken up the sport shortly before her retirement eight years earlier as principal of the Gore Bay elementary school, a post she had held for twenty years. Doreen grew up on the North Shore near Spanish, living part of the year on a farm. One day as she was hoeing onions she turned and saw a wolf sitting on its haunches, watching her. When she walked back to the house, it followed her. "I think it was actually a wolf-dog hybrid that a neighbor had raised and let go," she said. She was a little scared, but she felt an affinity with the animal, a beginning, perhaps, of her lifelong bond with nature. As a young woman she moved to Manitoulin to teach, fell in love with the island's beauty and people, and never left.

Doreen and her husband Leslie live on a large farm south of Gore Bay where the island pinches to its narrowest (a feature that channels many birds right through their farm). For a time she wrote a nature column for the Manitoulin *Recorder,* taking many subjects from her farm observations, like the ravens that plucked shedding hair from cattle in the spring for nest lining. In her brown GM pickup truck she was bouncing around all the back roads of Manitoulin, checking on the latest bird activity, and ignoring a painful case of gout. "My friends worry about me going all these places alone," she said, "but I don't give it a thought."

We went off in her pickup to explore the west half of Manitoulin. This being a "mild" winter, the snow was not deep, allowing us to get off the main roads and back into the woods. "We couldn't have done this last winter," she said, "we would have needed a snowmobile. We had forty below and a lot more snow. The ground froze down to six feet and broke a lot of water mains." The weather didn't keep her from birding that winter, though. And one day she was rewarded with a sight "southerners" like me will probably never see: a white gyrfalcon pursuing a snowy owl.

Basking in seventeen-degree weather, we looked out from the shore of Barrie Island at great blue heron nests in trees silhouetted against the sky on a small island to the west. It would be three months before the herons and other colonial water birds returned to these nesting islands. Near us, somewhere along the forested shore, snug cottages hid. Their owners, mostly German, come over from Europe in the summer to enjoy the remote lake shore, and at Christmas to enjoy the abundant snow. This Christmas hadn't met their expectations. Nearby, beside the road, we saw the parallel tracks of two otters, with long slide marks in the shallow snow between footprints.

At the western tip of Manitoulin, the short, sturdy Mississagi Lighthouse rose above the limestone shelves along the shore. Waves from the open Mississagi Strait crashed up against the ice-encased rocks, pushed by the wind that always blows here. A pair of red-breasted mergansers, unusual at this late winter date, rode the waves just offshore. North of the lighthouse we drove out to the dolomite quarry of the Lafarge Construction Materials Company. Quarrying had progressed from the shore inland, and now the crushed rock was brought shoreward on long conveyor belts to the dock. Though not in sight this day, ships carry their loads from here down to Detroit and elsewhere as long as the winter ice permits, sometimes past Christmas. Less than fifty miles to the southwest, ships from the huge limestone quarry at Rogers City, Michigan, do the same.

Most of the north side of Manitoulin Island was locked in ice, but the south shore, including many coves, was still open. A good-sized flock of herring gulls rested on Providence Bay, while goldeneyes and common mergansers pursued prey underwater. A few bald eagles, Doreen said, usually hang around the south shore as long as it remains open, hunting for dead fish, weak waterfowl, and any animal flesh inland, dead or alive, that they can find or capture. In winter a deer carcass is an eagle bonanza.

Doreen and her husband were looking forward to two weeks in Mexico with their friends Irene and George Purvis. George, as his father and grandfather were before him, is a long-time commercial fisherman, working out of Burnt Island (actually a peninsula) on the south shore. When the weather shuts down the fishing in December, George repairs equipment, finishes his bookkeeping for the year, and then takes that long awaited month's vacation before returning to the water in March. The day I was on my own I drove down to his fish station at Burnt Island. The weathered frame buildings stood silent in the forest. The mink pens lay scattered about, left over from the days when Purvis had a thriving mink ranch, before furs became immoral. The *Andave H., Chas R.,* and the larger *Blue Fin* lay at the dock, their bows pointed lakeward. No one appeared. It was quite a different scene than the one I had experienced several summers before. Men had been working around the dock, one cleaning algae from a net, and a gentleman had come from his cottage on Meldrum Bay to buy fish when the boats came in. Now I drove out through the forest, looking months ahead to the time when I could meet George Purvis and, I hoped, go fishing on one of his boats.

CHAPTER 4

# ICE

When I stepped out of our cottage at Port Sanilac in the morning, I never knew what to expect. Some days the lake was totally open, other days it was white with ice to the horizon. On still others, bands of shining floes alternated with strips of dark water. The varied combinations of temperature, currents, and wind could form ice, move it around, and melt it with astonishing speed.

Along the shore, a slower, more progressive process was at work. By early January, low shelves of ice had formed, with miniature cliffs a foot or two high where the waves had eroded them. When the wind was up, I could hear the surf at night. Later, after many days and nights of spray flying upon the shore and freezing, two parallel rows of ice dunes formed, looking like rounded little mountain ranges. As the lake built these "dunes," it also sculpted them. I could see cliffs and caves in the ice, and "fumaroles" and "volcanoes" where the water rushed in and sprayed up through openings in the top. Now at night, at the end of January, I could no longer hear the surf, muffled and dampened as it was by the irregular ice barrier and offshore floes.

Out on Lake Huron, as on all the Great Lakes, a general progression was occurring, although masked by the daily variations in any one area. Ice forms first at Thunder Bay on the north shore of Lake Superior—by mid-December in an average winter. Then it appears in shallow, sheltered spots at the west end of Lake Superior, in the St. Marys River—Superior's

Ice dunes at the cottage.

outlet—in the North Channel of Lake Huron and the eastern shore of Georgian Bay, the west end of Saginaw Bay, Green Bay in Lake Michigan, and Lake St. Clair, south of Huron. From these shoreline locations it gradually spreads along all the shores and outward until it reaches its greatest extent in late February. In an average winter, peak ice coverage on Lake Superior is 75 percent, 68 percent on Lake Huron proper, 90 percent in Georgian Bay, nearly 100 percent in the North Channel, 45 percent on Lake Michigan, 90 percent on shallow Lake Erie, where heat loss is rapid, and only 25 percent on deep, relatively small Lake Ontario, where heat loss is slow. In severe winters, such as those of 1979 and 1994, the ice coverage can approach 100 percent on all the lakes. Lake Huron was completely ice-covered twice in the winter of 1993–94, although only for a day or so each time.

As winter wanes, the pattern reverses, until ice remains only in the areas, like the St. Marys River, where it first formed. Lake Huron usually clears by the second week of April, except for the North Channel, where ice normally remains until the end of April.

Like the ice I watched from our cottage, much of the ice on Lake Huron is not a solid sheet but consists of broken floes. These do not stand still. Counterclockwise currents move this ice southward on the Michigan side of the lake, unless counteracted by southerly winds.

Occasionally the traveling floes carry surprising passengers. One winter in the early 1990s, Mike Hanson saw four or five moose on an ice sheet a couple of miles offshore north of Port Sanilac. "They were lying down," he said, "and would raise their heads once in awhile. They blew in with an east wind, then blew back out again." These may have been the same moose seen one March by Cecil Tubbs, my neighbor up the beach, although he described them as being only about one mile or less offshore. Since Port Sanilac is 200 miles south of the nearest moose territory, these animals must have had a long and harrowing ride.

One can imagine what might have happened. A group decides to cross the St. Marys River ice from St. Joseph Island to the upper Michigan shore. A section breaks loose in the current and they are carried down, past De Tour Village and out into the open water of Lake Huron.

Deer and coyotes, sometimes fleeing from dogs, get trapped on the ice, too, their carcasses later washing up on the shore. Mike Hanson thinks coyotes may go out there because, usually being lighter than the pursuing dogs, they can stay on thinner ice, but obviously this is a risky maneuver.

Under northerly winds, ice can build up rapidly at the south end of the lake. Here it either forms a barrier above the entrance to the St. Clair River—the lake's outlet—or moves on down the swift river. If it moves down, it meets the solid sheet on Lake St. Clair and piles up. Depending on the amount of ice coming down, the jam can extend ten or more miles back up the river. Such jams are especially frequent in March, when rising temperature is breaking up the ice on Lake Huron. Ferry boats to Harsens Island, in Lake St. Clair, and across the St. Clair River to Canada must then cease operation. As the ice builds down toward the river bottom, some of the water has nowhere to go but sideways, over the banks and into riverside towns.

This happened with a vengeance in mid-March 1987. One long-time resident of Algonac said it was the worst flooding he had ever seen. Six U.S. Coast Guard icebreakers and one Canadian were called in to try to break up the jam. It took twelve days, working sunup to well past sundown.

Such jams are also a concern for shipping. Closure of the Welland Canal and the Soo Locks, usually around January 15, prevents entry from Lake Ontario and the Atlantic and into Lake Superior from the lower lakes. But a small amount of shipping continues during the winter on Lakes Erie, Huron, Michigan, and connecting waters. The U.S. Coast Guard, often assisted by the Canadian Coast Guard, attempts to keep a channel open through the Detroit River, Lake St. Clair, the St. Clair River, Saginaw Bay, and the Straits of Mackinac. For this and other purposes, the U.S. operates five 140-foot icebreaking tugs, stationed at Cleveland, Detroit, St. Ignace, Sault Ste. Marie, and Sturgeon Bay, Wisconsin, plus the venerable 290-foot *Mackinaw* at Cheboygan. In the early spring they also help to maintain a channel through the St. Marys River and into harbors on Lake Superior.

So it was that on March 1, 1995, the U.S. Coast Guard icebreaking tug *Neah Bay*, out of Cleveland, entered the St. Clair River to work on the ice jam, which extended from Lake St. Clair ten miles or more back up above Algonac. Normally the *Bristol Bay*, stationed in Detroit, would have performed this duty, but she was undergoing winter maintenance and was unavailable. With the kind permission of the Coast Guard, I boarded the *Neah Bay* at dawn on March 2 at Algonac, to observe its work. She was a small but sturdy-looking vessel, attractive in her Coast Guard colors—white, with a red diagonal stripe at the bow.

This day the assignment has changed. Instead of routine channel opening, we are to help the *Samuel Risley*, a Canadian icebreaker/buoy-tender, get the tug *Mary E. Hannah* and her barge down through the river and across Lake St. Clair. Grinding, bucking, and shuddering through the piled-up, jagged field of ice floes, we round a bend and see the boats. The barge is empty and riding high, making it difficult for the tug to push it through the ice, which builds up in front of the barge and then stops it. Even at full power, the tug can't budge it. The *Risley*, 228 feet long and packing 8,000 horsepower, backs her low stern almost up to the front of the barge, attempting to churn the ice away with her twin screws. We make a pass around the stalled boats, trying to open space for the blocking ice to move to. After some minutes of this, the tug is able to move the barge fifty or 100 yards downriver, then comes to a halt again as ice piles up in front of the barge. The *Risley* repeats her patient backing and forthing, and again the barge makes a little headway.

Up on the bridge, our commanding officer, Lt. Fred Sommer, confers on the radio with the skipper of the *Risley*. It is decided that we could help most by making a track ahead, wide enough for ice to be pushed out to

The Canadian icebreaker *Risley* makes a path for the tug and barge.

the sides when the barge comes through. We grind down a few hundred yards, then turn around. Executive officer Lt. (jg) Mike Bush gives the orders. "Right full rudder." "Right full aye," the helmsman replies. Bush reverses the engines and we back across the channel, then turn right again to head upstream.

Meanwhile, the CO has been checking the navigational chart and establishing our position from minute to minute. The Army Corps of Engineers maintains a twenty-six-foot-deep channel through connecting waters like this on the Great Lakes, but it is only a few hundred feet wide. The *Neah Bay* works mostly on Lake Erie and Sommer is not very familiar with the St. Clair River. It wouldn't do to run the vessel aground on his first ship command.

Now we stop for several minutes. A problem has developed with the sea chest, through which water is taken in to cool the engine oil. So much slush has been sucked in from this fragmented "brash" ice that the pipe from the sea chest has been plugged up, creating an air pocket that blocks entry of the cooling water and causes the engines to overheat. We must wait until the slush in the sea chest melts and the cooling system operates properly. The chief engineer suggests taking on more ballast water to lower the ship a foot deeper and perhaps reduce the intake of slush, but this doesn't work. The slush is still sucked down along the hull and into the sea chest.

So we run a few minutes and stop a few minutes, slowly up and down the river all day ahead of the creeping *Risley,* tug, and barge. Over the radio we hear the gravelly voice of the tug captain speaking to the *Risley's* CO: "I appreciate your patience." Bosun's Mate Bradley says to me, "Yes, you do need a lot of patience for this kind of work." Patience seems in fact the prime requirement. "We could all move right along through plate ice," Sommer says, "but this brash ice is tough."

Though this ice frequently stops the barge, the *Neah Bay* has no trouble breaking through it. The bow of her steel hull is only seven-eighths of an inch thick and the rest five-eighths of an inch, but closely spaced ribs give her great strength. She can crash through ice ridges five to six feet high and move continuously through ice twenty-two inches thick. The "bubbler," a compressor that shoots a film of air along the hull, adds one to one and a half knots to her speed through ice. Still, the executive officer, Bush, is a bit envious of the larger *Risley.* "She's got better visibility from the bridge," he says, "not to mention 8,000 horsepower" (to our 2,500). Her high horsepower, low stern, and twin screws make a nice clean track through the ice, with vertical edges like curbs, whereas our higher stern and single propeller leave a less-defined track that fills in more rapidly with floes after we pass through.

Late in the morning an orange Coast Guard helicopter with a diagonal white stripe flies up the river, surveying the situation. This HH 65 Dolphin operates out of Detroit, making daily reports on ice conditions. Such surveillance from Coast Guard stations around the Great Lakes, coupled with satellite data, provide the information for weekly ice forecasts put out by the National Weather Bureau. We get the current word over the radio from the helicopter. "The brash ice extends down to Lake St. Clair. The lake is about 70 percent ice-covered, about six to eight inches thick. I think you can progress there OK."

By evening we have passed Michigan's Harsens Island, with its shore-line homes, and Ontario's Squirrel, Basset, and Seaway islands, with their gray woods and brown marshes, and have crunched out through the manmade St. Clair Cutoff into Lake St. Clair. Here we leave the jumbled brash ice and enter smooth plate ice up to ten inches thick. Cracks shoot outward as our bow hits it and then our hull and wake break the ice into floes. From a patch of open water mallards and a few goldeneyes watch our passing. Across the lake the western sky turns red. Far to the south the skyscrapers of Detroit rise into the clear air. An off-duty seaman on the deck below captures all this with his video camera. We turn around and move back up the ship channel to anchor for the night. The *Risley*, tug, and barge are out of sight around a far bend in the river. They will labor on until midnight.

Now there is more time to visit with the crew. Under the two officers are fifteen men—warrant officers, bosun's mates, and others down to two seamen apprentices. They all impress me with their intelligence and attentiveness to their jobs. I ask Seaman Apprentice Kauffman about his life. It turns out he's from Calgary, Alberta, but now has dual citizenship. "I majored in environmental science," he says, "and I'm finishing my bachelor's degree by correspondence. After that I want to get a master's. If I stay in the Coast Guard I'd like to get on one of the emergency environmental response teams, cleaning up oil spills and things like that." Meanwhile, he's learning basic seamanship skills, working on the deck and manning the helm. "It takes three months at sea to get certified as a helmsman," he explains. "So far I've had one month of it."

The cook is from Indiana. "My last duty was at San Francisco," he says. "I saw the West Coast from Alaska to Hawaii and Mexico. Now I'm getting to know the Great Lakes. That's what I like about the Coast Guard—you get around." I compliment him on the food, which is delicious, varied, and plentiful. "It's good for morale," he replies.

Some of the crew had served on the *Neah Bay* during the preceding winter, one of the severest in recent memory. No winter maintenance period for the Coast Guard icebreakers. No leave for anybody. Four solid months of icebreaking, pausing only to refuel every five to seven days. In April they were still breaking ice, first in the St. Marys River and then at Thunder Bay in Lake Superior.

"We thought we'd be breaking ice in Saginaw Bay for only two or three days," Mike Bush recalls, "but it turned out to be late December to mid-January. A couple of tugs and the freighters *Gemini* and *Saturn* were going in and out, mainly with heating oil. The ice fishermen were a big worry. They'd come right up to the edge of our track and drop their line in. We would just inch along, trying not to crack the ice away from the track. We'd tell them to back off and they'd only move their shanties back ten feet and start drilling. Last winter three or four fishermen went through the ice up there and drowned—not because of our icebreaking but just because of getting on thin ice."

Machinery Technician 1 Delp, an engineer, says their exit from Saginaw Bay wasn't too pleasant either. "We poked our nose out into Lake Huron and found ourselves in twelve-foot waves. So we went back into the bay and waited in the ice for four days until the weather calmed down." This was the wise thing to do. With her round, keelless hull, the *Neah Bay* rolls a lot, sometimes thirty degrees. "This ship doesn't turn very fast," Delp went on, "and we don't want to get broadside to the waves—she starts to roll more then. And if you've got three or four inches of ice on the ship it gets more unstable—that's dangerous."

I am curious to know how the men feel about Lake Huron. "I've been scared on Lake Huron," Bosun's Mate Schramm admits. "She lets us know she's there. You're either going north or south, usually broadside to the wind, and it's a long way. It's hard to maneuver. You've got room to maneuver on Lake Superior, and storms on Lake Erie don't last too long, or you can get in the lee of some land. But you just have to take what Lake Huron gives you."

"We call Huron the monster lake," says Mike Bush. "I just want to get through it. It seems like it's always rough either going north or going south."

Later, at the Detroit Station, I talked with Petty Officer Wood. He has spent many years on the Great Lakes, but now is restricted to shore duty because of softening cartilage in his knees. "That's what years at sea will do to you," he says philosophically. His opinion is that the east-west lakes—Superior, Erie, and Ontario—have the roughest water, because of the prevailing west wind.

Bad weather is a familiar occupational hazard in the Coast Guard. One wall of the *Neah Bay*'s messroom is filled with citations for the ship, many for brave work under adverse weather conditions. One citation in particular struck me. In the winter of 1981, one year after her commissioning in Tacoma, Washington, the *Neah Bay* was called on to go to South Bass Island in western Lake Erie to rescue an eleven-year-old boy who had severely cut his hand and nearly severed his index finger. Without treatment within twelve hours he would lose his finger or entire hand. The *Neah Bay* traveled from Cleveland to South Bass Island through shoal waters in dense fog and heavy ice, without benefit of navigational buoys, which had been removed for the winter. Maneuvering up to an eighty-foot, deteriorated dock in waters charted at less than the ship draws, the crew picked up the boy and got him help in time.

At 6:30 A.M. on March 3, the shaking of the vessel wakes me as it moves up the river toward the still laboring barge. We work around and in front of it and the *Risley,* and by late morning we're out of the brash ice and into Lake St. Clair. The *Risley* thanks us and heads back upriver. With no trouble we break ice across the lake, the tug and barge following steadily a quarter mile behind us. We go through open water at the south end of the lake, scattering thousands of diving ducks, and down the open Detroit River to the Coast Guard station opposite Belle Isle. The tug *Hannah* will stop in Detroit to repair a crack in the barge before proceeding to Toledo. The *Neah Bay* refuels. In an hour or two she will start to retrace her passage to help the freighter *Gemini* back up through the St. Clair River. The larger ship, I hope, will have an easier time of it.

During our trip across Lake St. Clair, I had been intrigued with the many patterns of ice: solid sheets in some areas, cemented floes in others forming all sorts of polygons and irregular shapes; three or four inches thick or up to ten inches; clear or clouded. One patch of ice had small round platelets throughout it.

An ice expert can read the history of the ice from such patterns and textures. For icebreaking purposes, Coast Guardsmen usually just distinguish between the broken, jammed-up fragments and slush—called brash ice—and smooth sheets of plate ice. I did enough reading to at least recognize some further stages and varieties of ice formation. Two basic types of ice occur in Great Lakes floes: lake ice and snow ice. Lake ice is formed when the water surface becomes supercooled. Needle-like or snowflake-shaped crystals develop and connect through branchlike growths, extending outward until an ice "skim" several millimeters thick is formed. This is called frazil ice. It looks like an oil slick. Several mornings from the cottage I saw smooth patches of frazil ice surrounded by the ruffled surface of open water. If the lake stays calm enough and the air temperature low enough, the frazil ice thickens until a solid sheet is formed.

Snow ice develops from snow falling onto the water at the time of freeze-up, from the depression of the ice sheet caused by the weight of snow, by water soaking into the snowpack through fractures, or by the thawing and refreezing of the snowpack during winter and spring thaws. It has a rougher or slushier appearance than lake ice.

During my walks along the shore I saw flotillas of small, almost circular floes with raised edges—one of those regular patterns you often see in nature that make you think somebody has been at work here. This was "pancake ice." It results from the break-up of ice sheets and rubbing together of the floes until the rounded shape is produced.

Plate ice, ball ice, and pancake ice.

Sometimes I saw large snowballs of ice floating in the water or resting on floes. This "ball ice," I learned, consists of slush and frazil ice that grows together and is rounded by turbulent water.

On quiet inland ponds the ice cover slowly thickens in a nice, predictable process until the warm air of spring breaks it up; but on the rough waters of the Great Lakes the process is anything but orderly. Many kinds of ice patterns, especially noticeable from the air, can develop. One of the most striking is thrust structures. These result when thin sheets of ice are pressed together by pack pressure, forming a series of parallel, rectilinear overthrusts alternating with similarly shaped underthrusts. The clean, right-angled lines contrast with the more irregular, rounded lines formed when the thinnest ice sheets are pressed together and override each other.

Along the shore, as I described earlier, an "icefoot" develops. This is composed of frozen masses of spray, brash ice, and ice cakes. Dramatic "ice ramparts" are often formed when the wind drives piles of ice floes up on the beach.

I sometimes wish I could have been here 14,000 years ago, when the thickest ice of all lay over the Great Lakes region. Imagine standing at the edge of that great blue and white slope or wall, perhaps a mile high, hearing the terrible thunder as huge slabs fall into the ponded water at the glacier's foot, sensing the immense weight that has depressed the earth's surface here and throughout the vast area covered by the ice sheet.

Our present Great Lakes are the result of glacial scouring and developments during the retreat of the last—the Wisconsin—ice sheet. Several major glaciations occurred over the past one million years, reaching as far south as the present Ohio River, but each wiped out most evidence of the preceding ice sheet. The Wisconsin reached its greatest extent 17,000 years ago, well south of the current Great Lakes and then, with intermittent pauses and temporary, local readvances, melted northward toward its origins around Hudson Bay. As it shrank, lakes formed from the meltwater and developed outlets at various points as the land, released from its massive burden of ice, slowly rebounded, at differing rates from one area to another. Geologists do not agree on all aspects of the extent, ages, and outlets of the many lake stages. I will follow the interpretation of V. K. Prest, who attempted to harmonize viewpoints, and will focus on the stages that led to Lake Huron.

Fourteen thousand years ago, the Huron glacial lobe was calving ice into Lake Maumee, which also collected water from the Erie lobe and drained southwestward through the Wabash River. As the ice lobes retreated farther into the present Saginaw area, this lake expanded (forming Lake Arkona) and found a new outlet through the Grand River to the lake south of the Michigan ice lobe. Several stages, with varying outlets, followed lakes Maumee and Arkona. Some of the better known are (1) Lake Whittlesey, followed by Lake Warren, both still draining through the Grand River; (2) long-lived Lake Algonquin, which sometimes included most of present Lake Huron, Georgian Bay, and Lake Michigan and at various times had outlets at Chicago, Port Huron, and southeastward from Georgian Bay; (3) Lake Stanley (in the main Huron Basin) separated from Lake Hough (in the Georgian Bay Basin), both of which drained eastward through Lake Nipissing and the Ottawa River to the Champlain Sea, which had invaded the St. Lawrence Valley; (4) Lake Stanley-Nipissing, still using the same outlet; and (5) the Nipissing Great Lakes, in which the Superior, Michigan, and Huron basins formed one huge lake in roughly their present shapes. This lake system had outlets at Chicago, Port Huron, and the Ottawa River about 6,000 years ago. Later uplifts closed off the Ottawa River outlet and raised the sill at Sault Ste. Marie, forming Lake Superior. Downcutting of the Port Huron outlet over the past few thousand years lowered Lake Huron to its present configuration.

Of today's five Great Lakes, Huron is fourth in maximum depth (750 feet), third in volume, second in surface area, first in land drainage area, and first by far in shoreline length (3,827 miles). The Bruce Peninsula and Manitoulin Island separate the lake into three very different sections: Lake Huron proper, Georgian Bay, and the North Channel. Each of these and its subdivisions has a somewhat different chemistry and biology, depending on the sources of incoming water, water depths, and other factors. Lake Huron's deepest basins lie in the north and north-central parts of the lake. Lesser, elongated basins run north and south in the southern half of the lake, and highly irregular basins wander about the floor of Georgian Bay. The North Channel, averaging less than 100 feet deep, has no major basins. Into all the basins muddy sediments have settled. Elsewhere, clay, sand, or glacial till and bedrock form the bottom environment. Like all the Great Lakes except Erie, most of Lake Huron is cold and deep; it is classified as oligotrophic, meaning it is relatively low in nutrients and high in dissolved oxygen. Saginaw Bay, averaging much less than fifty feet deep, is the only extensive shallow area.

This in a nutshell is the Lake Huron environment into which fish and other organisms returned after the last glacial epoch. The ice sheet had forced species that could migrate to follow drainage routes southward to

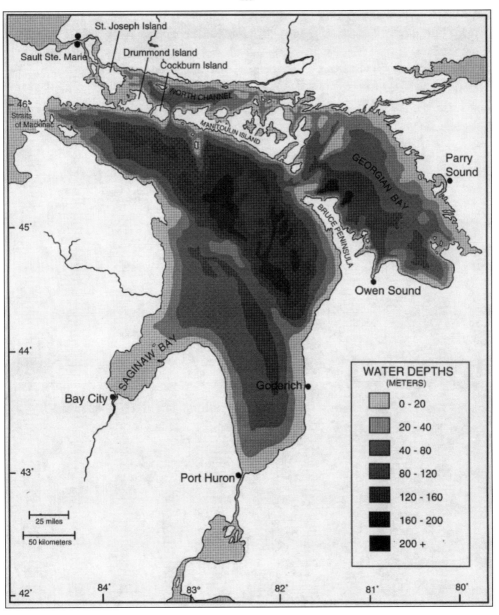

Water depths, Lake Huron.
(Sources: U.S. Lake Survey Chart No. 0; Berst and Spangler, 1973)
(Credit: Taina Litwak)

glacier-free waters. During the retreat of the ice, aquatic organisms had several outlets from the glacial lakes available to them for reentry. Thus, today, the Great Lakes have fishes from the Mississippi and Ohio river systems, and even from the Atlantic coastal plain, not to mention others that were deliberately introduced or that entered through canals or in ship ballast water.

So ice has been and is still a major player in the life of Lake Huron. On my winter rambles I tried to find out how the birds and fish and fishermen dealt with ice and the frigid water on which it lay.

# CHAPTER 5

# Fish and Birds in Winter

One day early in February, as I stood at the entrance to the St. Clair River, I saw the gillnetter *Doretta L.* coming in off the lake to the Purdy Fisheries dock across the river. Three herring gulls rode majestically on her bow, apparently anticipating a chance at some fish during the unloading. The boat's bow was encased in ice and icicles hung from the cabin.

Later I asked Milford Purdy, head of the Purdy fishery operation at Sarnia, what it was like fishing out there in the winter. "Well," he said, "it's not too bad unless you get trapped in the ice. If you're out there and the wind shifts and pushes the ice down into the funnel [where the lake flows into the St. Clair River], it's hard to get back through. This winter we got caught out there for three days. But they have good facilities on the boats. Both the gill-net boats have microwaves, color television, darts, and heaters. As long as everything works well and the food holds out we're all right. Of course, if the cigarettes run out—that's pretty serious! . . . Usually you just wait until the pressure shifts and opens up the ice. Sometimes the Coast Guard will come and help. The time we were caught for three days the *Risley* got us out.

"Ice on the boat can be a problem, too. You have to keep an eye on it—break it off if it gets too thick. We try not to go out if there's an ice warning from the Coast Guard—cold with a lot of wind and spray."

The main object of these somewhat risky trips is whitefish. Prices are higher in winter because few commercial fishermen go out at this season.

The Purdy boats, fishing in water up to 150 or more feet deep in winter, with gill nets, also catch a few lake trout and yellow perch along with the abundant whitefish.

Ice fishermen, being restricted to near-shore locations (if they have any sense), are usually dropping their lines in much shallower water. On Lake Huron, Saginaw Bay is a popular destination for ice fishing. It is shallow and therefore entirely freezes over. Most of it stays solid through the winter, but some parts may crack, deteriorate, or pull away from the shore. Then it gets dangerous.

Myles Willard of Mayville told me he had lost a friend out there. The fellow was an experienced outdoorsman who had spent many days on Saginaw Bay, but he hit the wrong spot on his snowmobile and went through. Dennis Schommer said he knew some men who carried two planks on their pickup truck when they went ice fishing there. If they came to a separation in the ice they just put their planks down and drove across. "Those ice fishermen are crazy," he said. He also told about some boys who had gone out on their snowmobiles in the early spring to fish. Coming back they discovered that the ice had pulled away from the shore fifty or seventy-five yards. "What they did was, they backed up their snow machines, they got 'em going as fast as they could, and they tried to glide them across the water. They didn't make it. They ended up in water up to their waist. It's a good thing they were big, strong farm boys, because they had to carry those snowmobiles through that muck to get to shore."

Wildfowl Bay, being sheltered by islands and Sand Point, has some of the most dependable ice on Saginaw Bay and is the setting for many of the events in Caseville's annual Ice Shanty Festival. I wasn't prepared for the sight that greeted me when I arrived here on a mild mid-February Saturday. Expecting to see mostly ice fishermen dotting Wildfowl Bay, going for one of the Festival's fishing prizes, I saw instead two large striped tents, hundreds of cars parked on the ice and along the access road, and several thousand people, most of them out on the ice watching something. This turned out to be ATVs racing around an oval, in the center of which stood a large, inflated Miller Beer can, and farther out, snowmobile drag races. Dozens of other ATVs and snowmobiles were tearing around on the wide frozen expanse of Wildfowl Bay, warming up for a race or just having fun. A fellow in a large grey Chevy was doing spins on the ice. The roar and whine of engines was overwhelming.

I watched the races for awhile and then ambled over to the Polar Bear Dip. A square section of ice had been chopped out and into this frigid pool jumped, one or two at a time, maybe eighteen "Polar Bears," two of them women. Some leaped right back out. Others frolicked in the water for a couple of minutes, demonstrating their extra hardiness. All the Polar Bears thawed out in a hot tub in the attending trailer. They each received a certificate to prove they had done the Dip.

The Coast Guard used this same pool for its ice rescue demonstration. A Guardsman in a wet suit slipped into the water. Soon an orange helicopter appeared over the trees along shore, circled the pool, and lowered a basket to the rescuee. He climbed in and was lifted to the hovering helicopter. Then they let him down again to the ice and the helicopter whirled over the crowd and out of sight beyond the tree line. In a real ice rescue I suppose your chances are good if you're on a floe, but if you're in the water help had better come quickly.

During all this activity near shore, some people were actually ice fishing. Half a mile out, where the ice was twenty inches thick over six or more feet of water, stood a cluster of ice shanties, automobiles, pickup trucks, and bent-over human forms. I walked out to see how they were doing. Three parties had piles of twenty or thirty small perch lying on the ice. Others had fewer or none, but all looked like they were having a good time, including one group with small children. Two days before I had seen a photograph in *Michigan Natural Resources* magazine showing a small boy with a large pike he had caught ice fishing on Saginaw Bay. It must have been a rare enough occurrence to warrant a picture. Today nobody had had such luck, but it didn't seem to matter.

I asked one man why everyone had gathered in the same area. It turned out I had asked the right person. "We got here first, around 8:30, and started catching fish. I guess the next group saw we had fish and came here too, and it just built up after that."

Out here it was more peaceful, more like Wildfowl Bay on a normal winter day. You could still hear the snowmobiles, but less plainly. Now and then a gull flew over, checking to see if the humans had left anything edible within safe reach. I walked back to shore, through the criss-crossing snowmobiles and the ever-increasing din. I was glad when I got back on a quiet road, into the farmland of the Thumb.

Mike Hanson, the conservation officer for Sanilac County, doesn't do much winter fishing on Saginaw Bay. "All those little fish," he says scornfully. He prefers the Port Sanilac and Lexington harbors, where brown trout and rainbows come in to chase minnows. He seems to be able to think like a fish. How else do you explain his catching more than 100 trout this particular winter, along with a few pike and walleyes?

Helicopter rescue demonstration at the Caseville Ice Shanty Festival.

Of course it also helps to have been fishing most of your forty-plus years and to have worked twenty years for the Department of Natural Resources, observing what other fishermen are catching and reading studies of fish. What are all those brown trout doing in the Port Sanilac harbor in winter? Going after the minnows that have moved in, he says. And why have the minnows moved in? "One reason they frequent the shore outside the harbor in winter," Mike says, "is because the turbulence stirs up food. The quiet water in the harbor may offer different benefits. Besides having possible spots of warmer water, the harbor usually stays ice-covered in winter. Fish seem to have learned that ice protects them from birds." Under the harbor ice minnows are at least safe from gulls and diving ducks, if not from hungry browns.

Mike catches few pike during his winter vigils over the round holes through the harbor ice. Where are they? "Most of the big pike are following the whitefish schools," he says. "The whitefish finish spawning in October–November and then they cruise around anywhere from shoreline to forty feet."

He doesn't catch many walleyes either. "The groups that are local are just cruising in and out. They come in at night, apparently, and feed around the harbors, wherever the minnows concentrate. Those are the ones that are here year-round. The rest of them have moved out of the area. They're in Lake St. Clair, the Detroit River. Some may be in Lake Erie. We're getting tags from that far."

Understandably, relatively little is known about the behavior of Lake Huron's fish in winter. Ice and winter weather make study difficult. Generally, the whole lake system slows down with the lowering of water temperatures. In the fall, water in the surface layers cools and becomes denser and thus heavier. As it sinks, warmer water rises to take its place. The eventual result of this "fall turnover" and mixing is near-uniform temperatures through most of the water column—about four degrees centigrade, the temperature at which water is most dense. The surface layer cools below four degrees and, being less dense, floats on top of the water below. When the surface reaches zero degrees it freezes.

With low water temperatures, low-angled winter sunlight, and ice cover on much of the lake that also reduces light penetration, the plant plankton (phytoplankton) on which the whole ecosystem depends reaches its lowest abundance. The animal plankton (zooplankton), having less phytoplankton to feed on, is also reduced, and many species overwinter as egg sacs. These developments reverberate on up the food chain to invertebrates and fish. Fish growth slows or stops entirely.

Studies of fish in the St. Marys River, whose channels wind among islands at the north end of Lake Huron, suggested what a few species were eating in winter. Stomachs of ciscoes (the sub-family including whitefish, lake herring, and chubs) contained mostly copepods—tiny crustaceans. Northern pike were eating fish all year, but in winter they ate less, and more of the stomachs were empty. Yellow perch appeared to congregate in shallow water in winter and feed mainly on insect larvae, such as mayfly nymphs. Of the thirteen walleye stomachs examined, eight were empty, one contained a single fish, and the other four held one or two leeches. In wintertime, one might say, the livin' is not easy.

Lake Huron's birds have the option of migrating to warmer climes in winter, and most species take it. A few kinds of ducks and gulls, however, stick it out. I had to admire the occasional buffleheads, goldeneyes, and common mergansers I saw feeding among the ice floes as I walked the winter beach by our cottage. They were diving in water less than five feet deep, where the bottom was sandy and scattered with round boulders. I couldn't see what they were finding, but all three species eat animal food primarily, the merganser eating nothing but that. The buffleheads—small ducks—could have been feeding on insect larvae and snails on the bottom. The goldeneyes may have been getting crayfish, insect larvae, mussels and snails, perhaps a few fish. And the mergansers, with their long, thin, sawtoothed bills, were mostly pursuing any fish they could catch and swallow. All three, however, may also have been feeding on zebra mussels, those tiny molluscs that in recent years have entered the Great Lakes and reproduced astronomically, attaching themselves to rocks, plants, water intakes, boat hulls, and any other firm surface. I haven't seen any zebra mussels on the underwater rocks visible alongshore, but farther out, beneath the reach of wave action and ice scour, they may be coating the rocks. They're out there somewhere, because the beach is often littered with their empty shells.

Most parts of the Great Lakes are nearly devoid of waterfowl in winter—anywhere that ice cover is heavy. But a few places where the water often stays open and provides adequate food are magnets for both ducks and gulls. One such place is the St. Clair River. Myles Willard and I headed there one overcast February day to look for the tufted duck, a European species, that had been reported at Sombra.

We didn't find the tufted duck, but we saw plenty else. Dozens of redheads and canvasbacks were flying up and down the river and feeding in rafts where openings in the ice remained. Mallards and Canada geese had gathered at various quiet backwaters along both sides of the river. Altogether, we saw twelve species of waterfowl.

Goldeneyes, the males strikingly black and white, were diving with their brown mates. Some of the males were courting, bending their heads back to their wings in one of those odd gestures that must mean something to the females. On the Canadian side at Sombra we drove across a small bridge to the ferry dock. A sign said the ferry was not running "due to ice." And it spoke truly. From here on down, the river was white, choked solid with upended, jagged ice floes. They made a rustling sound as the current tried to move them. But around the little bridge an open pool remained and on it a male goldeneye. Myles whipped out his Nikon with his new 300mm Sigma lens and began taking photographs. "I need waterfowl," he said.

Myles had retired from teaching fifth grade a year earlier and had taken up wildlife photography. He and his wife Marilyn go to art and craft shows all over Michigan, and he places mounted prints in several shops around the Thumb. But it's tough getting started in this business and he was wondering if he could make it. If success depends on knowledge of wildlife, however, he surely will. Born in Frankenmuth, south of Saginaw Bay, he has tramped the woods and fields since boyhood, studying and marveling at everything that lives. His home near Mayville, which he and Marilyn partly built, reflects this love of nature. Mounted ducks, geese, an Arctic fox, a bobcat, a fisher, and other animals adorn the walls of their two-story living room, along with Myles's painting of a cabin in the woods. Chickadees and goldfinches throng the feeders outside the window.

In the field, Myles's lanky, slightly hunched frame moves easily through the brush, his eyes seemingly seeing all that moves and his ears hearing everything within human frequencies. When I'm birding with him, I tend not to look very hard because I assume he will see whatever is there. So that day on the St. Clair River I concluded that the tufted duck was gone. Myles hadn't seen it.

Dennis Rupert, a long-time birder from Sarnia who died in 1996, probably followed the bird life on the St. Clair River more closely than anyone else. If there was a rarity around, Dennis probably would have known about it. It was he who told me about the tufted duck. One winter, he said, a gyrfalcon took up residence on top of the grain elevators near the Purdy Fisheries. Like the ones that often winter at Sault Ste. Marie, this one had ducks on the river and pigeons in town to feed on. Another winter a snowy owl stationed itself on top of these same structures and preyed on the same birds.

A herring gull gets a meal from a dead male common merganser. (Credit: Myles Willard)

During a more recent winter, a Ross's gull appeared briefly at the marina on Sarnia's side of the St. Clair River. This snowy white little Arctic gull (with some black markings in the immature) rarely gets this far south and to my knowledge has never been seen in Michigan. When one of these gulls appeared in Massachusetts a few winters back, birders from all over the country flocked to see it and the event was reported in *Time* magazine. The Sarnia bird did not give much time for a gathering of birdwatchers. It was seen only by Dennis Rupert and four others. (In the winter of 1995–96 he also saw, for the first time at Sarnia, an ivory gull, another Arctic bird equal in rarity to the Ross's gull at this latitude.)

The only common winter gull on Lake Huron is the herring gull, and, when ice closes in on harbors and shores, even this one can be rather scarce. Although herring gulls take eggs and chicks in waterbird colonies and catch baby ducks when they can, they are largely scavengers, especially in winter. At this season, with an ice foot covering the shore, it's difficult for them to find dead fish. So they often turn to human garbage.

I discovered a mob of herring gulls at the Carsonville landfill nine miles west of Port Sanilac. This giant mound receives trash from the whole three-county Thumb area. Trucks roll in through most of the day, ascend this long, flat-topped hill, and dump their loads in the current working area. At four o'clock the bulldozers start covering the trash with several inches of dirt, but before that time the gulls, along with dozens of crows and clouds of starlings, go at it, only momentarily being put to flight by arriving trucks. I see the gulls coming from the south and east, soaring above the landfill, and then alighting gracefully on the new garbage.

On my first visit, in January, I counted some 120 herring gulls. Most were adults, white with pale gray backs, but a few brown or mottled immature birds were among them (it takes four years for a herring gull to reach full adulthood). Two great black-backed gulls had also joined the feast. Largest of the North American gulls, the great black-backed is primarily a bird of the Atlantic Coast but is seen increasingly on the Great Lakes.

When I checked in February, the herring gulls had dwindled to fifty or sixty, but with them now was an adult glaucous gull, white below, with a very pale grey mantle, and white wing tips translucent with the sun shining through them. This is another Arctic gull that comes down in winter to the northern Atlantic and Pacific coasts and Great Lakes. The whiteness of the glaucous gull is striking, and the first-winter birds can be even whiter than the adults. One evening from the beach, because of their shining whiteness, I was able to pick out two glaucous among herring gulls soaring against dark clouds a mile from shore. Like the whiteness of Moby Dick, the whiteness of the glaucous gull seems almost supernatural, suggesting some kind of otherworldly purity. By human standards, however, this gull is anything but pure, scavenging and killing for a living like the herring gull.

I did not see any ring-billed gulls at the landfill that winter. Most members of this species, a smaller version of the herring gull that is abundant on the Great Lakes in summer, migrate toward the coasts or Mississippi River system in the fall, but a few linger on into the winter in the Great Lakes.

In winter, gulls take advantage of another human gift—warm-water effluent from power plants. This keeps the water near the plants open and attracts fish and their predators. The Consumer's Power plant at the mouth of the Saginaw River has been a magnet for fish, gulls, ducks, fishermen, and birdwatchers in past winters. Ron Weeks saw as many as 20,000 herring gulls there in January 1992 and Myles Willard reported 20,000 common mergansers in January 1991. But then the show stopped for a few years. "I think the alewives and gizzard shad disappeared," Myles said. These were the forage fish that attracted everything else. The power plant at Harbor Beach, in the Thumb, keeps part of that harbor open and draws gulls, along with wintering ducks. And the nuclear plant near Port Elgin, Ontario, is another winter destination for gulls and birders, with the added bonus, often, of bald eagles.

At our cottage, however, only a few gulls and ducks remained to give life to Lake Huron in winter. But as we moved into March I knew a great show was coming—something to make the cold winter wait worthwhile.

CHAPTER **6**

# Avian Highways

S pring on the lake is a long, drawn-out affair. On the shore of the
Thumb, I guess you can say it really begins in March and lasts until
sometime in June, depending on how you want to define it. Suffering
somewhat from cabin fever, I was looking for any little sign in February.
And, like the first, tentative notes of Aaron Copeland's "Appalachian
Spring," they came:

"February 12. 10:30 A.M. 0 degrees, but clear and sunny. A cardinal
sings briefly, testing his pipes."

"February 14. 7 degrees at 8:45 A.M. Clear blue sky. A house finch
and a mourning dove sang today."

"February 19. 9:45 A.M. 38 degrees. A fissure has appeared along
the outermost ice dune. In the space of a few minutes, a flock of eight
redheads, two pairs of goldeneyes, and six male common mergansers fly
by going north. Four Canada geese sit out on the lake. The first sign of
waterfowl migration?"

But then winter reasserted itself:

"February 25. 1:00 P.M. 22 degrees. Lake appears icy out to horizon."

"February 27. 9:30 A.M. 31 degrees. Freezing rain. Lake solid white
with ice and snow as far as I can see. Ice on trees."

"March 5. 8:00 A.M. 30 degrees. Raw morning. SE wind, light snow
falling. Lake mostly frozen. No ducks or gulls."

I was gone overseas the next three weeks, and when I returned on

March 25 I could see that spring finally had gotten the upper hand. Only a slight shelf of ice remained along the shore. Red maples were blooming. Two boats were trolling for salmon offshore. Back in the countryside, ring-billed gulls were feeding in plowed fields, male red-winged blackbirds were proclaiming their territories in field and marsh, and robins were everywhere. On March 26 I saw a freighter going down the lake, one of the first ships through the locks at Sault Ste. Marie, which had opened the day before.

Ships were starting to go south, but what drew my attention now was waterfowl going north. The show at the cottage was mostly mergansers. Some common mergansers had been around all winter when the water was open, but now many more appeared. With them came dozens—sometimes hundreds—of red-breasted mergansers, a more slender bird with rakish feathers flying off the back of its head, like hair that won't lie down. The males wore handsome, multi-colored plumages, with a dark green head, white collar, reddish-brown chest, and black and white wings. Most any spring morning I would see some diving in the surf, and often they congregated off the mouth of Liens Creek, down the shore, perhaps feeding on the smelt run, or what remained of it these days. The mergansers, like many of the spring migrants, didn't just move steadily north. I would see flocks going both north and south. Perhaps some were truly migrating and others were just looking for a good feeding spot as they lingered momentarily along this stretch of shore.

I found a more representative sample of the waterfowl moving north at Port Sanilac's sewage ponds, a mile west of the lake. The first pond here, no longer in use, has partly grown up in cattails. Peering over the rim of this pond the overcast morning of March 28, I saw ring-necked ducks, hooded mergansers, mallards, wigeons, a pair of Canada geese, and a bufflehead. The two open ponds held greater scaup, ring-necked ducks, and mallards. On a bank 130 Canada geese and five tundra swans were sunning themselves.

Such waterfowl diversity and numbers were present in spades on Saginaw Bay, the greatest concentration point on Lake Huron. In early April, among the many ducks, thousands of Canada geese rested along the south shore of the bay, from Quanicassee and Fish Point state wildlife areas to Wildfowl Bay. Flocks came and went from the fields inland, where they feed during the day or night. As the sun dropped on April 1, I drove out the Filion Road access to the shore of Wildfowl Bay, site of the snowmobile races two months earlier. It was much quieter now, except for the intermittent sounds of goose music. As far as I could

Migrating tundra swans pause at Saginaw Bay. (Credit: Myles Willard)

see down the shore southward, Canadas covered the water. Suddenly, startled by something, they all took off and flew farther out into the bay, their honking now becoming one concentrated din. Such abundance and exuberance were reassuring—samples of the former wildfowl multitudes of our continent remained.

In early April hundreds of tundra swans still lingered along Saginaw Bay, but their numbers had diminished from the thousands I would have seen in mid-March. These elegant birds were on their way from wintering grounds on the mid-Atlantic coast to nesting grounds on the Arctic coasts of northwest Canada and Alaska. Major stopover points for both swans and Canada geese include western Lake Erie, Lake St. Clair, Saginaw Bay, and the Shiawassee National Wildlife Refuge on the nearby Saginaw River.

To this list may be added a small but equally exciting concentration point—Thedford Bog, just inland from the southeastern shore of Lake

Huron near Ontario's Pinery Provincial Park. This former wetland is now mostly farmland, but so strong are swan traditions that these birds still stop there—up to 10,000 of them—feeding in the fields on leftover corn from the previous year. One farmer deliberately lets his land flood in spring to benefit the swans. As on Saginaw Bay, they are at their peak in mid-March.

Most people along the route of the swans are probably unaware of their passing, but if you know their call you can sometimes recognize their presence, even over cities. I have several times heard their high-pitched tooting at night above Washington, D.C., and one April night I heard a flock going over our cottage. Anywhere along the way the birds may descend to a likely looking field to refuel. Mike Hanson has seen fields near his house white with them. They feed on winter wheat and leftover corn, he says.

Someday the tundra swans may once again be accompanied by their even larger cousins, trumpeter swans, which once bred from northern Alaska to Indiana but with the settlement of our continent approached extinction. Under strict protection, they have recovered somewhat but are now restricted mainly to several areas in the West. Efforts are underway to reestablish breeding in several refuges farther east, including the Great Lakes region. One such place is the Wye Marsh Wildlife Centre near the southeastern corner of Georgian Bay. This privately operated sanctuary, once the domain of a hunt club, is breeding captive trumpeters and letting some of the offspring go free.

One problem sometimes encountered in the restoration work elsewhere, such as at Turnbull National Wildlife Refuge near Spokane, Washington, is that the swans reproduce but don't migrate in winter. If there's no open water then, as at Turnbull, they can't survive. Some of the captive-reared trumpeters at Wye Marsh have migrated to open water near Burlington, Ontario and returned the following spring. The others have been helped through the winter with supplemental feed. Introduced trumpeter swans at Seney National Wildlife Refuge, in the Upper Peninsula of Michigan, have reproduced well and migrate to nearby open water in winter.

The trumpeter swan's former winter range included the mid-Atlantic coast. With continued restoration efforts and good luck the birds may once again make this journey with the tundra swans and become a regular sight in the magnificent spring and fall flights.

Some of the waterfowl that travel the farthest to their nesting grounds bring up the rear of the spring migration, at least along the Thumb. Mike

Hanson is out on the lake in his patrol boat throughout the fishing season, which may begin in March after a mild winter, so he gets a good look at the waterfowl. He says that oldsquaws, beautiful black and white, long-tailed sea ducks, don't appear until late April and early May. I was with him on May 5 and sure enough, two or three miles offshore we encountered rafts of these ducks totaling two or three thousand. He said that scoters (chunky sea ducks that, like oldsquaws, winter mainly in salt water, although some winter on the Great Lakes) come through a little later in May.

The white-winged scoters—the only common scoter on the Great Lakes—are headed for western Canada and Alaska, the oldsquaws even farther—to ponds in the Arctic tundra atop the continent. The oldsquaw's lateness makes sense. Those ponds don't thaw out until May or June. The white-winged scoter, though usually not traveling as far as the oldsquaw, is nevertheless North America's latest nesting duck.

All through April and May, Bonaparte's gulls, loons, and cormorants moved up the lake along with the waterfowl. The small Bonaparte's gulls, with white fore-edges on their wings flashing, flew in small groups, strung out single file low over the water when they faced a serious headwind. The black cormorants, sometimes in flocks of fifty or more, did the same. The loons, more individualistic perhaps, came usually in ones and twos, close in, far out, high or low, their long necks arrowing ahead and long legs trailing behind.

People have very different feelings about these birds. Only the bird-watchers and observant fishermen, I suppose, are even aware that Bonaparte's gulls exist. They are not aggressive scavengers like the larger gulls and are enjoyed for their lightness on the wing. Loons, the very symbols of wilderness, are much loved for their strange calls and interesting ways. Concerned people in many states and provinces are monitoring their nesting success as summer cottages and boaters spread ever more extensively onto the loons' northern lakes. Cormorants, knocked down by persistent pesticides in the 1940s and 1950s, have rebounded amazingly and now nest by the thousands around the Great Lakes. Fish-eaters, they have become the scapegoat in many minds for the decline of yellow perch. We'll look into this question in chapter thirteen ("Colonial Waterbirds").

While the waterfowl are moving north over the water, some of the landbirds are paralleling their flight at the edge of the water. Many of these are hawks, eagles, and vultures, pushed to the shore from their inland routes by wind. The migrations of these birds, known collectively (along with owls) as raptors, can be quite spectacular where weather and geography collaborate to concentrate them. Spring raptor flights, like those of many other birds, are heaviest on south winds ahead of warm fronts. Not liking to fly over water, whose coolness does not produce rising thermals of air that assist their flight, most raptors stay over land. If the land gives out and a broad expanse of water confronts them, such as at the tip of the Thumb, the birds bunch up and then follow the shoreline east or west until they once again find a northward passage over land.

In the Thumb, a westerly component to the wind pushes raptors to the shore, which they follow southward to Port Huron and then northward up the Ontario shore or, more frequently, they fly northward to the tip of the Thumb. At the cottage I saw a few hawks and vultures progressing overhead, but the exciting place to be was Port Crescent State Park, up at the tip. Here, near the dunes alongshore, in an open area that affords a wide view of the sky, one can watch hawks coming low over the forest that borders the Pinnebog River or circling high above in thermals.

On March 26 I found Monica Essenmacher, Myles Willard, and others building an observation platform for hawk-watchers on a low dune. Monica, who owns a cottage nearby and founded the Huron Audubon Club, organized hawk counts here and the annual Hawk Fest, when visitors can see and learn about hawks. Later, I asked her about all this. "People have noticed the spring hawk flights here for decades," she said. "An old man told me that as a boy he watched men shooting hawks along the shore right in Port Austin." But only in the last few years has the magnitude of the hawk flight been recognized and measured. Myles Willard and Ron Weeks, experienced birders from the area, saw large numbers of hawks migrating along the Saginaw Bay shore in the spring of 1989 and alerted other birders. Among them was Monica.

"In 1990, at Eastertime, I sat down on a dune," she said, "and had about a thousand broadwings come over that day." That inspired her to begin making regular counts the next year, and with the help of others she continued them each spring. Each succeeding year, for several years, the hawk-counters put in more hours, producing a generally upward-trending total count. The peak year so far was 1994, when 10,573 hawks were recorded. How many were not seen can only be guessed. The numbers seen per hour compare favorably with those recorded at Whitefish Point on Lake Superior, a better known, better studied location, one of several other spots around the Great Lakes where hawks are counted in spring or fall.

The hawk spectacle is ever-changing through the spring. "March is slow," Monica said, "and April is hot. The earliest birds are rough-legged, red-tailed, and adult red-shouldered hawks, sometimes a golden eagle. Often these hawks are a mile inland, over farm country, where the air is warmer than over the cold lake. In April it just keeps getting better, with lots of sharp-shinned hawks appearing. In mid-April we usually hit our first 1,000-plus day, if a big broad-winged hawk flight comes through." Things quiet down some in May, but "usually about the end of May you get a flight of broad-winged and red-shouldered immatures." By early June it's over, with a few turkey vultures, sharp-shins, broadwings, red-tails, and maybe a bald eagle or two straggling through at the last.

Altogether, fifteen species of raptors are seen nearly every year, the scarcest being peregrine falcons, golden eagles, and goshawks. Once in a long while a real rarity appears. On May 1, 1992, Monica was watching alone when a large buteo came over the distant trees, flying low. "It came right overhead," she said, "almost hovered, and gave me a good chance to see all its field marks." It was a ferruginous hawk, a pale western species seldom seen in Michigan. Two springs later, down the shore near Bay Port, Myles and Marilyn Willard saw a Swainson's hawk, another western species. Birders began hoping for southern rarities, such as a black vulture or Mississippi kite. Some said it is just a matter of time until these, too, are spotted.

The weather has a big effect on hawk flights. "If you have a good strong front pushing in from the southwest, with a strong, steady southwest wind—that's the best," said Monica. "East and north winds are both bad. And rain effectively stops the flight. So does snow."

Five times in April I tried to pick a favorable day and went up to see what was happening. I spent my days at Port Crescent State Park with Tom Heatley, who was banding hawks here throughout the month. Tom is a retired high-school science teacher from Macomb County, in southeastern Michigan. A very sharp birder, he is the first person to see at least 50 percent of all the bird species recorded in each of the forty-nine continental states. Raptors are a special love of his.

"I think the banding started back in 1972," he said, "when Sergei Postupalsky [then at the University of Michigan] asked me if I'd like to go up to northern Michigan and help band eagles. When we finished the eagle season I got to help him with ospreys at various floodings." That fall Tom got his own banding permit from the U.S. Fish and Wildlife Service. For several years he banded migrating hawks, owls, and other birds at Whitefish Point on Lake Superior. In 1994, when "I knew I was going to retire, I looked for another place where I could set up a raptor banding station." Monica sent him her data showing the peak migration time and he set up his station at Port Cresent State Park. The first year was successful, so he returned in 1995.

Tom's station was situated at the edge of a clump of young jack pines. His wooden blind looked out on a small open space enclosed by three lines of mist nets. Within this space, when I first arrived, sat a very unhappy-looking starling—the lure bird—wearing a leather vest attached to a long string. If Tom saw a hawk approaching, he explained, he would jump into the blind and pull the string, making the starling flop around and look injured. If the hawk saw it and was interested, it would dive at the bird and, if the angle was low enough, hit one of the nets and become entangled. Then Tom would jump out, remove the hawk from the net, band it, record its species, sex, and age, and then release it.

On this and subsequent visits, I saw a nice variety of raptors flying over, and a few captures. The sharp-shins and Cooper's hawks—long-tailed bird-hunting accipiters—usually came low over the forest beyond the river, but sometimes they soared higher against the clouds. The buteos—hawks with broad wings and tails—red-tails, broadwings, rough-legs, and red-shouldered hawks—usually began appearing in midmorning, when the sun had started the thermals of rising air they like to ride. They would circle ever higher and then glide on to the southwest, where they would seek another thermal and repeat the process. Once in awhile, they were joined up there by a bald or golden eagle, majestic in its imposing size. The small falcons—kestrels and merlins—usually flew so low that you had to be very alert to spot them coming. The rare peregrines, Tom said, tend to travel right along the shore of the lake. Strong fliers, they and the merlins are the only ones that regularly cross large bodies of water. Ospreys, large fish-eating raptors, often appeared; sometimes one would land in a dead tree along the Pinnebog, as if considering a meal before it continued on its way. And always there were turkey vultures, circling lazily on their tilted black wings.

Banding hawks and other birds contributes to knowledge about their age and where they go. When a banded bird is caught or found dead, it can be identified by the number on its band and information about it can be obtained from the U.S. Fish and Wildlife Service, which keeps the records. Tom had caught several banded hawks here himself. One had been banded the previous fall at Hawk Cliff, on the Ontario shore of Lake Erie. Another—a Cooper's hawk—had been banded only two days before, near the Lake Huron shore north of Port Huron.

Besides the contribution to science, there's pure excitement in it. "You see a hawk going across," Tom said, "and all of a sudden you see it turn when it sees that lure bird. You see it come down near the ground, level off, the wings go back, the feet come out, and bang!, you've got 'im." I understood how he felt one slow afternoon when I was standing outside the net watching the far tree line. "Freeze!" Tom yelled, and I froze. A sharp-shin came tearing in low over the ground and hit the net. I jumped to wrap more net around it, and Tom extracted it. According to the manual, it was a female past its first year but not yet fully adult. It had the brownish-red barring of an adult on the breast but not brownish feathers on the rump. After banding it, Tom handed the bird to me to release. As I held it by the legs, the hawk's reddish eyes turned up to look at me, fiercely. I tossed her up toward the pines and she flew away eastward, circling higher, maybe to see what the heck had happened to her.

The starling huddled on the ground, no doubt glad the hawk was gone. It didn't need to worry. The net would stop most attackers, and those that came in over or under the net would be scared off by Tom, who hoped they would hit the net on the way out. The starling would soon get a rest, food, and water in its cage with the other starlings, next to the cage with pigeons, used to lure larger hawks like red-tails.

The Hawk Fest, held the last Saturday in April, was a roaring success. Under blue skies, seventy-five or more people gathered to dedicate the new hawk-watching platform, hear talks about raptors, see the hawk-banding operation, and watch hawks sailing overhead. And see them we did—more than 400! Among the many sharp-shins and red-tails were a few harriers, a late rough-leg, a goshawk, two or three bald eagles, and a golden eagle. This last bird, king of the world's raptors in the estimation of many, made the day for me. Though not really rare, it was the first I had ever seen in Michigan, in many years of birding.

Hours of watching hawks at the state park also gave me a wonderful window on other spring migrants at this bit of Lake Huron shore. Ducks came and went from the Pinnebog River, which flowed out into the lake through high dunes. Once Tom pointed out a rare Eurasian wigeon in a flock of American wigeons, its red head obvious among the greenish heads of the Americans. Another day three huge tundra swans landed briefly on the river, then flew out westward past us. Tree swallows, which would nest here in boxes put out for them, were constantly in sight, swooping after insects. Overhead, the passage of sandhill cranes, announced by their throaty "karruck!" sometimes enlivened our watchful waiting. Or a loon came over, heading straight across the mouth of Saginaw Bay. Or a big V of Canada geese passed, likewise continuing north. A reminder of winter twice appeared in the form of a glaucous gull flying along the dunes, its whiteness arresting among the greyer wings of the herring gulls.

Hawks apparently think some water bodies are crossable and others not. At the top of lower Michigan, where the Straits of Mackinac produce a four-mile water gap, hawks make the leap. I ran into some people in May who had in one day seen around 2,000, mostly broadwings, crossing over. At Tobermory, a town at the tip of the Bruce Peninsula, hawks cross the fifteen-mile opening of Georgian Bay, perhaps emboldened by the presence of islands along the way. But the crossing of Saginaw Bay from Port Crescent State Park is some twenty-five miles, here an island-less gap too intimidating for most hawks. Where they go from here is still a mystery. They seem to head southwestward and disappear, presumably to head northward again at the west end of Saginaw Bay.

While the hawks are migrating by day, most of the smaller landbirds are traveling at night, guided by landforms such as rivers and coasts, the position of stars, the earth's magnetic field, and perhaps other means. When the sky begins to lighten, they drop down into likely looking feeding areas to refuel for the next night flight. If the winds are strong, these little migrants—warblers, thrushes, flycatchers, and others—may find themselves over the water at dawn, in which case they head for the nearest shore. This phenomenon makes for good birdwatching along many shorelines of the Great Lakes, depending on the wind direction and strength. In the Thumb, strong west winds can bring this result. At the cottage our yard is often crawling with birds, both spring and fall.

If the wind has been very strong, or if fog confuses them, small birds may find themselves too far out over the lake and, wearied by their long flight, fall exhausted into the water. The shore is sometimes littered with their bodies. But if they're lucky, they find a boat to land on. Any size boat will do. Mike Hanson, out on the lake in his small patrol boat on a foggy morning, has often been visited by little migrants. They are too tired to be afraid of humans. "One warbler," he said, "crawled up on my shoulder and went to sleep."

I saw this phenomenon myself on the *Grayling,* a research boat heading out to Six Fathom Bank in the middle of Lake Huron to conduct lake trout surveys. We had fog on the way out and by the end of the four-and-a-half-hour trip had collected two savannah sparrows, two kinds of warblers—a northern waterthrush and a black-throated green warbler—and a tiny ruby-crowned kinglet. These birds stayed with us a long time, hopping around the fishing gear at the stern getting midges and spiders, or just riding atop the pilot house. When the fog cleared we were out of sight of land, which I suppose was a further inducement for them to stay put.

Our skipper, Cliff Wilson, told me about larger birds landing on the boat on various trips—turkey vultures, a great horned owl, and two kestrels (small falcons). "The owl perched on the railing in front of the pilot house, hunched over facing the wind. The kestrels came on board another time in the fog near Goderich [on the Canadian shore]. One of them huddled under some gear on top of the pilot house and the other sat right out on the bow. They rode all the way across to Alpena [Michigan] and then flew off."

Birds out over the lake have more to contend with than weather, I discovered. Our small riders occasionally took a short flight away from the boat and then came back. If they went out very far the herring gulls that always followed us chased them. One of our savannah sparrows went too far. In one swoop a gull forced it down into the water, snatched it up in its beak without landing, and swallowed it whole like a small piece of bread.

I knew herring gulls were predatory and once had seen one attempt to catch a duckling, but I didn't know they would go after large prey until a great egret came flying by. This large white heron apparently had overshot its normal nesting range and was wandering farther north up the middle of the lake. Unaware of the danger, it flew right over the 200 herring gulls resting on the water. Many of them gave chase, trying to force it down into the water. Each time they nearly succeeded, the egret stabbed upward with its long yellow bill, momentarily backing them off. Through binoculars I watched this fearsome drama until I lost the birds about two miles away. Ten gulls were still pursuing, and I had no doubt they would win if they kept it up much longer.

For many birders, myself included, warblers are the stars of the spring migration. These brightly colored mites sometimes appear in great numbers and amazing variety. It is possible to find a dozen species feeding in a single tree. May is their month. I started a trip northward, expecting to find a lot of warblers at various points along the shore. But Tobico Marsh, at the head of Saginaw Bay, was quiet. I was sure Tawas Point, a southward projecting peninsula on the north side of the bay's mouth, would be better. Birds flying across the bay often drop down onto the first land they see—the point—and the trees and shrubs there can be alive with warblers and other small birds soon after dawn. Unfortunately, it rained the night I stayed there, which discouraged bird flight, and in the morning intermittent rain and a cold northeast wind added to the poor conditions. I didn't see much. Farther north the warblers were still few and far between.

My ultimate destination was Manitoulin Island. One of the reasons: the numbers of warblers and other small migrants are often spectacular at the ends of the island and on Great Duck Island to the south of it. All of these places were planned destinations of the Sudbury Ornithological Society, which I was going to accompany. Things didn't work out quite as planned, but they did indeed work out.

I arrived in mid-May and checked in at the Janet Head campground, at the mouth of Gore Bay. The only camper, I picked a site facing the North Channel and set up my small blue tent. Just a few weeks earlier, the North Channel had been frozen, but now it echoed the muted calls of gulls and the eerie wail of loons. Snaky-necked cormorants flew back and forth, and mergansers dove along the shore. Many of these birds would no doubt be nesting nearby, the herring and ring-billed gulls and cormorants on islets in the North Channel, loons on some of Manitoulin's many inland lakes, and the mergansers along shorelines of any of these waters. I reflected that I might have seen some of these very same birds winging past our cottage in April.

When I met Doreen Bailey to go birding a couple of days later, I asked her if she had found her fifty species of birds in January and beaten Terry Land. She couldn't remember. Now she was hell-bent to get 200 species on the island this year. She was up to 175. I tried mightily to help her add to the list that day, but the birding was slow and I thought we would be unsuccessful. Then, in late afternoon, came one of the birding highlights of my life. We were driving slowly down a rural lane near her farm when we spotted a hawk-like bird ahead, circling directly over the road. It seemed a little odd—didn't look quite like any hawk I knew. After being blocked momentarily by a school bus and me fretting that the bird would get away, we saw it right above us. I jumped out and yelled at Doreen—"Get out here and look at this bird!" It was a Mississippi kite, pearl gray with a whitish head, circling and gliding on its long wings and tail and now and then suddenly diving to catch an insect in the air. A bird of the South, it wasn't supposed to be north of southern Illinois but for reasons known only to itself had kept on going. Doreen Bailey and Napier Shelton were ecstatic to have been at the right place at the right time and to have seen the first Mississippi kite ever recorded on Manitoulin Island. Species number 176 for Doreen!

The next day I joined the Sudbury group at South Baymouth, where the ferry leaves for Tobermory on the Bruce Peninsula and where migrant birds often land in great numbers after making the trip in the opposite direction. Chris Bell, leader of the group, explained that "on clear nights the birds tend to overfly the island, but fog and other bad weather puts them down here." We had had a relatively clear night and saw only a sprinkling of warblers among the houses of South Baymouth. We stopped at other places along the south shore and next morning worked the pines at the Mississagi Lighthouse, on the western tip. Still no big influx of birds.

Ah, but surely Great Duck Island would produce. The island constantly appears in the species accounts in John Nicholson's *The Birds of Manitoulin Island.* On various individual May days of the past, observers had seen (alive, or dead at the foot of a microwave tower) 269 wood thrushes, fifty-six red-eyed vireos, 1,500 Tennessee warblers, 500 Nashville warblers, 1,500 bay-breasted warblers, 200 common yellow-throats, 330 Baltimore orioles, plus unusual western strays such as the scissor-tailed flycatcher, Say's phoebe, and sage thrasher. Alas, George Purvis decided he couldn't take the group out this year. A liability case against a commercial fisherman in southern Lake Huron had convinced George's lawyer that George shouldn't do it, because of the possibility of an accident.

One strategy remained for finding big bunches of warblers—look for them along the north shore of Manitoulin, where they would tend to congregate if they fed northward across the island. So I checked Indian Point, where a thin neck of land leads to a bridge across the North Channel's entrance to Lake Wolsey. As early morning light struck the south side of the point, I walked along its shore. Thousands of midges were dancing in the sun among the trees and bushes, and warblers—many of them—were snatching the insects up. In my short walk I saw eleven species of these feathered jewels, flitting about at point-blank range.

Evening sunlight provided the best show of all. One day as the sun dropped toward the hills beyond the North Channel, I drove out the East Bluff Road flanking Gore Bay. Four hundred feet above the water, I looked down on tiny boats and far across to my campground at Janet Head. Approaching the headland, I saw small birds and stopped. Again, midges were swarming around every white cedar, and warblers were frantically pursuing them, stoking up for the night flight into the immensity of Canada.

Usually, it seems, warblers feed back in the foliage where all you get are tantalizing glimpses of a yellowish head here or white tail spots there. But these birds were feeding at the tips of branches on the dense cedars, in the full glow of low-angle sunlight. Each bird seemed to be a different species, and each more beautiful than the last. I focused on a black-throated green warbler, with its jet-black throat and bright yellow face; then a bay-breasted warbler, with creamy buff behind a black mask, and chestnut crown and sides; next a tiger-patterned Cape May warbler, its heavy black stripes below accentuating a chestnut cheek framed with yellow, followed by a blackburnian warbler, its fiery orange throat burning against the dark green of the cedars. And many others.

It all seemed a gift, here at land's end on an island in the northern extremity of Lake Huron—a God-sent conclusion to the search for migrant birds coming up the great lake.

CHAPTER 7

# THE BASE OF THE PYRAMID

While life on and around the lake was awakening and moving, so too was life within the lake, as the water warmed and the higher sun shot its rays farther below the surface. All of us around the lake were aware of the fish and bird activity, but few of us gave a thought to the minute, to us invisible, life in the water that sustains all the rest—the drifting plankton and the organisms that dwell on the bottom of the lake.

All these were experiencing the spring acceleration of life, beginning with the multiplication of phytoplankton—tiny or microscopic plant life composed of single-celled or colonial algae, bacteria, and fungi. The algae and some of the bacteria were using carbon dioxide, water, and the sun's energy to produce carbohydrates, and also were absorbing nutrients from the water. They are the primary "producers" that directly or indirectly support all the other life in the lake. The other bacteria and the fungi were absorbing nutrients from other organisms and decomposing dead organisms into their constituent elements, which were thus returned to the watery environment.

In Lake Huron, as in the other Great Lakes and the ocean, the dominant type of phytoplankton is diatoms, golden-brown, microscopic algae of great beauty and all sorts of configurations, many being round, oblong, pencil-shaped, or rectangular. Collections in 1971 and 1974, using fine-meshed plankton nets, showed that diatoms constituted 50 to 95 percent of the phytoplankton biomass (dry weight) at most of the collecting stations in Lake Huron, including Georgian Bay and the North Channel. Life in the lake thus is built mostly on diatoms, because much of the zooplankton (minute animals) feeds on diatoms, small fish feed on zooplankton, and large fish on the smaller ones. As one botany textbook puts it: "As all flesh is grass, so all fish are diatoms."

The one area of Lake Huron where diatoms were not the dominant group of phytoplankton was Saginaw Bay. Here, blue-green algae were prevalent. The blue-greens require large amounts of nitrogen, an element that is (too) abundantly supplied to Saginaw Bay through run-off from farms and deposition of nitrogen oxides from polluted urban air.

Drifting around among the phytoplankton, smaller numbers of zooplankton feed on the diatoms, other algae and bacteria, and on each other. The smallest are the one-celled protozoans, which "graze" on (or, more accurately, filter) the phytoplankton. More numerous and larger, multi-celled crustaceans feed on the protozoa, as well as on phytoplankton. Predominant among these are copepods, tiny shrimplike creatures some of which move around by beating their legs. In a 1988 study, copepods were found to constitute three-fourths of the zooplankton biomass in Lake Huron. Nematodes, threadlike worms, are also extremely abundant, but their abundance is hard to measure because many are so tiny they pass through the mesh of plankton nets.

When they hatch, larval fish also become part of the drifting plankton—they can move but not strongly enough to counteract the power of water currents and turbulence. Many other members of the plankton can also move, using hairlike cilia, whiplike flagella, or tiny legs, but they, too, are not strong enough to go wherever they choose. Gravity tends to pull plankton downward, especially in fresh water, which is less dense than sea water, but the plankton are usually saved from this fate by certain features of their anatomy and environment.

One adaptation is reduced weight. Diatoms have very delicate shells. Planktonic crustaceans have outer coatings much thinner and lighter than larger, bottom-dwelling crustaceans such as crayfish. Many diatoms, rotifers (minute animals with a wheellike ring of cilia at the front end), and protozoa carry lighter-than-water oil droplets as food reserves. Some algae make gas bubbles that are contained within the plant. Many kinds of plankton have a large surface in relation to body volume. This increases friction and slows descent. Irregular shapes, like ridges and spines, have the same effect. Some diatoms, and desmids (green algae), have sticklike elongations on their bodies that, when held horizontally, slow their descent. And some copepods have antennae they

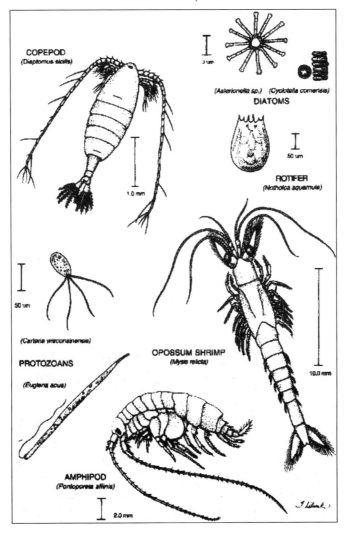

Some of the planktonic inhabitants of Lake Huron.
(Credit: Taina Litwak)

can use like a parachute. Still, all these aids to buoyancy would not ultimately win the battle against gravity were it not for turbulence of the water. Storms, currents, sinking of cold water and the consequent upwelling of warmer, lighter water stir and move the plankton, most frequently upward.

Under favorable conditions, many kinds of plankton actually make vertical migrations, using their various means of locomotion, upward at night and downward when dawn comes. Scientists still debate the reasons, but light is generally considered the main factor. Certain light conditions are most favorable for photosynthesis by the chlorophyll-bearing phytoplankton, and some zooplankton presumably follow them for food.

These vertical migrations are usually no more than ten to twenty meters, but one organism, the opossum shrimp, *Mysis relicta,* makes longer and more regular journeys, following the same daily pattern. This little crustacean is found in cool depths of the Great Lakes and other deep lakes of northern North America and northern Eurasia. Studies of the opossum shrimp in Lake Huron found it most abundant at depths from 125 to 200 meters, where it feeds on detritus, phytoplankton, zooplankton, and a bottom-dwelling amphipod crustacean, *Pontoporeia affinis.* (*Pontoporeia* reaches a length of one-third of an inch, but the one-half to one-inch-long *Mysis* can consume it.) Its abundance and traveling habit make the opossum shrimp an important link between bottom-dwelling and planktonic elements of the lake ecosystem, and also an important food for fish.

Life on the bottom of Lake Huron consists in large part of the amphipod *Pontoporeia,* with segmented worms, fingernail clams, and midge larvae accounting for most of the rest. In one study, the benthic organisms averaged around 1,200 per square meter, with a maximum of 10,556. In water less than twenty-five meters deep, *Pontoporeia* and midge larvae were the most abundant organisms. Where such water is polluted, as it has been in the inner part of Saginaw Bay, tubifex worms and midge larvae, both pollution tolerant, are especially prevalent. The invading zebra mussel has become a major member of the bottom fauna in shallow water during the 1990s, and the quagga mussel, which can live in deeper water, is expected to invade the upper Great Lakes as well.

One of the most interesting and ecologically important bottom-dwellers in shallow water is the nymph of the burrowing mayfly, also known as fishfly and sandfly. There are many species of mayflies around Lake Huron, but this one, *Hexagenia limbata,* is especially abundant in nearshore waters less than about sixty feet deep. The nymph excavates a U-shaped burrow in muddy bottom and lives there about a year, molting as many as thirty times as it grows, eating plant food. In some places there are up to 500 burrows per square foot. These "wigglers" are highly prized as bait by ice fishermen and collectors can command a good price for them.

Growth of the nymph halts in winter but resumes when the water rises above fifty degrees. During the summer, with a peak in July, the nymphs rise to the surface in the evening and transform into the winged "sub-imago," a delicate-looking insect with net-veined wings and a long forked tail. In some areas the numbers can be so great that snowplows have to be called out to remove the masses of mayflies from highways. They are also attracted to lights at night. Lake St. Clair and the St. Clair River have especially good habitats for the mayfly nymph, and residents along these shores witness an annual invasion. A restaurant hostess in New Baltimore, on Lake St. Clair, complained, "We get it so bad in our parking lot. The smell is unbelievable."

One to three days after emergence, the sub-imago molts to its final adult, imago stage, with transparent wings and fully developed reproductive parts. In the evening the males swarm in the air, rising up and down, making a rustling sound like wind in the leaves. The females fly through the swarm, are seized by males, and the pairs slowly sink through the swarm. After mating the females fly to the surface of water and deposit yellow packets containing up to three or four thousand eggs. These sink and are dispersed along the bottom. In about two weeks the eggs hatch and the little nymphs start burrowing. The female insects die after laying their eggs and the males, having landed on vegetation, also die.

The swarms along shorelines may be a nuisance to people but they are indicative of a healthy aquatic environment. Pollution in western Lake Erie and Saginaw Bay virtually exterminated the mayflies there in recent decades. Although they have now returned to Lake Erie, Saginaw Bay still was largely barren of mayflies in the mid-1990s. They became scarce at Port Sanilac, too, but in a recent summer I saw clusters around the lights at the Exchange State Bank, and two mayflies somehow made their way into our cottage. Maybe they are coming back around the Thumb, too.

This is a good sign. The fish will be happy, because they devour the mayfly at every stage of its existence—as nymphs on the bottom, as the sub-imagos emerge from the water, and as the dying female deposits her eggs on the surface. Near shore, the mayfly is thus a leading citizen in the natural economy of the lake.

Although the nutrient levels and numbers of plankton and bottom organisms in cold, deep Lake Huron are low compared with those in warm, shallow lakes, they are nevertheless high enough to sustain large populations of fish. Those small organisms form the base of the lake's pyramid of life. For each pound of fish there must be ten to 100 pounds of plankton and invertebrates.

After I researched all this I saw the lake in a new way. I saw not just blue or green or purple waves, but in my mind's eye a lake floor crawling with life and water dancing with all sorts of wonderful little creatures. Let us praise small things.

# CHAPTER 8

# Fishing for a Living

S pring on the lake has its human as well as natural signs. People begin putting their boats in the water and some go out fishing. The harbor at Port Sanilac normally doesn't lose its ice until April, but this year the ice went earlier. In spite of a north wind and forty-degree temperature, two boats were offshore trolling on the afternoon of March 25. By March 27, the *Miss Port Sanilac*—a doughty, former perch-fishing boat—and one sailboat lay at their slips in the harbor. As April progressed, more and more boats were taken out of drydock, and increasing numbers of people went out fishing, especially on late April weekends, when salmon/trout tournaments began.

The increasing warmth was triggering changes in the water as well. During the winter, the coldest water is at the surface, with the densest water, a few degrees warmer, just below. Now the surface water was warming to maximum density and sinking, starting mixing. Convection currents would add to this mixing, producing the "spring turnover." Eventually a new equilibrium would be reached, with summer temperatures in the upper layers ranging from ten to fifteen degrees centigrade, with the highest temperatures near shore, and decreasing to four degrees below about 150 feet.

Heat drives the engine of life. As temperature rises, biological processes speed up, and growth begins, or increases. The phytoplankton multiplies to a spring peak of biomass in May and June that may be four times what it was in winter. Zooplankton feeds on the plant plankton and multiplies. In early summer many insect larvae overwintering in the bottom sediments will metamorphose into adults and leave the lake. The emergence of mayflies from the water is perhaps the most dramatic and noticeable example, but midges, swarming and dancing in the air around all shorelines, are even more abundant. (Recent research indicates that northward migrating warblers at the North Channel are almost entirely dependent on the newly hatched midges for food.) The larger caddisflies and stoneflies also appear and reproduce.

In spring fish become more active. During April, suckers, smelt, and trout run up streams to spawn. People dip the smelt (though with much less success than formerly), spear the suckers. Mike Hanson is out on the Sanilac County streams at night, making sure people don't spear the trout as well.

All around Lake Huron these things are happening. Many people are fishing for sport, but some are fishing for a living. Of course, Milford Purdy down at the south end has been fishing for much of the winter, and a few commercial fishermen have set gill nets under the ice, but most of them must wait until the melting of ice frees harbors.

One of these is Forrest Williams, who with his brother and a friend owns the Bay Port Fish Company, on Saginaw Bay. Early in April I had seen one of their boats going out on their first fishing day of the company's 100th year, dodging the few remaining ice floes in Wildfowl Bay. Early in the morning on April 21 I returned to go out myself, weather permitting—they never know until the last minute. This morning a light rain was falling, blown by a southeast wind. Dozens of people lined the banks of channels leading into the lake, catching perch that had moved into the warmer shore water to spawn. An hour later, Forrest gave the go-ahead, and I stepped aboard the *Patsy,* a forty-foot trapnetter captained by barrel-shaped Denny Root, one of the company's owners. The rear three-quarters of the boat was low and open, giving room to handle the net and fish. At the bow was a small pilot house, into which squeezed Denny, myself, St. Clair (Bill) Young—a short, middle-aged man with a dark, curly mustache—and a young fellow who sat in a corner and tried to catch a few more minutes of sleep.

As we chugged out across Wildfowl Bay in rain and fog, Denny set our course by Loran and plotter. We were headed for the north side of Sand Point, a long finger of land that protects Wildfowl Bay from northerly blows. I never saw the point as we passed it, but the waves grew bigger and choppier, and we began to roll.

84

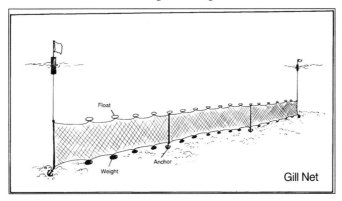

Gill nets and trap nets are the principal types of nets used by commercial fishermen on Lake Huron. Pound nets and seine nets (not shown) were frequently used in the past. (Credit: Taina Litwak)

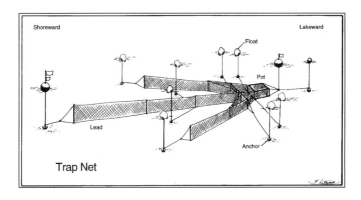

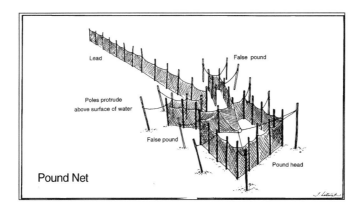

Soon a buoy topped by a red and white flag appeared out of the mist. We stopped beside a nearby float and Bill pulled in the line to which the float and an anchor were attached. Denny started a motor, the arm supporting the winch swung out over the side, and rope began winding up on the winch. In a minute or two a large, box-shaped contraption about ten feet long on a side broke the water and hung at the side of the boat. Framed with stout sticks, its sides were net. At the bottom of this "pot" squirmed a mass of fish.

The pot—the trap end of the net—had been resting on the bottom in seventy feet of water for four days. Fish had been guided into it by the "lead"—a net set perpendicular to the shore that directed them between two "wings" that then funneled the fish into an opening in the pot through which they couldn't escape. The fish didn't get caught in the guide nets because they were fine meshed and the fish could see them.

Denny untied an opening in the side of the pot and began scooping up fish with a long-handled net and dumping them in a box on the deck. The other two men sorted the fish. Whitefish went flopping into one box, sheepsheads—a hump-backed bottom feeder—into another, "white buffalo" (quillback, or quillback carpsucker) into another. Some of the yellow perch were tossed into a box and some went into a tank of water, which would keep them alive for sale to an aquaculturist. All the channel cats—many of them five- to ten-pounders—and two burbots—another large, homely bottom feeder—were thrown into another tank, sending spray over me and the pilot house. Small carp were dropped in a box but large ones, for which there was no market at the moment, went over the side to resume their vacuuming way of life on the bottom of the bay. With them, too, went an amazing number of large walleyes, illegal for non-Native commercial fishermen because this is a major gamefish as well as popular restaurant fish (Michigan restaurants can buy walleyes from Indian fishermen). With the sheepsheads and catfish, the walleyes formed the principal part of our catch. No doubt the men saw a lot of dollars going over the side with the walleyes. We caught a few salmon and lake trout and these, too, had to be thrown back. That's the virtue of the trap net, as opposed to the gill net. It keeps fish alive, so unwanted or illegal fish can be returned healthy to the lake. It also benefits the fishermen, because if prices are low for certain species, they can be kept alive for two weeks or more in the net if prices are expected to rise. But the Bay Port Company seldom does this.

When all the fish had been scooped out and sorted, the trap and its attached lines were winched back down, the anchor going out last. Then

Forrest Williams, on board the *Patsy,* scoops fish from a trap net.

on to two more trap nets set closer to Sand Point in shallower water. These were more difficult. The wind had shifted from south to west to northeast and then back to northwest. "I haven't seen it so variable in a long time," Denny complained. We found ourselves on the upwind side of one net, pinning the boat against the trap and making it hard to lift above the side of the boat.

I felt suspense as each net rose, wondering what would be in it. These last two contained mostly the same kinds of fish as the deeper one, except they lacked whitefish, which prefers deeper water most of the year. One net yielded three long-nosed gar, a strange-looking long thin creature with a needle nose. The gars are regarded as "living fossils" because nearly all their relatives are extinct. Denny showed me one walleye with large tumors on its tail and fins. "We see a few of these," he said. "They think it's due to a virus."

87

I was interested, too, in the behavior of the herring gulls that followed us closely, waiting for the occasional dead fish that had to be thrown overboard. They ignored one small yellow perch, perhaps disliking its spiny dorsal fin. But they pounced eagerly on a silvery little fish of some sort. A gull had half swallowed this fish when another bird jumped on its back and forced it to regurgitate. Different gulls in turn tried to take possession, until one adult gull, apparently dominant in the hierarchy, took possession unopposed.

On the way in, Denny pumped oxygen into the tank of live perch. The tough catfish didn't need it. At one o'clock we pulled up to the open door at the side of the packing house and began unloading our catch. The workers inside disdainfully threw our small carp in the water. No market for even the small ones, they said. With a crane they hoisted the blue boxes of iced fish and the tanks of live catfish and perch. Immediately, with the help of our crew, Forrest and others began gutting and filleting the perch and whitefish that would be sold locally. They packed the sheepsheads and white buffalo iced, in fifty-pound boxes, to be shipped whole to markets elsewhere. The live catfish and perch went into big aerated tanks, the catfish destined for fish-farmers in Ohio, Indiana, and Illinois, the perch for one in Holland, Michigan.

"How come you can't sell catfish here in Michigan?" I asked Denny. "Well," he replied, "for some reason people in Michigan don't eat catfish much, but as soon as you cross the line into Ohio, they do." Maybe it had something to do with much of Ohio being in the Ohio-Mississippi river watershed, I thought, a southward-flowing drainage perhaps encouraging southern traditions.

Denny thought our catch was below average, though it appeared that we had two or three thousand fish. He figured they were worth about $800–$900, the catfish accounting for the majority of it. The Bay Port Company had one other trap net boat out that morning—the *Osprey*—which would perhaps double the day's income.

On many a day, the crew would go out again in the afternoon, but not today. Maybe the wind was going to be too tricky for lifting. At $5.00–$5.50 an hour, the wage workers would have thin wallets. I wondered how they could do it, getting up at 5:00 A.M. day after day, going out in all kinds of weather, handling tons of fish on a rolling deck—all for low pay. Our youthful crew member was training to become a diver for a salvage company in Port Austin, but Bill Young had been fishing for fifteen years. It looked like he would be doing it for fifteen more. Maybe he was just glad to have a job, or maybe fishing was in his blood.

88

Forrest Williams's office occupies the second floor of a weathered frame building looking out at the packing house, the twine shed, and Wildfowl Bay. Papers clutter his desk, account books and manuals line the shelves behind it. Red-haired, fortyish, and quick of speech, Forrest gives me the big picture of his business. The Bay Port Fish Company has been in operation exactly 100 years, he says, with a succession of owners. He, his brother Tod, and Denny Root, a college friend, bought the company in 1977. He had always liked to fish, but had no experience with commercial fishing. At the time, he was a manager at a Holiday Inn in Detroit, Denny was working at a home for delinquent boys near Detroit, and Tod was "cowboying" out west. They weren't particularly happy with their jobs and saw promise in the fishing business. Saginaw Bay was getting cleaner, whitefish were coming back in the lake, and fish prices looked strong. They decided to give it a try.

It's a medium-sized operation, as Lake Huron fish companies go, but has a great variety of facets. "Right now we're running five boats here and one at Sebewaing, all trapnetters. When we're going full blast we have twenty-five or thirty people, between on the boats and in the packing house. Including what we catch and what we buy, we're up to about a million pounds a year. Most of our fish go to the big markets—New York, Detroit, some to Los Angeles, Miami. But we sell a lot of fish right here—people come in the door."

Among the fish sold are walleyes bought from Indian fishermen up north, who are allowed to fish for this game species. The diversity of fish in the bay and lake makes for flexibility in the business. The commercial catch includes whitefish, channel catfish, yellow perch, white perch, sheepsheads, suckers, carp, "white buffalo," crappies, and burbot. "In 1977 we were more into rough fish like carp and suckers. We used to seine carp. But the carp market is low now [except for the Jewish market during holiday seasons]. We make most of our money from whitefish and catfish."

"There's all kinds of ways to sell the fish. We bought a machine that minced suckers, like fish hamburger. We still use that to make fish sausages out of suckers and buffalo. . . . We marketed whitefish gizzards in Taiwan, and we're trying to work out something now with whitefish livers. We save the roe out of whitefish because there's a good demand for that. There's a guy in northern Michigan that buys whitefish roe from us and makes caviar from it. And we're aquaculturing yellow perch—there's so much demand for perch."

89

Their permits allow them to fish at various times in ten by ten-mile grids scattered from the middle of Saginaw Bay to its mouth. Their season usually runs from about April 1, if the ice is out, until Thanksgiving. "Then the ice starts coating nets and anchors. It's just a lot of work and no fish. It seems like when the lake turns over in the fall the fish skedaddle anyhow. You can't catch anything."

In spite of public pressure on commercial fishing, coming mostly from sport fishermen, Forrest sees a good future for his company. "We're in an upward growth. The whitefish and catfish are doing great, and the perch price has really gone up. When we started, perch fillets were $2.00–$3.00 a pound. Now it's in the $8.00 range. Health-conscious Americans are eating more fish, and the contaminants in the fish here in Saginaw Bay have gone down to nothing [a wishful exaggeration, however, in the light of current Michigan health advisories]. We can sell as many fish as we can catch."

Up on Manitoulin Island, George Purvis is doing well, too, thanks to the whitefish renaissance of the past two decades. One sunny day in mid-May I go out aboard his seventy-eight-foot gillnetter, *Blue Fin,* to see how gillnetting is done. A northwest wind is blowing at 10–15 knots, but here on the south side the island cuts it down some, making the waves only two to four feet. As we progress out of the harbor at Burnt Island the four crew members gather in the attractive wood-paneled pilot house. They haul out their coffee thermoses and Igloo coolers for salad and sandwiches and swap stories about local doings. Forty-five minutes later we have passed the Duck Islands and reached an area several miles off Murphy Harbour where Cameron (Cam) Thibault, the captain, wants to set the nets. I ask him how he determines his position in poor visibility. "By Loran," he says. "Right now it's being repaired. I hope they get it fixed before we have fog."

Everybody gets into their rubber boots and overalls and moves to the stern. Like most Great Lakes gill net boats, the *Blue Fin* is totally enclosed, with sliding doors at the stern and sides for paying out or pulling in nets. We have sixteen tubs—8,000 yards—of monofilament four-and-a-half-inch mesh net to put out. One man pulls net from a tub. Another stands at the roller on the stern, making sure the net doesn't tangle on its way out. A third carries up new tubs, ties nets in succeeding tubs together, putting on an anchor every two or three tubs, and throws hot water on the net to make the fuzz lie down, to "tame it," he says. Cam maintains a slow forward speed to make the net pay out correctly. In an hour the job is done. Two days later they will return to lift this string of nets, set 140 feet down on mud bottom, which, Cam says, is what whitefish like.

The gillnetter *Blue Fin* at Burnt Island.

Then we move on to pick up nets set yesterday. This is done mechanically through an opening on the port side of the bow. The net, holding whitefish every few feet, comes in over a roller and around a horizontal revolving lifter. One man feeds the net into a tub, two others pick out the fish and throw them into boxes. This involves first sticking a handheld hook into the fish's belly to deflate the air sac, which inflated when the fish was pulled up from the bottom, then using the hook to peel net back over the fish's head, and finally hooking the fish's head and pulling it through the net.

All this time, for three and a half hours, the skipper has constantly adjusted the boat's direction and speed, and slowed or stopped the revolving lifter when there are too many fish to handle at one time. Once he has had to stop everything while they untangle a massive snarl around one of the net anchor ropes. Cam also watches the incoming net to scoop up any loose fish that are about to fall out.

91

After this long, intense operation, we stop for lunch. Most of the men heat food in a microwave oven. They eat well.

Two chores remain—to set another string of nets and clean the fish. This time two men set nets and Randy Clarke—the youngest—cleans fish, almost all of them whitefish one to one and a half feet long. He slits the belly of each, scrapes the guts through a hole in the cleaning table into a box, and tosses the cleaned fish into another box. I time him—ten seconds per fish—and all the while he is keeping up friendly chatter with me. His pay depends on the catch, he says. "I usually make about $140 a day [Canadian], but one day I made $900. We were cleaning fish most of the night."

Mark Witty, a technician on contract with the Ontario Ministry of Natural Resources (OMNR) has another job—sampling and recording the catch. He records the number of each species (except whitefish) as they come in and then takes a sample of fifty whitefish, weighs them, measures their length, scrapes off a few scales and puts them into an envelope for later determination of age, and checks for lamprey wounds. Most aren't wounded, but one has a big hole in its side. He follows the same procedure for the few lake trout we have caught. One is a magnificent specimen around fourteen pounds—probably about eleven years old, he says. It has run the gauntlet of lamprey predation and survived to spawning age. "Lampreys are ten times more numerous in the North Channel," he says. "There was a big increase of wounding there last fall, and this spring the nets picked up a lot of dead fish."

The OMNR puts such people on fishing boats around Manitoulin Island eighteen days each month, two of those days on Purvis Brothers boats. Their data will help assess the trends of fish populations and catches so appropriate quotas can be set the following year.

We've had a good day: seventeen boxes of whitefish—about 1,700 pounds. Cam radios the news to the fish station at Burnt Island. The boat crews work on commission only. Purvis gets 60 percent, the crews 40 percent. At $1.00 a pound, today's catch is worth $1,700. The crew will get about $680, averaging $170 for each man. They're going home tired but happy. I didn't hear how the other gill net boat, working westward out toward Mississagi Strait, has done. Cam says the moon affects the catch— "the more moonlight the smaller the catch; they can see the net in bright moonlight." But last night we had a fairly bright moon and still did well. According to Mark Witty, we have also caught six lake trout, which we keep, and twenty-one smelt, forty-eight chubs, and eleven burbot, which were all thrown back.

Purvis has a loyal crew in these men. Cam Thibault has worked for him thirty years, Philip Harper for twenty-five, the other two four or five years. Randy Clarke, the youngest, is just getting started at four years. "I like this work," he says. "You're out in the fresh air. And it's not hard work, just long." I wonder what he thinks *is* hard work. I ask what he does in the winter. "I work for the government," he says, "drawing unemployment insurance. And I go skimobiling."

When we pull up to the dock the impressive bulk of George Purvis emerges from his office. He looks pleased that the catch was good and that I enjoyed my day.

The Purvis family has been fishing around Manitoulin Island since 1877, when Will Purvis, an immigrant from Scotland, received a government appointment as lighthouse keeper on Great Duck Island. Like most lighthouse keepers in those days, he also fished. His five sons incorporated as Purvis Brothers and started fishing operations in Gore Bay, Providence Bay, and at Burnt Island and Great Duck Island. Three sons in the next generation continued the business, which is now run by George Purvis— the fourth generation. *His* son, Drew, is the fifth. From 1936 to 1990 the family also had a mink ranch at Burnt Island—a logical companion business since the mink could be fed fish entrails. They quit raising mink when the price went too low, because of oversupply George thinks.

Purvis Brothers has licenses to fish all around the eighty-mile-long Manitoulin Island. Although Burnt Island is their headquarters and main port, they move their boats around according to the zones they are fishing in. The OMNR sets annual quotas for each commercial species for each zone, so if George has reached his whitefish quota for one zone, or if the fish seem to have moved, he shifts operations to another zone.

The *Blue Fin,* the fifty-eight-foot *Andave H.,* and the fifty-two-foot *Chas R.* set gill nets, and the *D.D. Purvis* sets trap nets. George prefers gill nets. "The trap nets aren't very successful. You can't cover enough water. And you can't get deep enough in the lake with a trap net. Right now we've got one trap net in 110 feet of water, and that's as deep as we want to go with it. If you want to get fish you have to go to 180 feet of water. You'll never winch trap nets up out of that kind of water, or it's hard, and you'll kill fish doing it. You'll bloat them if you bring them up too fast. If the trap's full of small fish you can't release them, they'll be dead and go to the gulls. That doesn't happen with a gill net. With a gill net everything you catch is the right size [because of the four and a half-inch mesh], and you can set them deeper and move them around easier, depending on where the fish are. With a trap net it's either feast or famine—it only does well when the fish are in shallower water—late spring and late fall."

Almost all his catch is whitefish. Purvis Brothers trucks the fifty-pound boxes to Espanola or Sudbury, from where trucking companies carry them to markets in Toronto, Montreal, Chicago, Boston, New York, sometimes to Los Angeles and Miami. The price, as usual in a market economy, depends on supply and demand. Early and late in the season, when fewer people are fishing, the price goes up. "But as soon as they start pumping those trap net fish in out of Lake Michigan, the market won't stand the saturation. The bottom falls out of the price. They blame it on us and we blame it on them. We weren't producing cheap fish until yesterday, when all of a sudden they had two or three big truckloads out of Michigan, and the price fell twenty cents a pound."

The price also fluctuates with the Jewish holiday seasons, since most of the Purvis Brothers' catch goes to the Jewish market. "We ship the whitefish undressed at holiday times," Irene Purvis told me. "That makes them kosher." The fact that they are scaled also makes them kosher, as are such fish as carp and suckers. The Jewish faith forbids eating of unscaled species, like catfish.

Weather is not as big a factor in fishing as it was when men were going out in rowboats and doing their own weather forecasting. With bigger, motorized boats, modern navigation equipment, and (mostly) accurate forecasting, today's fishermen can usually stay out of trouble. "Our gill net boats go out when the wind is under forty kilometers per hour," Irene said. "The trap net boat can only work in less wind. If it looks like high wind will continue, the gill net boats will try to lift their nets, especially if they're in shallow water, where they could get tore up on the rocks. . . . We know a lot more about the weather nowadays. When high winds are forecast, we can set nets in sheltered places. And the radios are better than they used to be. The old Marconi radio only worked one quarter of the time, but VHF radio works real well."

Purvis Brothers sells not only their own catch but also fish they buy from about ten other fishermen operating between Blind River, on the North Shore, to Britt, at the north end of Georgian Bay. Two or three of these men are Native Americans on Manitoulin Island. One of the whites there is Murray Hore.

Murray lives on Campbell Bay, on the north side of the island. His yard is full of equipment. The interior of the house looks well lived in—thanks to six young children. Murray began fishing in 1984, following his father, who began in the 1920s. Murray keeps his forty-foot boat, the

*Charlie H,* at Cook's Bay, some twelve miles to the west. He leaves the dock at 7:30 in the morning, with his two helpers sets 6,000 yards of net, and then lifts the net set the day before. On the way home they clean the catch, arriving around 6:00 P.M. if they've been a long way out. (Murray has a permit to fish anywhere in the North Channel, except for a few bays reserved for sport fishing.)

Whitefish and perch are the mainstays of his operation. Now in mid-May, when I visited, he is fishing for whitefish. Next week he will set in shallower water—fifteen to forty feet—for perch. "The perch price is pretty stable," he says, "around $2.00 U.S. Whitefish varies a lot, anywhere from $3.00 to seventy-five cents Canadian, depending on the Jewish holidays. The highest price is at Passover, in early April, if you can fish through the ice. . . . I catch a few lake trout and pickerel [walleyes] too. Once I caught a 110-pound sturgeon. Suckers have a very low price—they're not worth it—and I don't bother with ling [burbot] and menominee [a different species of whitefish], there's not much market."

Unlike the Purvis Brothers, who have open water on the south side in March, Murray has to wait until late April for the ice to go out of the North Channel. Unless he's met his quota earlier, he usually fishes until early November, going out in almost any kind of weather. When you have six young mouths to feed, you don't take many days off.

Purdy Fisheries in Point Edward, Ontario, at the south end of the lake, is the largest fishing operation on lower Lake Huron. This is not surprising considering its location on the most productive part of the lake, nearness to large markets, and long history. A visitor senses this success almost immediately. Tucked in Sarnia Harbour on the St. Clair River, just downstream from the lake, fishing boats line the docks and rest on shore. Flanked by twine and packing sheds, a retail store welcomes the fish-buying public. A briskly cheerful woman behind counters of neatly displayed fish explains what is available today—an array ranging from whitefish they have caught to salmon from the east coast. It is a bright, attractive place—surprisingly so amidst the usual clutter of a busy fishing operation.

Upstairs in his pine-paneled office, Milford Purdy describes how they get the fish. Mostly they use trap nets, he says, set anywhere from near shore to eighty feet of water. Trap nets for walleyes (called pickerel in Canada) lead first into a funnel with a two-by-two-foot opening, then into one with a fourteen-inch opening, into gradually darker areas with smaller mesh. Trap nets for whitefish, he says, are bigger, with larger mesh, "because whitefish don't like going into a dark area. The net is green rather than black."

In winter they use gill nets set in deeper water, usually 100 to 140 feet but sometimes down to 230 feet, for whitefish. Up to Grand Bend, their permits allow gillnetting beyond five miles from shore, and all the way to shore from Grand Bend to Bayfield. Their zone extends out to the international boundary, where depths reach more than 200 feet.

The fishing has been good for some time now. "In the last ten to twenty years, everything is up, except possibly perch. Whitefish have really rebounded—we've had the best fishing for a hundred years in the last five to six years. But it's been increasing ever since 1977. Everybody has a different idea why it's getting better, but my opinion is it's because of banning DDT in 1970. Before that the fish weren't reproducing very well. It's been going up even for pickerel. There used to be a lot of fluctuation in the catch. But we've caught our quota of pickerel ever since quotas began in 1984, which means the fishing is real steady. And whitefish quotas, which are based on yearly assessments by the MNR, have been going steadily upward."

But nothing stays the same in the fishing business. Markets change, the rules change, and fish move. "It seems that ever since the zebra mussel the fish are going deeper all the time. The shore fishery is not as good as it was, say, four years ago. I think one reason is because of the clarity of the water. I thought it was just affecting the pickerel at first. Then we noticed the whitefish are going more out into the central part of the lake. We used to get muddy water for five or six days with a wind, sometimes all spring. Now it clears up in a day or so. Pickerel don't like clear water—the sunlight. And you get more weeds and moss growing—things that are undesirable for fishing. I didn't know perch didn't like clear water either, but for some reason they're going deeper, too. Perch used to always be along the shore. Now they're in 100 feet of water. Maybe there's less food for minnows near shore because of the zebra mussels eating so much of the plankton."

The Purdy family has been successfully meeting such challenges since around 1900, when Milford's grandfather began fishing with hoop nets in Sarnia Bay on the St. Clair River. He moved his fishing out to the lake in 1912, switching to pound nets fastened to wooden stakes driven into the bottom. Milford's father Ron took over next and now, at eighty-three, was still going out on boats a couple of days a week and was doing other jobs around the fish station. The Purdys started using gill nets in 1947 and trap nets the following year, abandoning pound nets. Milford, in his late fifties, has been fishing for forty years. Though he doesn't claim so, he is the de facto chief of operations. Two of his sons work in the business, and his sister runs the retail store. Two of Ron's great-granddaughters work there, too, making the present fishery a four-generation operation. The Purdys oversee twenty to thirty people and run two gill net tugs and nine trap net boats. Within two fish-processing rooms in the main building, machines trim off fins and heads and scale and fillet fish. Some are smoked. The store sells not only fish Purdy boats have brought in but also some obtained elsewhere, such as Atlantic salmon bought from fish farmers in Nova Scotia.

It's a carefully run business, but more than a business—it's a vocation infused with love for the lake and family tradition.

Jimmy Preseau's operation, in northern Michigan, is a far cry from the Purdys' big business. Like many other Native Americans, he fishes from a small (twenty-five-foot) open boat, in all weathers except thunderstorms and high wind. I talked to him one June morning at Hammond Bay harbor when winds around 30 mph kept him ashore. The boats of other Chippewa fishermen were inactive here that day, too. There were three enclosed tugs—his cousin Tod Preseau's yellow boat, Vern Alexander's white boat, and the largest, Joe Laceque's sixty-five-foot boat—as well as an open trap net boat owned by the Sault Ste. Marie Chippewa tribe, and a small brown outboard owned by "Boon," a man from the Bay Mills Indian Community on Lake Superior who still pulls his nets by hand.

Jimmy, a member of the Sault Ste. Marie Tribe who lives in Cheboygan, begins his summer days at 4:30 A.M. He picks up Tom Phillips, his helper, and, towing his boat, arrives at Hammond Bay by 5:30. They were currently fishing three and a half miles offshore in 160 feet of water where the temperature was around fifty-five degrees—what the whitefish like. The gill nets come in over a roller at the bow and around a circular, horizontal Crosley lifter, where they pick the fish out. By 11:30 they're back in. Jimmy sells his fish to the Big Stone Bay Company at Mackinaw City, where they are processed and shipped to Chicago, New York, and other markets.

Fog sometimes makes his work dangerous. His nets are in the shipping lanes, and without radar he can't see those 600- to 1,000-foot freighters coming. "The other day," he said, "I was out there in the fog and I could hear a ship blowing its fog horn but couldn't tell where it was. My radio was off so they couldn't call me. The ship passed me just 300 or 400 feet away, and I could see someone looking down at me. The front end disappeared in the fog while I could still see the back end." Jimmy moves out of the way when he knows where a ship is, because they can't turn very fast. This one apparently had to miss *him.*

Fog is an occupational hazard that Jimmy can deal with, though one seven-day stretch of continuous pea soup with all those freighters coming through it definitely tested his fishing resolve. But thunderstorms are another story. When you're riding on the only piece of metal out there the lightning may seek you out. One beautiful June day with flat water a storm suddenly came up. Jimmy and his helper were in a twenty-four-foot aluminum boat loaded down with twenty-four tubs of fish. Lightning flashed. The winds went up to 50 mph and waves started coming over the bow. They headed for the Cheboygan River but then decided it was too far. They would have to beach the boat at Duncan Point. "I was scared," Jimmy said. "I wanted to get back to Mother Earth." To run higher in the water they dumped their day's catch overboard—all 2,400 pounds of it—and ran full speed up on the shore. "The bottom wrinkled up so bad we had to send that boat to the junk yard." But they were safe.

Jimmy Preseau began fishing with his father when he was eighteen—right out of high school—in a sixteen-foot outboard, pulling the nets by hand. He used this method from 1979 until 1990, when he bought a lifter. This made the work easier, but his body remembered the earlier days. "That's probably why my back's out of it half the time," he said. At thirty-seven, blondish and still youthful-looking, and on his own since at least 1987, when his father died, he continues to fish by boat from ice out around the end of March until the first week of December. He takes time out only from November 7 to 30, when it's illegal to fish for whitefish because they're spawning. Sometimes in winter he'll push the sixteen-foot boat across the ice to open water. Some of the fellows with tugs go out all winter, whenever a southwest wind has blown the ice out of Hammond Bay. In winter Jimmy sets gill nets under the ice at Cross Village, on Lake Michigan. "There's a good price for whitefish then," he said, "$1.50 to $2.00 a pound, because there's not many people fishing." Now in June it was forty-five cents per pound.

This summer he was putting out 9,000 feet of net—almost two miles. His catch ranges from around 200 pounds—the breakeven point—to 2,000 pounds once in awhile. One thousand pounds is a good day. His best day came three years earlier, when he hauled in 4,000 pounds. "My hands were sore from picking that day," he said. He's making a decent income, enough to buy a second, $12,000 motor a year or so earlier, "but I'm still living in my trailer in a trailer court. I want to fish long enough to see my son [Jimmy Jr., then four] grow up and do it. He wants to go in the boat now but I'm waiting for a nice calm day."

A lot of Chippewa Jimmy's age were working in factories or casinos, but "I like fishing," he said. "It's quiet out there. No factory whistle. No twelve o'clock lunch bell. Just the sound of water and seagulls."

Fishing is pretty peaceful for Mike Meeker, too, on Manitoulin Island's Lake Wolsey. But Mike walks to get his fish. He's an aquaculturist. Most of his fish are rainbow trout living in ten fifty-by-fifty-foot net cages thirty feet deep on either side of his dock. Each year the Coldwater Company of Barrie, Ontario, supplies him with more than one million three- to four-inch fingerlings. He raises them to two or three pounds, on a diet of fish meal made from Peruvian and Chilean anchovies and east coast herring byproducts. "It's a natural diet," he says, "and the fish taste good because of this and the clean environment." Between one June and the next Mike harvests 750,000 to 800,000 pounds of rainbow trout for the Coldwater Company.

The clean environment is provided by the circulating waters of Lake Wolsey, which has a direct connection to Bayfield Sound in the North Channel. "There's a strong current moving in and out," Mike explains. "My nets are always hanging one way or the other in the current. The waste is taken care of by this current and fish and other organisms around the nets."

He also raises Arctic char, which he buys as fingerlings and starts out in a shed, near his house, through which lake water is circulated. Bacteria break down the fish waste into nitrogen that bubbles off. When they've grown some, Mike transports the char to a shed owned by George Purvis at Burnt Island, where Mike raises them to market size. Here they get the colder water, pumped in from Lake Huron proper, that this species needs. "There's a good market for Arctic char now," Mike said. "It's a novelty that expensive restaurants like to put on the menu."

Mike and his wife, an American from St. Louis, came to Manitoulin Island in 1984. "We decided Manitoulin would be a good place," Mike said, "because it's on the fringe, out in the boonies. My wife didn't know how she would like this kind of life that her crazy Canuck husband wanted," but apparently she did. They bought a 200-acre farm near Lake Wolsey, which they liked because of its sheltered location and clean water with a short flushing time—important for the fish farming they intended to do. Mike worked at the Gore Bay hatchery and sold maple sugar and firewood from his farm while establishing the aquaculture business. A local farmer gave him access to the lake, where he started with fish cages in the middle, working them by boat.

"We made the cages ourselves," Mike said, "from wood cut on our property, sewed the nets, used rubber from tires. It was hard to get financing. We lived on a shoestring. And we were pioneering. There was no one to talk to about it. At first we tried chinook and Atlantic salmon and char in the cages, but the water was too warm for them. Finally, we found that it was OK for domestically raised rainbow trout."

Eventually, they obtained venture capital from a finance company that liked their prospectus, and they were able to buy shoreline property with 1,600 feet of frontage. With assured support from the Coldwater Company, the business is well established now, but of course it is not worry free. "There are problems in spring when the ice is breaking up," Mike said. "Two cages were damaged this spring and I lost a few thousand fish. For that three-week period about all you can do is pray, and chop ice."

Predators are a less serious but more continuous problem. "I put a fine-meshed net over the top of the net cages in summer to keep predators out. This stops gulls, and cormorants don't come around the nets, but great blue herons do, and they're smart. They have learned their weight pushes the net down to the surface of the water and they can spear fish through the net. Mink will climb over top of the net cage and drag fish out over it. If there's a net over the top they will chew a hole and go through. If I have to, I trap them with a live or dead trap. Muskrats will chew a hole in the net just to get through and then chew another hole on the other side where they want to go out."

Thirty-seven years old in 1995, Mike looked forward to many more years of fish farming, perhaps adding more cages in the middle of Lake Wolsey and perhaps offshore in the North Channel or Lake Huron proper. "I've been looking at a cage system on the east coast that is submersible," he said. "It's spherical, with triangular aluminum plates and a net inside. You pump feed into it. When a storm is coming or winter ice is forming, you can submerge it. I'm working with a guy now to make these cages."

With the inherent uncertainty in trends of wild fish populations, and tribal treaty rights on Lake Huron clouding the future for nontribal fishermen, Mike Meeker may have made a wise choice by turning to aquaculture. Mike knew of only a half dozen other fish-farming operations on Lake Huron. But even here the competition could get tough if many tribal members, who can receive government funding to get started, went into it. "You can't compete with a company that has no bottom line,"

Mike complained. As always, commercial fish production is at the mercy of human decisions as well as the dictates of nature.

Rob Taylor doesn't *have* to fish. In his early forties, he has a good, if noisy, job at the die factory in Sebewaing, on Saginaw Bay, stamping out automobile parts for General Motors. But in a sense he does have to fish. His grandfather was a commercial fisherman, and somehow the trade got into Rob's blood and he can't stay off the bay. He's one of four men in Sebewaing who have licenses to set lines for catfish. Most afternoons in the spring and early fall at three o'clock, when he gets off work, Rob heads for his fish shed by the Sebewaing River, gears up, and climbs into his sixteen-foot aluminum Starcraft to visit his catfish lines.

One windy day in late September I joined him, replacing his black Labrador retriever, who usually goes along. Encased in dark green rubberized overalls and hooded slickers, we pounded across the three-foot waves toward Lone Tree Island, two or three miles offshore, near which Rob had set five 550-foot lines. As we passed the "island," now only a few small willows with their feet in the water, Rob talked of the days when the island was bigger and had a tarpaper shack on it, and of the much earlier days when the first settlers to Sebewaing were stranded here for a time while the local Indians decided whether to carry them onward to the mainland. He talked, too, about rescuing sport fishermen whose boat had capsized in a storm and drifted all night, and of finding the body of a duck hunter who had tried to wade ashore in the cold water after his boat capsized, and didn't make it.

Motoring up to the flag on the farthest line, Rob cuts the outboard engine and tilts it out of the water, momentarily ties the line to the bow, and cuts his frozen smelt bait into pieces. "Fresh fish is better," he says, "but I can't get any right now." Sitting in the bow and untying the line, he pulls along it, baiting or rebaiting each No. 5 catfish hook, which dangles down a foot from the main line. This would be harder if he had to pull against the wind, so he has set the lines parallel with the prevailing winds, which are northwest this time of year. Anchored at each end, the lines have been lying on or near the bottom in four to nine feet of water. Today a north wind blows us down the line as we bob on the breaking waves.

The first line, with 100 hooks, has no catfish on it, but it does have a perch or two. "I would eat these," Rob says, "but they're dead now." He hasn't been out for a couple of days because the fishing has been slow. If the perch were alive when unhooked, they would go on the family table. One of the perch has been swallowed by a northern pike, which has hooked itself in the process. "First time I ever saw that," Rob says. He can't get the hook out so has to cut it off. The pike—perch, hook, and all—swims away. Pike cannot be sold by U.S. commercial fishermen.

Partway down the next line, I see a pale shape thrashing underwater. "See that catfish pulling back on the line," Rob says. "For some reason they don't pull forward like other fish do." It's maybe a five-pounder, and gets thrown into a tub of water in front of me. A short distance down the line, a couple more catfish are on. They swim in schools, so tend to get caught in clusters.

But by the end of the fifth line, Rob has caught only eleven catfish. The catfishing is not nearly as good in the fall as it is in the spring, he explains. In spring they seem to come into shallower water when it warms up, then go deeper in summer and fall. Rob quits in summer—the fishing's too poor in the shallow water and the deep water is too far out to be safe. He resumes in September, when the fishing becomes modestly profitable. In October he quits for the winter.

"In the spring I go out when the ice goes out, as early as March 27 one year. At first it's not so good. Maybe the catfish aren't feeding. But it really gets going about the middle of April and stays good through May. One day last May I caught 1,898 pounds." The Bay Port Fish Company, to whom he sells his catfish, couldn't pay the usual forty-five cents a pound and had to lower the price to thirty cents that day, but Rob still got $569 for the day's effort.

Besides wondering how much of a catch he will have, the fisherman is always curious about what sort of creatures he will find on the line. Rob's record catfish—twenty-five and three-quarter pounds—must have been an impressive sight. And in the early 1990s he caught a fifty-inch, forty-seven-pound sturgeon. The sturgeon is rare in the Great Lakes these days, and such a catch often warrants a newspaper story.

We motor slowly up the Sebewaing River to a weathered grey frame fish house and tie up. With a long-handled net Rob scoops the catfish from their tub into another on the dock. Then he dumps them into a tank of aerated water in the fish house. "Do you know how to tell if a catfish is happy?" he asks. I don't, so he scoops one out of the tank and shows me. "If his eyes are not looking down, just staring straight out, he's not feeling so good." This one, with a face only a mother catfish could love, I am thinking, is looking down. Rob hopes they all are looking down. He wants his catfish to feel good and not die because he sells them alive to the Bay Port Fish Company, which in turn sells them live to fish farmers.

The catch today: eleven fish totaling fifty-nine pounds. There were 489 empty hooks. "I guess I made around $2.50 today," Rob comments wryly, "after the cost of gas and bait." But on other days and in other months, he does better. A $2,000 check at the end of last April enabled the family to travel to San Diego for a vacation. And I see Rob's twenty-two-foot sportfishing boat parked on his lot.

There are, of course, other, more fundamental compensations. There's the mystique of fishing, the suspense. "If you knew what you were going to catch," Rob says, "they'd call it catching, not fishing." And he likes the fact that people call on him and his knowledge to help when somebody's in trouble on the bay. Today we have found a boot floating in the water and retrieved it. "I'll call the sheriff to see if something happened," Rob says. And he just likes being out on the bay, connecting with all the local history he knows so well, and thinking his own thoughts in the quiet—just him and his black Lab.

Some commercial fishermen practice their profession just to make a living. Russ Herrick, who lives in a mobile home court up the shore from us, retired from fishing the Thumb area in 1972. He fished because a factory job wasn't available at the time and it was the family occupation. He hated lifting those heavy trap nets by hand. And he worried about the dangers—mechanical as well as natural. His brother lost a finger, and his father a leg.

But other fishermen are wedded to their work. They wouldn't think of doing anything else. Russ Herrick's father got a wooden leg and kept on fishing. Lake Huron fishermen from Milford Purdy, with his eleven-boat operation, down to Jimmy Preseau and Rob Taylor in their small open boats, are permanently hooked by the family tradition, the independence, the mystery of fish that can fill your nets or your lines one day and leave them empty the next, and the great lake itself, with its peace, its beauty, and all its ever-changing moods, even those that threaten death.

It's all part of the lure.

# CHAPTER 9

# MANAGING THE FISHERIES

L eonard Dutcher is one angry ex-commercial fisherman. When I called to arrange an interview about the fishing business, he roared, "*What fishing business!*" And when I arrived at his De Tour Village home his first words were a string of expletives aimed at the Michigan Department of Natural Resources and the federal government.

Leonard is another fourth-generation fisherman. His father fished Saginaw Bay and the Thumb. Starting at sixteen, Leonard fished with him around Port Sanilac and in 1963 moved his own operation to the Drummond Island area at the north end of Lake Huron. His ire arises from the Department of Natural Resources' (DNR's) curtailing of commercial fishing to benefit sport fishermen and, especially, the establishment of exclusive fishing zones for Indians by the DNR and federal government. One such zone includes most of Leonard's former fishing area. He ended up selling his fishing rig to some young Natives.

Leonard was still fighting the DNR in court for additional compensation but, at sixty-three, probably wouldn't fish again, even if it were possible. "I've got a bad back from lifting fish out of trap nets," he said. When I left I wished him a good life. "I've *had* mine," he answered. "I'm too old to do any fishing now." Fishing *was* his life.

The issues behind Leonard Dutcher's unhappy exit from fishing began in the 1960s and still are not totally resolved. Up until the early 1960s there had been few restrictions on commercial fishing—just those shared with sport fishing, such as allowable size, seasons, and species. But several developments led to a fundamental policy change by the DNR. Stocks of many valuable fish species had been declining for decades, especially since 1940. The Great Lakes were overrun with alewives, an exotic species that periodically died off in great numbers, producing windrows of stinking carcasses on the beaches. Gizzard shad and rainbow smelt—two other exotic species—had also proliferated. And chemical control of the sea lamprey, scourge of lake trout and whitefish, now appeared to be feasible.

These were the major reasons for certain far-reaching steps taken by the Michigan Department of Natural Resources in the late 1960s. First, Howard Tanner, then chief of the DNR Fisheries Division, and Wayne Tody, an associate in the division, jointly decided to introduce Pacific salmon (beginning with cohos in 1966) into Michigan waters of the Great Lakes to reduce the populations of alewives and other exotic fish and provide a new sport fishery. This turned out to be, in the words of one Michigan manager, "Probably the greatest piece of fisheries management in the continent, if not the world." The salmon gorged on the alewives and other exotic fish and sparked a sportfishing frenzy when they made their first fall spawning run, in 1967, to the Lake Michigan streams where they had been released as yearlings. This was the beginning of a multi-million-dollar recreational industry on all shores of the upper Great Lakes, including waters of Lake Huron, where stocking of cohos began in 1967 and of chinooks in 1969. An expanded stocking program that includes rainbow and brown trout as well as salmon continues today.

Meanwhile, with lamprey control beginning to take hold, the U.S. Fish and Wildlife Service had been stocking hatchery-reared lake trout in Lakes Superior and Michigan to try to restore this once-dominant predator. To protect these stocks, commercial fishing for lake trout was banned in U.S. waters of Lake Superior in 1962; in Lake Michigan in 1965; and in U.S. waters of Lake Huron in 1967. However, studies showed that a large number of stocked lake trout were still being caught in gill nets set for whitefish. In 1968 an amendment to the Commercial Fishing Law of 1929 allowed the director of the DNR to establish new conditions for licensing commercial fishing and to determine the number of licenses.

Nineteen seventy was a pivotal year. Only those licensees who, over two of the three previous years had fished for at least ten to fifty days, depending on type of gear, were relicensed. This dropped the number of licenses in Michigan waters of the Great Lakes from 483 in 1968 to 188 in 1970. This was also the year the DNR established zone management in Michigan waters of the lakes, designating all of Lake Huron, except for

Saginaw Bay and a few isolated areas, exclusively for recreational fishing. In 1974 the department eliminated nearly all permits to use large-mesh gill nets, the type used for whitefish and most other commercial species. The commercial fishermen fought this in court but lost, and the rule went into effect in 1984.

Success of the salmon introductions and concern for lake trout and whitefish populations had led to a DNR policy that clearly favored sport fishing over commercial fishing. Recreational fishermen vastly outnumbered commercial fishermen and outweighed them economically as well (in 1985, expenditures by sport anglers were estimated at $2 billion, while the commercial catch in the Great Lakes was valued at $41 million). The DNR figured it was opting for the greatest good for the greatest number. Licensing of commercial fishing was frozen at its 1970 level. No new licenses would be issued.

Then a new development further complicated the picture. Indian tribes in Michigan had been conducting subsistence and commercial fishing for generations. Like the non-Indians, they had been required to buy commercial licenses from the state and to follow state regulations. But they believed that their ancestors had reserved fishing and hunting rights on all their lands in the Treaty of 1836, which ceded large areas to the U.S. government and restricted Indian homes to fourteen reservations, in exchange for various financial rewards. When the state banned gill nets and started confiscating Indian fishing gear for violations of the new fishing regulations, the tribes went to court. They lost the initial cases, but then the federal government, in an effort to settle the vexing question of treaty rights, stepped in. The United States, joined by the Bay Mills Indian Community, the Sault Ste. Marie Tribe of Chippewa, and the Grand Traverse Tribe of Ottawa and Chippewa, filed a case in the federal court for the western district of Michigan, seeking to prevent the State of Michigan from interfering with treaty fishing. The State of Michigan, joined by sportsmen's groups, presented its case through the efforts of the Department of Natural Resources and the attorney general's office.

*U.S. vs. Michigan* was a long, complex case accompanied by nasty conflicts outside the courtroom. According to Charles Cleland, an ethnohistorian who testified in the case, "Outdoor writers and television hosts warned the public that 'blue-eyed Indians' were raping the lakes with 'killer' gill nets. . . . Indian fishermen were . . . subject to attack by angry mobs of 'sportsmen' who took it upon themselves to destroy their nets, boats, and trucks; they were also constantly harassed by conservation officers. . . . [Indian] children were constantly taunted in school as 'gill netters' and were humiliated by shouts of 'Save a lake trout—scalp an Indian.'"

In May 1979, Judge Noel Fox issued his decision affirming the rights of Indian fishermen under the Treaty of 1836. The state appealed and lost and the U.S. Supreme Court refused to review the case, making the Court of Appeals decision final. This did not end legal conflicts about Indian fishery practices, however. These were eventually resolved by agreement between or among the tribes, the state, and the U.S. Department of the Interior to a joint management plan that became the basis for the Order of Consent in 1985. The management plan, good until the year 2000, provided for the establishment of zones within the treaty waters in which the tribes had exclusive commercial fishing rights, including some zones in which the tribes could use "impoundment gear" only (not gill nets), zones in which commercial fishing would be conducted under state regulation, and three lake trout refuges. Sportfishing regulations, except in the lake trout refuges, were not affected by the agreement.

The 1836 treaty-ceded waters lie in parts of Lakes Superior, Michigan, and Huron centered in the Sault Ste. Marie-Straits of Mackinac region. In Lake Huron, these zones occupy the Michigan portion of the northwest corner of the lake, north of Alpena. Leonard Dutcher found himself on the shore of a tribal fishing zone, with a lake trout refuge immediately to the east. Along with twenty-six other fishermen, he lost his license as a result of the new zoning. Sixteen of them, the smaller operators, settled with the DNR. Leonard and ten others went to court, charging that the DNR had taken their property without just compensation. In June 1996, the State of Michigan and the eleven fishermen reached a settlement that required the state to pay the fishermen $3.1 million.

Today, some resentment lingers among white commercial fishermen, such as Leonard Dutcher, and among sport fishermen as well, who think the tribes may be overfishing, but the situation is relatively calm. Most tribal fishing is conducted under regulations developed by the tribes in cooperation with the U.S. Department of the Interior and enforced by tribal conservation officers. In most treaty areas, they can use gill nets and can take lake trout, walleye, and salmon but can't take rainbow or brown trout. It is hoped that the new agreement taking effect after the year 2000 will be negotiated with a minimum of conflict.

The Michigan DNR says it has always accepted commercial fishing as a legitimate component of the total fish harvest, although it wants no expansion from present levels. "Essentially we have held the line on the amount of gear out there," says Jim Baker, district fish biologist in Bay

City. "The only way that someone new could get into the fishery would be to buy an existing license." Commercial licenses specify the boats used, ports where the licensee can land his fish, types and numbers of nets, where they can be set, and, for some species of fish, seasons, size limits, and catch limits.

Jim says that state-licensed commercial fishing, as now regulated, occupies a niche that doesn't conflict significantly with sport fishing. Except for yellow perch, it takes species that are seldom sought by sport anglers, such as whitefish, catfish, sheepshead, and carp. The use of impoundment gear (trap nets, seines, pound nets) allows any game fish caught to be returned to the water alive. Set hooks for catfish are allowed, as are eight-inch gill nets for carp, which are taken mostly in Saginaw Bay under the ice. In 1995, there were just thirty state-licensed commercial fishermen on the Michigan side of Lake Huron, twenty-six of them in Saginaw Bay and one each at the tip of the Thumb, Tawas, Alpena, and Rogers City.

Still, sport anglers continue to complain about the commercial fishermen, and they get a sympathetic ear from the DNR. There was, for instance, argument over who got to fish in the summer in an area of Saginaw Bay known as "The Slot." "The walleye trollers wanted to fish in The Slot," Baker said, "because it's the deepest water close to shore. The trollers were constantly hanging up their boats and their lures in the commercial nets, and a great deal of bad feeling ensued over a period of several years. Ultimately we were able to get the commercial fishermen out of The Slot during June, July, and August [when the sport fishery is most active], but that was only accomplished through litigation. In most cases when we attempt to impose another rule or restriction on commercial fishermen, they take us to court and the state and commercial fishermen fight it back and forth until one side or the other wins. It takes a lot of time, the lawyers get rich."

Of course, the commercial fishermen have legitimate gripes about the sportfishing fraternity, on the Canadian side as well as the American. One Canadian commercial fisherman said to me, "The sportsmen complain and bitch about us catching all the fish. They get a little obnoxious. We tell them over the radio where our nets are but they'll run over them anyway. We're thinking about putting up a gate on the road in here and just give the key to local people. We want to discourage sport fishing around here. We tell them the fishing's not very good."

Commercial fishermen in Canada enjoy more governmental support than they do in the U.S., according to Jim Baker. "For us the commercial fishery is secondary to the sport fishery. For now, the Province of Ontario takes a different approach. Their commercial fishery is foremost. The sport fishery is just an adjunct. This is a philosophy that has developed over many years. They tend to look at their natural resources differently than we do. They look at them in terms of economic benefit to commercial interests, whereas we tend to look at them in terms of the greatest benefit to the greatest number of users."

The Ontario Ministry of Natural Resources (OMNR) would probably state their philosophy in less black-and-white terms. I doubt that Canadian commercial fishermen feel favored over sportfishermen. In any case, commercial fishing in Ontario, as in the U.S., is closely regulated. Licenses specify boats, co-fishermen on the license, where and when fishing can occur, and annual harvest limits. Most of the 100 or so licensees on the Canadian side of Lake Huron use gill nets only, but a few operators use large trap nets.

Most importantly, the OMNR attempts to keep the catch below levels that would reduce fish populations, through a system of species quotas within management areas. This system, instituted in 1984, divided the Canadian waters of Lake Huron into seventeen management areas: two in the North Channel, nine in Georgian Bay, and six in the main basin. Each year, within each area, quotas (by weight) are established for channel catfish, chub (composed of several species, but mostly bloater), lake sturgeon, lake trout, lake whitefish, northern pike, walleye, and yellow perch. Twenty or so other species caught commercially have no quotas because the catch is small or there is no concern about the size of the species' population. You'll note that four of the quota species—lake trout, northern pike, lake sturgeon, and walleye—are not legal in the Michigan non-tribal commercial fishery. Canadian fishermen cannot sell the introduced salmon (except for pink salmon) and brown and rainbow trout. Because most of these fishermen use gill nets exclusively, any salmon or introduced trout caught die. (They are supposed to be given to charity or surrendered to the OMNR.) These species, however, generally live in mid- to shallow water, whereas the gill nets are usually set on the bottom in deeper water, targeting whitefish or chubs.

The quotas are based largely on data from the commercial harvest and from annual index fishing conducted by the Lake Huron Management Unit of the OMNR. They can be adjusted up or down depending on information such as the catch per unit effort and the size of year classes within species.

The OMNR feels the system is working rather well, and many commercial fishermen do, too. One said to me, "You can plan ahead. You know about how much money you will make. You can catch all your quota in May and June if you want, or adjust the fishing to the market, put out different amounts of net." But no such system is perfect. Besides the difficulty of estimating fish populations in a body of water as large as Lake Huron, there are incongruities between fish behavior and area boundaries, which are laid out along lines of latitude and longitude. This can present problems for fishermen.

George Purvis on Manitoulin Island says, "It's a bit of a problem if the fish don't stay in those zones as much as they think they do, and you're trying to follow them and you can't do it. That's what they found in the [North] Channel. One year, all the fish would be in the west end of the Channel. The next year they'd all be in the east. I don't know if it's winds or currents or what it is, but they move the full length of that Channel, back and forth. If you're trying to chase fish and they're all in the wrong end of the Channel, you're in big trouble. It was causing grief, because, say, if you had a hundred thousand pound quota and you had to take fifty thousand pounds in the west end of the Channel and fifty in the east, and all of a sudden you had your east end filled, but all the fish were in the east and there was nothing in the west, you could fish forever in the west end for another fifty thousand pounds and never catch it. We finally prevailed on them to do away with that zone line [and make the main North Channel one area] because the fish didn't know where they were.

"It's the same in Lake Huron [south of Manitoulin Island]. In the north end here the zones are real small. We've already filled one zone at the west end [of the island]. We can't fish anymore in it and we'd like to. It costs us a lot of extra money to move around, but I suppose it balances the catch. We had a bad zone out here for years. There weren't a whole lot of fish out here in 4–2 and we had to take most of them from 4–1 and 4–3. I don't know why the fish weren't in 4–2. It made a problem for us because then you can't go to the other zone to take that 4–2 quota. This year there's lots of fish in 4–2. Another problem is that between 4–2 and 4–3 there's a shoal. If you're on one side of that shoal you're in one zone and on the other side you're in the other. Those are all the same fish. You just go around the end of the point and all of a sudden you're in the other zone, and you've got to chalk it up to the other quota. . . . Computer lines."

George Purvis's comments imply a feeling common among commercial fishermen: they know as much or more about the fish populations than the OMNR does. As Bryan Perks down in Snug Harbour put it, "I don't have any hook knowledge, but I do have practical knowledge. I know about how many fish are out there as well as the MNR. If you want to know about farming, talk to a farmer. If you want to know about logging, talk to a logger. And if you want to know about fishing, talk to a fisherman."

Any unhappiness about Ontario's zone management may be a small matter, however, compared with the issue of Indian fishing. Twenty-five First Nations live on or near the Ontario shores of Lake Huron and occupy much more territory than do the tribes in Michigan. From 1785 to 1923, treaties were made with those Nations or their predecessors, for whom fish was a staple food and an item of trade. Since 1982, the courts have been affirming existing aboriginal and treaty fishing rights.

On the Bruce Peninsula, a decision in 1993 indicated that there is a native priority right of access but that the province retains jurisdiction for management. The Indian interpretation is that they are not subject to provincial regulations, and they make their own. Non-Indian fishermen, subject to provincial area quotas, say the native fishermen are putting too much pressure on the fish stocks because their take is in addition to the OMNR quotas. Those taking the native viewpoint say it is a matter of fair allocation rather than overharvest. The government has offered to buy licenses from willing non-Indian sellers to reduce the pressure. Most don't want to sell, but if the stocks become depressed, there won't be a reason to keep one's license, they say, so they feel economic pressure to sell. As an alternative, the provincial government has also been leasing quotas from non-Indian commercial fishermen on a yearly basis from around the Bruce Peninsula.

When you talk to non-Indian fishermen you feel sympathetic toward them, and when you talk to Indian fishermen you feel sympathetic toward *them.* One day at the dock on the Cape Croker Indian Reserve, on the east side of the Bruce Peninsula, I met Marshall Nadjiwon beside his pickup truck as he cleaned the last of the whitefish he'd caught that day. A lean, handsome fellow with a ponytail tied at the back of his head, he was hardly the stereotypical stocky, broad-faced Indian. "Indian fishing rights are in the Canadian constitution and Queen Victoria's treaty with my tribe," he said. "We want to live here at Cape Croker, but we have to be able to make a living." He had a rather expansive view of Indian fishing rights. "We want halfway across Lake Huron [from the Bruce Peninsula] and halfway across Georgian Bay." His opinion of the OMNR went a bit further than that of white commercial fishermen. "They messed up the ecology of the lake," he said. "They don't understand it like we do." Listening to him, I sensed the Indian closeness to the environment, and I wondered if he was right.

On Manitoulin Island, the natives have quotas, like other commercial fishermen, but they are not inspected by OMNR officials. One contract catch sampler said the OMNR was discussing going out on the Indian boats to inspect and sample the catch, "but I think the natives would be difficult about this. And there's not much room on their boats." (Most of them are eighteen-foot skiffs.)

As more natives enter the commercial fishery in Canada, consternation rises among other commercial fishermen, as well as sport anglers and natural resource officials charged with the management of fish stocks. One hopes that all these parties can come to the table with open minds and reach agreements that successfully address the needs of all, as well as of the healthy fish populations they all desire.

Whatever sector of the fish harvest might be primary in the mind of the OMNR, sport fishing does get a lot of attention. The Lake Huron Management Unit (LHMU) keeps tabs on trends in recreational fishing through creel surveys, and it stocks rainbow trout, brown trout, and lake trout. (Lake-brook trout backcross hybrids were stocked until 1995.) One species—the lake trout—dominates its research efforts. As the unit's annual report for 1994 says, "Rehabilitation of lake trout . . . is the top management priority in Lake Huron." The lake trout was once the dominant predator and a major component of the commercial catch. Through stocking, research on lake trout biology, control of the sea lamprey, and careful regulation of the commercial and recreational take, fishery managers hope to see a resurgence of the lake trout in the years ahead.

In most years, the Lake Huron Management Unit stocks over two million fish—the vast majority being lake trout—but stocking by private clubs, under the Community Fisheries Involvement Program, is even greater. These groups concentrate on chinook (king) salmon and pickerel (walleye), species the LHMU doesn't stock, but the clubs also stock substantial numbers of rainbow and brown trout, species the LHMU is gradually phasing out. No one knows how the stocking of predators is affecting the prey populations, but Lake Huron fisheries managers are working on a computer model that will help answer this question. Until the predator-prey relationships and the carrying capacity of the lake are better understood, targeted Canadian and U.S. stocking levels will be held below the total 8.33 million fish that were stocked in 1990–91.

A fisherman plays a salmon at the Port Sanilac harbor.
His catch—a ten-pound female chinook.

On the Michigan side, nearly all stocking in Lake Huron and its tributaries is done by public agencies. The majority of the stocked fish are spring or fall fingerlings (SF, FF); the rest are yearlings (Y), with occasional very small plantings of adults. The 1995 stocking (in rounded numbers) shows the relative emphasis among species: chinook salmon, 3,829,000 (SF); lake trout, 801,000 (Y); walleye, 718,000 (SF, FF); rainbow trout, 625,000 (Y); brown trout, 325,000 (Y); Atlantic salmon, 42,000 (Y); splake (a lake trout-brook trout hybrid), 38,000 (Y). You'll notice that coho salmon, the introduced Pacific species that started the fishing renaissance in the late 1960s, is not on the list. It was found that, though cohos do well in Lake Michigan, chinooks fare much better than cohos in Lake Huron. The small planting of Atlantic salmon is conducted with the assistance of a Lake Superior State University hatchery at the Edison power plant at Sault Ste. Marie (site of my winter gyrfalcon). Most raising and stocking of lake trout is done by the U.S. Fish and Wildlife Service (the other species by the Michigan DNR). The yearling lake trout are planted around potential spawning reefs, from a boat christened "Togue," a commercial fisherman's name for the species.

The numbers of fish species stocked partly reflect the relative pop-ularity of the various species among sport anglers. I got a sense of the popularity contest while fishing with Mike Hanson and Tom Muer on Tom's thirty-one-foot Bertram out of Harbor Beach. We had found a window of opportunity between very windy spells in late September and were trolling straight out from the harbor in waves still running three to five feet high, with six lines on downriggers and off a planer board line. Conversation over our radio indicated slow fishing that day, but out around two miles, in seventy to eighty feet of water, Mike yelled, "Fish on!" Since I was the guest, he handed me the twitching rod. It wasn't what you'd call a fight, just ten or fifteen minutes of work reeling the fish in. The first time I got it near the boat it spooked and stripped off line speeding away. The second time Tom netted it—a slender, silvery rainbow trout around six pounds that measured twenty-seven inches. A beautiful fish, and one that tasted good that night. But not exciting on the line.

"I was hoping we'd hook a king today," Mike said later, as we headed back to the harbor. "They run up to thirty-five pounds, and they're strong and unpredictable. One may jump and another one head for the bottom. You never know." Mike and Tom reminisced about kings they had caught in the past, including one that had taken an hour to bring in.

Mike had another opinion of lake trout. "I'd rather not catch one," he said, "they're oily." A similar view was held by Alexander Henry back in the eighteenth century. Comparing the whitefish and lake trout caught around Sault Ste. Marie, he wrote that the flavor of whitefish is "perhaps above all comparison whatever. Those, who live on them for months together, preserve their relish to the end. This cannot be said of the trout." A fisherman on Lake Superior once complained to me, "They don't fight much. It's like pulling up a log." And you usually have to fish deep for them, unlike the mid-water-inhabiting salmon. From the manager's perspective, the lake trout, unlike the fast-growing salmon, has the added drawback of slow growth to spawning age, by which time, in Lake Huron, it is likely to have succumbed to sea lamprey predation. But the federal fisheries people, like the Ontario MNR, favor it because it's a native, adapted over millennia to the Great Lakes, and it occupies a key niche at the top of the food chain. The Michigan DNR recognizes this role and sees a place for the lake trout as a sport fish, but is happy to let the feds do most of the stocking and research on it.

My own view of the lake trout is colored by my National Park Service background and a personal experience in the Adirondacks. National parks are places where native species are protected and exotic (non-native) species that threaten the natives are removed, if possible. As a strong supporter of the national park idea, I tend to favor such natives as the lake trout over exotics such as salmon in the Great Lakes. However, I recognize the salmon's value and the fact that Lake Huron is not a national park. (The natives-versus-exotics argument has gone on for some time but, as explained later, a compromise management plan has been reached.)

My first encounter with the lake trout occurred on a chilly summer morning on New York State's Saranac Lake. The father of one of the boys at my camp was taking me and another kid lake trout fishing. Bumping my line on the bottom far below, I suddenly felt a heavy tug. Our host soon took over, but when the fish neared the boat it broke away—it had bitten through the copper snelling. "Felt like about fifteen pounds," the man said. That summer in the Adirondacks I began a life-long love of the North Woods and their cold, deep lakes. As the wolf is a symbol of northern wilderness, the lake trout is a symbol of those northern lakes.

The DNR's stocking program has been a trial-and-error affair, seeing what works and what doesn't, what species and genetic strains do best in various environments. The fisheries people are currently experimenting with brown trout at Port Sanilac and rainbow trout at Lexington, ten miles down the shore, to see whether concentrated plants of these species at specific ports improve returns to the fishery. The same sort of experimentation with trout goes on at numerous other stocking points up the shore of the lake. Chinook salmon, like brown and rainbow trout, are stocked at many places from the Thumb to Sault Ste. Marie, but not inner Saginaw Bay. Capture of chinooks that were tagged or fin-clipped at the hatchery has shown that they travel all over the lake and into Lake Michigan, tending to move north in summer and south in winter. The mature salmon return to their stocking sites in spawning season and most then die, although a few actually spawn in streams before dying.

The walleye, a native species, is another favorite sport fish that gets a lot of attention from the DNR. Saginaw Bay once produced a commercial harvest of one million pounds of walleye yearly, but overfishing and pollution of spawning grounds in the Saginaw River and the inner bay caused a collapse. Since the mid-1980s, with greatly improved water quality in the tributaries and an aggressive stocking program, an excellent sport fishery has developed and the catch has rebounded to about a third of its former level. (Walleye are prohibited in the commercial harvest.) Jim Baker and his DNR associates would like to see a full recovery based, if possible, entirely on natural reproduction, as is the walleye fishery on the Ontario side of southern Lake Huron and in western Lake Erie, which is the best in the Great Lakes. To determine the level of natural reproduction, the DNR wanted to omit stocking in three alternate years (1993, 1995, and 1997) to be able to compare those year classes with classes from stocking years. This was done in 1993, but subaverage year classes in both 1992 and 1993 led to a decision to wait until 1996 to omit stocking again. Another gap in stocking was planned for the future, when the DNR finds that year classes prior to the non-stocking year are at least average or better.

Though the U.S. and Canadian natural resource agencies charged with managing the fisheries of Lake Huron have their individual biases, they recognize that the lake is an ecosystem and that fish don't observe political boundaries, which leads to the necessity for lakewide management consensus. International cooperation began at the federal level in 1956, when the Great Lakes Fishery Commission, headquartered in Ann Arbor, Michigan, was established under a U.S.–Canada treaty to find means to control the sea lamprey and improve fishery resources. Under its aegis, a Strategic Great Lakes Fisheries Management Plan was developed, and a committee for each lake was formed to establish principles and set goals for management of that lake's fisheries.

The Lake Huron Committee, composed of a representative from the Chippewa-Ottawa Treaty Fishery Management Authority, one from the Michigan Department of Natural Resources, and one from the Ontario

Ministry of Natural Resources produced "Fish Community Objectives for Lake Huron" in 1993. These objectives cover habitat, genetic diversity, species diversity, and the major fish species. The overall objective for the following two decades is to "restore an ecologically balanced fish community dominated by top predators and consisting largely of self-sustaining, indigenous and naturalized species and capable of sustaining annual [commercial and sport] harvests of 19.6 million lbs. (8.9 million kg.)." This figure was the approximate annual harvest of all species from 1912 to 1940, a stable period, and one that the committee thinks is the lake's potential, given its particular physical characteristics. The goal for salmon and trout is a sustained harvest of 5.3 million pounds, of which lake trout would supply approximately three to four million pounds. "There is international consensus that the lake trout should be the dominant salmonine. . . ." The goal for whitefish and ciscoes, the foundation of the commercial fishery, is 8.5 million pounds. Other objectives are set for species ranging from walleyes and channel catfish to the numerous smaller prey species as a group. All the objectives "are predicated on a high level of sea lamprey control," a challenge that U.S. and Canadian scientists are struggling to meet.

The hard work behind this plan fell to the Lake Huron Technical Committee, composed of scientists from the various agencies represented on the Lake Huron Committee, plus the U.S. Fish and Wildlife Service, National Biological Service (now a division in the U.S. Geological Survey), and the Canadian Department of Fisheries and Oceans. The Lake Huron Committee told them what it sought, and the technical committee came up with information and recommendations. On Lake Huron, as on the other Great Lakes, fisheries management is based on the studies and surveys of numerous scientists and technicians, collecting data in rough weather and calm, and many long days spent analyzing and interpreting.

The science done and reported seems unemotional and must, as far as is humanly possible, be objective and true to the evidence, but behind the work of a natural scientist usually lies a love for nature and a very human being. Jim Baker's career, for instance, began with an early passion for hunting and fishing. "I knew in high school," he says, "that I wanted to go into fish or wildlife work." One reason he chose fisheries was his love of hunting and the fact that fisheries work usually slows down during the fall and winter, the hunting season. "Some of the most avid hunters," he says, "are fish biologists." He also remains an avid angler, fishing on average once a week. Jim is a member of the Lake Huron Technical Committee and puts out his share of scientific reports, but he prefers writing for the local fishermen on Saginaw Bay—"Joe Six Pack and Joe Lunch Box. Those are the kind of people I grew up with."

Much of fisheries management is carried out through regulations addressed to sport and commercial fishermen, and these regulations must be enforced to be effective. The Michigan DNR has conservation officers who check on the activities of commercial fishermen, and others who enforce the recreational fish and game laws. One of the latter is Mike Hanson, who covers all of Sanilac County. Most of the fall and winter he's pursuing deer poachers and other miscreants within the hunting fraternity. And most of the spring and summer he's watching over the fishing. I joined him on patrol one early-May morning on the lake.

As we motored at "no-wake" speed out of Port Sanilac harbor, I donned a red survival suit labeled "Michigan Conservation Officer." The lake was pretty calm, but the surface temperature was thirty-eight to forty-four degrees. And though the north wind was light, it felt cold when we speeded up. Powered by two 200-hp. engines, Mike's small "Pursuit" boat could reach 50 mph. We headed north with the sun behind us. "They can't see you coming as well when the sun's behind you," Mike explained.

I admired his technique. This was the day before a weekend salmon/trout derby and a lot of boats were on the water. Mike knew many of these people from hundreds of days on patrol, and he could pass most with just a friendly wave or inquiry about the fishing. But once in a while he spotted something suspicious: a man who might be taking an illegal line out of the water, or guys who looked furtive.

We approached one such boat and Mike began with his usual question: "How's it going?" One of the two men spread his arms out, palms up, signifying no fish. After a few questions, it turned out that neither had a fishing license with him. Mike told them to keep moving ahead so the lines wouldn't get tangled. He tossed them a plastic bottle and asked one man to put his driver's license in it. The man did so and threw the bottle back, Mike wrote a ticket using the license information, and tossed him the bottle with ticket and license. The man took them out and returned the bottle. Just one of the men had been given a ticket. Mike felt the point had been made.

"I knew he was lying," Mike said as we pulled away. "He kept looking down at his feet. And he didn't answer my questions right. He said his license was in his car, but he didn't know the cost and some other things. They passed six places on the way up where they could have bought licenses. This ticket will cost him $85." Most conservation officers use metal containers for the document transfer, but Mike switched to plastic

119

Mike Hanson, DNR conservation officer for Sanilac County.

"because metal can nick the paint on a boat. I figured plastic would be better public relations."

He gave out two other tickets that morning, for having too many lines in the water. "They're allowed two lines for each license," Mike explained, "and they all know it." We patrolled thirty miles up to Harbor Beach and back, talking to a few other fishermen along the way. The successful happily held up their big brown trout. To the unsuccessful—the majority—Mike gave advice on lures and depths to try. He greeted a middle-aged, bushy-bearded fellow going by in a weathered old craft. "I know he sells some of his fish," Mike said, "but I haven't caught him. Pleasant to talk to, though. He's a good fisherman."

Two or three miles offshore we passed huge rafts of long-tailed oldsquaw ducks, pausing en route to their tundra breeding grounds. Near shore Mike showed me a bouldery stretch of bottom where walleyes would come at night to hunt crayfish, when the water warmed up. It was an interesting morning—a privileged look into the life of a man at the legal end of fisheries management.

CHAPTER **10**

# LAKE TROUT AND LAMPREYS

High-bowed and low-sterned, the sturdy, seventy-five-foot *Grayling* pushed her way out of the Thunder Bay River at Alpena and into the foggy waters of Lake Huron. She carried seven of us: Chuck Bowen, fish biologist from the Great Lakes Science Center of the U.S. Geological Survey; his assistant Richard Stickel; Margie Chriscinski, an invertebrate specialist; Renee Mroczek, a biology student at the University of Michigan; engineer Bill Boyle; our captain, Cliff Wilson, and myself, a volunteer. We were headed for Six Fathom Bank, four and a half hours away in the center of the lake. Our mission: to find out if the lake trout stocked there over the past ten years had again reproduced, and to collect samples of the fish and invertebrates on the bank. We hoped the weather would behave long enough for us to accomplish our work. It might give us anywhere from two to seven days.

Our journey was one small part of the long, difficult effort to restore lake trout to Lake Huron. Once the abundant top predator in the lake, it had been reduced first by overfishing and then, in the 1940s and 1950s, virtually exterminated by the invading sea lamprey. Restoring the lake trout requires a detailed knowledge of the species' biology and response to human exploitation. These make a saga of epic proportions.

One can only speculate about the origins of the lake trout, *Salvelinus namaycush*. We know that during the last glacial advance it was forced south into the Mississippi River system and other refugia and that during glacial retreat, which began about 17,000 years ago, it spread north. Today the species occupies large, cold lakes from Alaska to Labrador and south to northern New England, the Great Lakes, and British Columbia. It has been stocked in many lakes of the West.

Over its vast range the lake trout has developed many different strains with varying body sizes, shapes, and habits. Most populations are fairly low in fat, with a streamlined body, but for instance the siscowet, one of the forms in Lake Superior and perhaps formerly in Lake Huron, is extremely fat and oily, and it typically lives at depths greater than 300 feet—deeper than most varieties of lake trout go. Slow-growing and late-maturing, but also long-lived, lake trout have been known to reach an age of thirty-seven years and a weight of 100 pounds. Their color varies; most fish have gray or olive bodies mottled with light gray or whitish spots. The lake trout was the dominant predator in each of the upper Great Lakes and was the only predator that occupied the entire lake from shore to shore and surface to bottom. Altogether it was, and is, I think, an impressive animal.

The lake trout's decline probably began long before the arrival of the sea lamprey. Centuries of fishing by native peoples had little known effect, but fishing by European settlers during the nineteenth century undoubtedly did. Commercial gillnetting by settlers near shore began on Lake Huron in the 1830s. Growing numbers of settlers and fishermen, and technological developments in the fishery, put increasing pressure on the lake trout. Introduction of the large, seaworthy steam tug in 1860, for instance, allowed fishing far from landmarks that the rowboat and sailboat fishery had relied on for finding their nets. Declining catches of lake trout were reported in the 1870s. The peak landings of lake trout in Lake Huron—over seven million pounds annually—occurred from 1891 to 1893, but no records of fishing effort were kept at that time, so we cannot know if catch per unit of fishing effort was actually decreasing. (Such information on fishing effort was not required until 1927 in Michigan and until 1946 in Ontario.) Improvements in gear, which made catching fish easier and more efficient, also could have obscured the picture. In any case, the total catch showed a slow decline after the 1890s and a precipitous decline after 1940. By 1947 the lake trout was commercially extinct in the main basin and by 1955 in Georgian Bay.

The final collapse was undoubtedly due to the arrival of the sea lamprey, an ugly, eel-like fish with a round mouth supplied with rows of sharp teeth on a disc of fleshy muscle. In the center is a rasping tongue. The lamprey attaches its suction-cup mouth to the side of a large fish, rasps a hole with its tongue, and, aided by an anticoagulant in its saliva, draws blood and other bodily fluids out of the fish, leaving it weakened or dead.

The sea lamprey is a species native to the Atlantic Ocean that, like salmon and sea-run trout, typically spends its juvenile life in fresh water and its adult life in salt water, but spawns in streams and is capable of living in fresh water indefinitely if there is enough food. (Several other species of lamprey are native to the Great Lakes, but none of these is a threat to the fisheries.) The sea lamprey made its way from the Hudson River into Lake Ontario by way of the Erie Canal ten years or less after its completion in 1825. (The first sea lamprey was positively identified in Lake Ontario in 1835.) It may, however, have reached the lake much earlier by fighting up the rapids of the St. Lawrence River. By mid-century, if not much earlier, the lamprey was well established in Lake Ontario and had moved up the connecting rivers to the Finger Lakes in New York State. By 1900, the lamprey was abundant enough, along with continued fishing, to reduce lake trout and whitefish to low numbers and cause the extinction of Atlantic salmon in Lake Ontario. Sea lampreys increased rapidly because of abundant prey and forest practices, such as clearing along streams, that caused stream temperatures to rise to levels favorable to lamprey reproduction.

The four other Great Lakes might have been spared this disastrous newcomer (as well as some of the other alien invaders) if it weren't for engineering changes on the Welland Canal. Prior to 1919, the canal was watered partly from the Grand River, whose current attracted anadromous fish like the lamprey. In 1919, this source was cut off and all the flow came from Lake Erie. Swimming against this current, sea lampreys entered Lake Erie, where it became established in the 1920s. From here it was a clear shot to the three upper lakes.

The presence of sea lampreys in Lake Huron was inferred in 1932 from wounds on fish and was confirmed in 1937 by actual observation of a lamprey. A rapidly rising lamprey population soon drove lake trout to commercial extinction and decimated other large deepwater fish—burbot and large chubs. It then turned to remaining species such as whitefish, ciscoes, suckers, and walleyes. The lamprey wrought the same devastation in Lake Michigan and the lesser, but still serious, decline of the large native fish in Lake Superior, where conditions were not as favorable to the lamprey. In Lake Huron in the late 1950s, only two small populations of native lake trout remained, in Georgian Bay. Things looked bleak for the lake trout, as well as for the fisheries in general.

In natural resources management, as in so many other areas of human life, it often takes a crisis to get remedial action. Here was an obvious crisis. The response was frantic activity by fishery agencies around the lakes to find a solution to the lamprey problem. The need for coordination was met in 1955, when the U.S. and Canada signed the Convention on Great Lakes Fisheries. This created the Great Lakes Fishery Commission (GLFC), with responsibility to coordinate fishery research and management, to advise governments on measures to improve the fisheries, and to develop measures and programs to control the sea lamprey. This last task has taken most of the GLFC budget since 1958, and most people would say it has been money well spent.

The primary lamprey control method used now was discovered through sheer long-term persistence in the face of doubt. Elsewhere people were trying weirs and lamprey traps, destruction of spawning beds, or electroshocking during spawning runs to capture adult lampreys— all with minor success. But at Hammond Bay, Michigan, a Bureau of Commercial Fisheries research laboratory under the direction of Vernon Applegate had been experimenting with chemicals since 1950. Ten-liter jars were filled with water, lampreys and rainbow trout were put in, and the chemical to be tested was added. After seven years and more than 6,000 experiments, during which time bored workers resigned and had to be replaced, a chemical was discovered that killed the lampreys but not the trout. This chemical was too expensive for widespread use, but a cheaper one in the same family was found to have the same effect. It was 3-trifluoromethyl-4-nitrophenol (TFM for short). After tests in artificial streambeds and in nearby Elliot Creek, TFM was applied in twelve tributaries of Lake Superior. Ninety-eight percent of the lamprey larvae in those streams died, and other organisms didn't. It looked like safe lamprey control was possible.

Beginning in 1958, U.S. and Canadian federal fisheries personnel, coordinated by the GLFC, applied TFM and, later, Bayer 73 (2',5-dichloro-4'-nitrosalicyanilide, another chemical known to kill lampreys) in lamprey spawning streams throughout the Great Lakes (except for Lake Erie, where conditions supported only low lamprey populations). Treatments were completed on Lake Superior tributaries first, then those of Lake Michigan. In 1970, the first round of treatments was completed on the 102 Lake Huron lamprey spawning tributaries. Overall, lamprey populations were reduced by about 90 percent.

Meanwhile, as the lamprey treatments progressed, state agencies, coordinated by the Great Lakes Fishery Commission, began restocking lake trout. The original brood stock was selected and cultured at the Marquette State Fish Hatchery. This continues today, but the eggs taken from them are reared to planting size at the Jordan River National Fish Hatchery in the northern Lower Peninsula of Michigan, at another hatchery in the eastern Upper Peninsula, and one at Iron River, Wisconsin.

The goals were to improve the sport fishery for lake trout and to establish naturally reproducing populations. The first goal has been met, but progress toward the second has been good to nonexistent, depending on which lake you look at. In Lake Superior, repeated stocking has succeeded in reestablishing reproduction, large-scale stocking has been stopped, and restoration was declared a success in 1996. In Lake Michigan, the success rate has been zero. Fish biologists are unsure whether the problem is egg predation, siltation on the spawning reefs, toxic chemicals, or all of the above factors.

In Lake Huron, lake trout once spawned on many reefs and shoals around the margins of the lake and on offshore reefs, including two in the middle of the lake—Yankee Reef and Six Fathom Bank. The lamprey wiped out all these stocks except small populations in Georgian Bay's Parry Sound and upper McGregor Bay. Restocking, now at the rate of over one million yearlings a year by the U.S. and over two million by Canada, has established some reproduction at Thunder Bay, near Alpena, and some at South Bay, Manitoulin Island. A Canadian fisheries technician told me there was also some at other sites on the south side of Manitoulin Island. The problem is that few lake trout, whether stocked or naturally reproduced, live to spawning age. The lampreys get them. As a result of reduced budgets for stream treatment with lampricides and flourishing lamprey reproduction in the St. Marys River system, which is too large for total treatment, lamprey populations have rebounded in Lake Huron. Probably because the main source is the St. Marys River, lampreys are most abundant in the northern part of the lake and dwindle southward.

One approach to this problem has been to try to find strains of lake trout that are more resistant to lampreys. The lake trout from Seneca Lake in New York may turn out to be such a strain. It has coexisted with the sea lamprey for at least 150 years and possibly much longer, and therefore may have evolved characteristics that give it some protection. An experiment was set up to test its resistance. Beginning in 1985, nearly equal numbers of Seneca and Marquette strains were coded-wire-tagged and stocked in the North Lake Trout Refuge, adjacent to the mouth of the St. Marys

River, and on Six Fathom Bank, far to the south. An additional strain taken from Lewis Lake, Wyoming, but originally introduced there from Lake Michigan, was also planted on Six Fathom Bank. As of 1993, among lakewide recoveries of lake trout stocked on Six Fathom Bank and longer than 632 millimeters (about twenty-five inches), Seneca-strain trout were four and a half times more abundant than the Marquette strain and three times more abundant than the Lewis Lake strain. Among trout of that same size from the North Refuge, Seneca fish were more than forty times more abundant than the Marquette strain. The two strains from the North Refuge showed similar lamprey wounding rates among fish more than 632 millimeters long, but the Seneca fish below 532 millimeters (about twenty-one inches) had a much lower wounding rate, indicating that they might be attacked less frequently than the Marquette strain during their earlier years and therefore might have a better chance for survival.

If more fish of the Seneca Lake strain can survive to reproductive age (five years for males and eight years for females), might it be one answer to establishing reproducing lake trout populations in Lake Huron? That was the main question that sent Chuck Bowen and his helpers out to Six Fathom Bank that foggy May morning, a trip that Chuck had been making for most of his dozen years of lake trout research. We wanted to find out if the lake trout had reproduced that year, as they had for the past two, what strain or strains were reproducing, what was the makeup of the lake trout population out there, and what was the status of prey organisms on the bank. We would collect fish and record data. Renee Mroczek, with Mary Curtis, her scientist supervisor back at the Great Lakes Science Center, would try to identify through genetic analysis the parentage of any lake trout fry we might find.

Cormorants and loons skittered out of our way as we headed out into the lake, the *Grayling* rolling hard from the seas. A few miles out, a tug and barge appeared on our radar. Our skipper, silver-haired Cliff Wilson, radioed the tug captain we would go behind him. We passed within a quarter mile but never saw them in the fog. Other unseen boats appeared and disappeared on the screen. "One trip on Lake Superior," Cliff said, "we had fog for seventeen days. We never saw land." He had piloted the *Grayling* on all three upper Great Lakes since 1977, and before that had been a commercial fisherman on Lake Superior. Cliff had seen a few things.

We reached Six Fathom Bank at 11:30 A.M. Time to go to work. "Get your yellows on," Chuck barked. With a crane Bill Boyle, the engineer, lowered a small beam trawl off the stern. He had made it himself—vertical parallel steel bars at the mouth, a thirty-foot fine-meshed bag trailing behind. We dragged it twelve to twenty-five fathoms down (the highest point on the bank being six fathoms) over the rough limestone bedrock. One man kept his hand on the cable to feel if the trawl needed to come up or down.

Twenty minutes later Bill pulled it up. In the lab we scooped out a small part of the contents of the bag into shallow pans. Mostly there were clumps of brown and green algae, Swiss cheese chunks of limestone, small pointed snails, and tiny translucent opossum shrimp (*Mysis relicta*). There were also things we were looking for. We picked out the sculpins so Margie could later check their stomach contents, and the caddisfly egg cases so she could identify the species. (There are two species of flightless caddisflies that are unique to this bank, Chuck told me.) And we looked for lake trout fry. After some minutes one was found! Joy reigned—reproduction had once again occurred! The tiny fish was about one inch long, very slender with a big head and dark eyes, its body light colored but speckled. From seven trawls in three locations we recovered fourteen lake trout fry, enough to tell us that a significant amount of reproduction had occurred. Many more must have been down there in the crevices of the rock.

I tried to imagine the events that had led to the birth and growth of these little fish: the gathering of spawning adults in October, males first, rubbing and fanning algae and debris from the rocks; after dusk, males pressing against the sides of females; the shedding of eggs and milt; the eggs—several thousand per female—drifting down into crevices among the rocks; the birth of larvae a few months later, barely half an inch long, with big mouth and yolk sac, which supplies them food, as do zooplankton and tiny insects later on; when the yolk sac was fully absorbed, the fry descending to deeper water to avoid predators. Our fry had absorbed their yolk sacs. "We were just in time to catch some," Chuck said. "Last year a lot of them still had the yolk sac. The warmer winter this year must have led to earlier hatching."

From 5:30 to 7:00 P.M. we put out 8,100 feet of gill net, two people standing at the stern spreading the net to avoid tangles as it went out over a roller. We set the nine nets, each tied to the next, across the reef, covering a range of depths. Each net has mesh sizes ranging from six inches down to two, to capture lake trout of different ages. We anchored near the spar at one end of the string of nets and settled down for the night. So did seventy-five herring gulls, floating nearby. They knew this boat meant food. It was a beautiful evening, peaceful, in the middle of Lake Huron, out of sight of land.

During the night, we each had to stand one and a half hours of watch. We were not in the shipping lanes, but you never know what might happen—a stray boat, a dragging anchor, even—God forbid—a fire. I drew 11:30 to 1:00 A.M. I watched the radar and the global positioning system (GPS), which gives your coordinates accurate to several decimal places. As the boat swings on its anchor, the GPS numbers change slightly, but not like they would if the anchor were dragging. A blip or two appeared on the radar, but too far away to be of concern. One o'clock came sooner than expected. It's amazing how fast time moves when you're half asleep (but also half awake, Captain).

The morning, too, was beautiful, with light wind. First order of business: pull in the gill nets. The net came in through an opening in the starboard side of the bow and wound around a net lifter as in a commercial fishing boat. Bill coiled net into a box and he and Chuck picked fish out of the net. They sorted them by net number and mesh size to indicate what part of this transect of the reef they were caught on.

Altogether, the net yielded about 200 lake trout of various sizes up to fifteen pounds or so and ages from three to ten years. "We haven't been able to catch one- to two-year-old fish," Chuck said. "They must get down in the rocks where they're hard to catch." We also caught a few burbot, whitefish, and alewives. The fish were placed in labeled bags and boxes, iced, and taken to the lab near the stern for examination. The lake trout got the most attention. Chuck measured their length and weight, noted any lamprey wounds (there were just a few), their sex, whether the fish were immature or mature, and any prey species in their stomach (nearly all identifiable prey were alewives). The guts and heads of some went into ziplock bags for a parasite study. One of us recorded the data Chuck called out and another moved an electronic detector over the trout's snout. If it beeps, which it usually did, there's a tiny wire tag in the snout. "Don't drop that thing," Chuck cautioned, "it cost $4,000." He cut off the top of the snouts that had tags inside and placed them in a compartmented plastic box.

Those tiny wire tags, only one millimeter long and the width of a human hair, had been injected with a hypodermic needle into the yearling fish before it had been released. A number on the tag, which can be read through a microscope, identifies the source, including the date of stocking, the strain (Seneca, Lewis Lake, or Marquette in this case), and the hatchery from which the fish came. All is vital for determining the relative success of various strains in the effort to establish reproducing populations. If the

Chuck Bowen pulls up the water sampler on the *Grayling* at Six Fathom Bank.

day is reached when many of the lake trout on Six Fathom Bank *don't* give off a beep, we'll know they're coming back on their own.

While Chuck, Renee, and Margie processed our lake trout catch, we started deep trawling to find out what sort of prey populations were down there for the lake trout to feed on. These trawls, fished at the same locations each year, are conducted with a long, small-meshed net held open at the mouth by heavy wooden runners, called doors, that run along the bottom. While examining trout, Chuck had commented on the large amount of fat on many of them. "There's a lot to eat out here," he had said. Pulling up the net, we had to agree. After a trawl, we counted and weighed the fish, but the second trawl caught so many we had to just take a sample for recording. Ninety-five percent of the fish were alewives, the rest small smelt and an occasional whitefish, chub, or burbot. Chubs are increasing in Lake Huron, but on that day, in that place, alewives were dominating their level of the food pyramid.

On the third trawl, the net caught on something and tore. We had to replace it with one of the two spare nets. Then we had to pull up the fourth trawl early because it was getting into rocks. It was now 4:30 P.M. Gale warnings were up for the next evening. Chuck and the captain decided to go in. Chuck could finish processing the remaining five boxes of trout in port and wait for good weather to go out again.

Nearly everywhere in Lake Huron, as I mentioned, the lamprey wiped out the native populations of lake trout, including the Six Fathom Bank spawners, and non-native strains must be used in the effort to rebuild reproduction. But in two locations in Georgian Bay, small remnant populations survived the lamprey onslaught. The Ontario Ministry of Natural Resources is trying to protect and build these populations. The most promising one spawns in Parry Sound, known locally as Big Sound, on the eastern side of Georgian Bay. Here, in 1979, eggs were collected from wild fish and the resulting yearlings were stocked in the sound. Later, a brood stock was developed to continue supplying yearlings.

To further protect the Big Sound lake trout, a Public Advisory Committee, composed of representatives of the main user groups, was established in 1993 to make recommendations. After numerous committee meetings and several public meetings, the committee recommended new lake trout regulations for the sound, which were adopted in 1994. They set up three zones. The innermost has the longest harvest season, including one in winter for ice fishing. The next zone has a shorter fishing season. Part of the seasons in both of these zones is catch-and-release only, and lake trout fishing is closed during the fall spawning period. A third zone, at the mouth of Big Sound, is a lake trout refuge where no lake trout fishing is allowed. The daily catch and possession limit in the two open zones are one fish only, and any lake trout over twenty-four inches long must be released, to protect the adult fish. Two studies have shown that most lake trout caught and released survive. Anglers are given information on how to release lake trout with least effect on them. So far, support for the program has been good and the number of wild fish seems to be increasing.

The other surviving pocket of native lake trout is tucked way up in the northwest corner of Georgian Bay, at the far north end of McGregor Bay, a famous fishing area. Back in through narrow channels lies Iroquois Bay, and here small numbers of lake trout continue to spawn successfully, perhaps protected by their remote location and lack of adjacent lamprey spawning streams. Competition with chinook salmon on the spawning shoals may be a problem, however, and stocking of other lake trout strains in the 1970s may have diluted the native strain. The OMNR did some stocking of the local strain here in 1989 and conducts research but has not instituted any special fishing regulations, other than closure of ice fishing in a refuge area. Perhaps when more is known a program similar to the one at Big Sound will be considered.

So the battle for the lake trout is two-pronged: find and establish strains that are resistant to the sea lamprey, and find a way to hold lamprey numbers at a low level. Chuck Bowen is one of those who has given a large chunk of his life to the first effort. Others are dedicated to the second.

Roger Bergstedt is a lamprey researcher. I'm not sure what a lamprey researcher should look like, but Roger reminded me of a middle-aged former professional football player—a tight end perhaps. Though white-haired and needing bifocals, he said, he was still an active outdoorsman. The evening before I met him at the Hammond Bay Biological Station, he had gone out in the snowy woods, shot a deer with his muzzle loader, and dressed it. He was a bit tired in the morning, but not too tired to brief me on the lamprey situation.

"I used to do the kind of work Chuck Bowen is doing now, on lake trout in Lake Ontario. But I decided it was more important to go into lamprey control research. There's no future for the lake trout unless we can control the lamprey." At Hammond Bay he was continuing the research of Vernon Applegate, who had worked out the main stages of sea lamprey life history and discovered an effective lampricide when the station was run by the Bureau of Commercial Fisheries (it's now under the U.S. Geological Survey Great Lakes Science Center, but most of its research is directed and funded by the Great Lakes Fishery Commission). Bergstedt and his colleagues were seeking more detailed knowledge of the lamprey's life cycle and refining control methods to find those that are most effective and affordable.

Sea lampreys migrate to tributary streams in the spring and early summer, seeking gravel riffles for spawning—the same kind of spawning beds used by Pacific salmon and rainbow trout. There they lay some 70,000 eggs and then die. After the eggs hatch, the larvae drift downstream and burrow into sand or silt. Here they feed on detritus carried down by the current and on a slimy organic film on rocks until they grow to about six or seven inches. This can take anywhere from three to twelve years, and possibly up to seventeen years in rare cases. Five years is about the average,

Bergstedt said. "In a very infertile stream it may take longer." At this point they metamorphose into adults. This process usually begins in June or July. "Starting, say, in July, they would not be feeding and the energy for that transformation is fairly substantial. They develop eyes and a different gill arrangement," since water cannot be taken in through the mouth when they're attached to a fish. "All of this transformation is fueled by stored fat. A large number of the animals that metamorphose during the summer leave the stream during the fall, generally in November and December—once the water temperature drops below about fifty degrees. There's another peak of migration out of the stream during the spring runoff.

"A typical weight when they enter the lake is about five grams. They go from that to an average of around 100 grams by the end of the following September. They then double their weight to around 200 grams in October and the first half of November, a period when most of the damage is done." They remain in the lake for twelve to twenty months and grow to about one and a half feet. During this parasitic phase each lamprey kills about twenty or more pounds of fish, selecting the largest prey available. There are currently an estimated 250,000 to 500,000 lampreys in northern Lake Huron, and are thus removing some five to ten million pounds of trout, salmon, whitefish, and other large fish during their one to two years in the lake. This is roughly half of the total annual commercial and sport harvest in Lake Huron.

"There are only a couple of points when the sea lamprey is vulnerable," Bergstedt said. "One is when they make their spawning migration in the spring." The other is during the larval stage. "They can be killed at any time in the larval stage. When we do a stream treatment we expect to kill all year classes [ages]." A treatment is preceded by study of the stream's rate of flow and volume, finding application sites, and tests to determine the proper concentration of lampricide—one that will kill lampreys but do minimal harm to other aquatic organisms. During application of the lampricide the stream is periodically analyzed at many locations to ensure proper concentration, and dead lampreys are collected to provide information on lamprey populations. In the rare case where large numbers of larvae survive, the stream is scheduled for retreatment.

The other point at which sea lampreys are vulnerable is during the spawning run. Control methods used during this stage or being tested include specially designed low dams; release of sterilized males into spawning streams so that eggs will be infertile; trapping; and odor-producing materials that attract or repel lampreys and thus confuse them in their efforts to spawn.

Before leaving the station, I was shown a few of the research animals. Bergstedt stirred up the sand in one tank and several-inch-long larvae came wiggling up, then burrowed back into the sand. In another tank swam much larger, metamorphosed lamprey, with their disk-shaped mouths and pores for intake of water. A specimen bottle contained a saltwater, sea-run lamprey, largest and ugliest of all. A very unpleasant adversary, this animal.

The Sea Lamprey Control Centre, on the Canadian side of the St. Marys River rapids, is responsible for the Canadian part of lamprey research and control in the Great Lakes. Here Rod McDonald explained the efforts to solve the St. Marys River lamprey problem. "The St. Marys is considered the largest known sea lamprey larvae population extant in the Great Lakes," he said. "Estimates made from mark-recapture studies were six million [larvae]. . . . Of these, it's possible that up to as many as 8 percent transform into adults each year."

Low dams cannot be used because they would block navigation, and one treatment of the whole St. Marys River system with TFM would cost at least $20 million—an unacceptable amount—so alternate approaches are being investigated. All rely on knowledge of the distribution and density of larvae in the river. Using newly developed deepwater electrofishing gear, geographic positioning systems, and satellite information systems, researchers mapped that information. They learned that most of the larvae are concentrated in distinct patches, such as the North Channel, backwater areas, small side channels, and the gravel beds under the power plant tail races at the Sault rapids. Application of TFM and a bottom-release lampricide—granular Bayer 73—to such areas may prove to be cost effective. Release of sterile males at major spawning areas is also being tested.

Trapping may be the cheapest and one of the most effective methods. "We've been trapping lamprey in the river since 1975," McDonald said. "Our trapping has gradually improved to the point where we now believe we're taking as much as 40 percent of the run." The traps have mesh sides and a funnel leading in from either side, but offset so they can't swim out the other one. They are placed at the base of power plants on either side of the river at Sault Ste. Marie, which most of the lampreys visit as they search for spawning sites and where much of the spawning actually takes place. "We catch as many as 13,000 in the course of one season in our trap on the Canadian side. We truck the males to the research center at Hammond Bay. They sterilize them and bring them back to the river. So we're getting a double effect: we're not only removing the animals, we're reducing the reproduction of females that remain in the river. The ratio of sterile to fertile males we're achieving on the spawning beds is .6 or .7 to 1.0. This year we got nearly the same ratio with the eggs. With the sterile-male program thrown on top of the trapping, we're getting about 65 percent control. But we're still not sure if that's enough to do the job. We're looking for new places to catch lamprey."

Knowing how to control lamprey is one thing. Getting the money to do it is another. The federal governments on both sides of the border reduced the lamprey control budgets in recent years and ground was lost. The number of juvenile sea lamprey caught by Canadian commercial fishermen north and south of Manitoulin Island jumped in 1983 and rose until the early 1990s, when it stabilized. The rise in the 1980s, ironically, was thought to be due to cleanup of the St. Marys River, which improved the spawning environment, but later budget cuts undoubtedly boosted the rise. On Georgian Bay, where lampreys had earlier been relatively scarce, a commercial fisherman told me in the summer of 1996 that 70 percent of his whitefish had old or new lamprey scars. In the late 1990s some budget improvement occurred.

One hopes that the legislators understand the situation: without adequate budgets, the tremendous investment in lamprey control and salmonid stocking may have been wasted and the fisheries may once again collapse.

# CHAPTER 11

# RESTORING THE LAKE

The fish fauna and populations of Lake Huron in 1615, when Samuel de Champlain reached its shore, were much different from the ones we know today, because of the human influences that followed. In pre-settlement days, abundant lake herring and deepwater ciscoes supported great numbers of the top predator, lake trout. Huge schools of whitefish moved seasonally from the depths to shallows, and lake sturgeon up to seven feet long cruised the shoal waters and spawned in tributary streams.

Since those days, overfishing, introductions of fish and invertebrates, both intentional and unintentional, and toxic contamination have changed the fish community forever. The slow-maturing lake sturgeon, considered a nuisance because of its destructiveness in nets, was reduced to near extinction by fishing. Four species of deepwater ciscoes are now regarded as extinct and two others are seldom seen. Lake herring are only a minor element in the Lake Huron fish community. And as we have seen, Huron's native lake trout nearly disappeared. Aldo Leopold, the great American wildlife manager and conservationist, wrote, "The first rule of intelligent tinkering is to keep all the parts." We came within a hair's breadth of losing several of Lake Huron's major parts. "Tinkering" to restore stability begins from a narrow base. Total restoration of the original magnificence is impossible.

Complicating the picture are some parts that have been added, many of them unintentional and unwanted. The deliberate introductions—

most of them species of salmon and trout—were all intended to enhance sport fishing (and solve the alewife problem, in the case of salmon), and for the most part they have done that. First to Lake Huron came brown trout, at the end of the nineteenth century, from plantings in Lake Michigan, followed by rainbow trout in 1904, which made their way to Lake Huron after introduction to Lake Superior in 1895. Rainbow trout now spawn in most major tributaries of Lake Huron except those draining Canada's Precambrian Shield. Small populations of brown trout have also become naturalized in a few tributary rivers.

The salmon experiments began much later: Kokanee salmon in 1965 by the Ontario Department of Lands and Forests; coho salmon in 1967, chinook salmon in 1969, and Atlantic salmon in 1972 by the Michigan Department of Natural Resources. Pink salmon, originating from an accidental release in Lake Superior in 1956, were discovered in Lake Huron's Carp River in 1969. The pink salmon, considered an inferior sport fish and lowest quality food among the Great Lakes salmon tribe, has established some spawning runs but seems to have decreased from earlier levels. The chinook also reproduces in Lake Huron but is maintained largely by annual stocking, as are brown and rainbow trout (although natural reproduction maintains rainbow populations in parts of Canadian Lake Huron), along with relatively small plants of Atlantic salmon at Sault Ste. Marie and the Carp River. Stocking of kokanee salmon ended in 1972 and the species has not been seen in recent years.

The introduced salmon and trout, bolstered by continued stocking, now constitute a large proportion of the top-level predators in Lake Huron. To ensure more stability of the lake's ecosystem, as described earlier, the fishery agencies on the lake, along with U.S. and Canadian federal agencies, have agreed to try to restore the native lake trout to a dominant role among the salmonids (salmon and trout), but the road to this goal looks long and hard.

One other deliberate introduction has been cause for regret, although it does contribute marginally to the commercial fishery. The carp, native to Asia but introduced widely elsewhere, was esteemed as a food fish in Europe and was brought to the United States in 1831. Successful plantings in Lake Erie in 1883 led to the fish's spread to Lake Huron about 1900 and then Lake Michigan. Unfortunately, the carp feeds voraciously on invertebrates and the roots of aquatic vegetation and stirs up great quantities of sediment, muddying the water and perhaps interfering with the spawning of perch and other fish.

Introduction of the rainbow smelt, a slender silvery fish reaching, at most, fourteen inches, has been a mixed blessing, on balance negative. Native to the Atlantic coast, the St. Lawrence River, and Lake Ontario, it was planted in Crystal Lake, near Lake Michigan, in 1912. It soon spread to Lake Michigan and in 1925 reached Lake Huron, with Lakes Superior and Erie soon to follow. The immense schools of smelt became a target of commercial fishermen, especially in Lakes Michigan, Superior, and Erie. Landings in Lake Erie reached twenty to forty-five million pounds in the 1980s. The smelt was a smaller component of the Lake Huron catch, fading to insignificance in the 1990s. Tasty and pleasantly crunchy when deep-fried, the smelt also became the target of armies of dip-netters during the spring spawning run in hundreds of streams around the Great Lakes. Smelt populations dropped in the 1940s, then rose again, and in recent years have been fairly stable in Lake Huron. The smelt remains a major prey species as well as predator on eggs, invertebrates, and small fish in Lake Huron.

The smelt's unwelcome effect has been its impact on native fish species, including some of major ecological and economic importance. Declines of whitefish and other ciscoes, including the lake herring, were seen after the arrival of smelt in Lake Huron in the 1920s. Competition for food is the presumed cause, although not proven. After the Lake Huron smelt population suffered a collapse in the winter of 1942–43, the greatest year class of whitefish recorded to that time got its start the following spring. Other ciscoes also reversed their decline. Arrival of smelt on lake trout spawning reefs in the spring, just when trout "swim-up" fry are emerging from the rocks, could be one reason lake trout reproduction has been so low in Lake Huron. The fry would make excellent smelt food. It may be more than a coincidence that lake trout numbers soared along the North Shore of Minnesota, in Lake Superior, just as smelt populations bottomed out.

Not far behind the smelt came the alewife, another saltwater native. It had reached Lake Ontario by 1873, but was not known in Lake Erie until 1931, perhaps stymied by the same current directions in the Welland Canal system that seem to have held up the lamprey. The first alewife in Lake Huron was recorded in 1933. By the 1960s alewives had become abundant, perhaps constituting the majority of fish biomass in the lake.

The rise to dominance by alewife and smelt can be attributed to lamprey predation accompanied by changes in commercial fishing targets. When lampreys proliferated in the lake in the 1930s and 1940s, they virtually wiped out lake trout and severely reduced the populations of burbot, large chubs, whitefish, ciscoes, and suckers. Commercial fishing shifted toward large chubs after the decline of lake trout and whitefish, further reducing chub numbers. Released from predation and competition for food, alewives and smelt had the lake pretty much to themselves. The result, as we have seen, was gleeful smelt dip-netters, rotting alewives on the beaches, and the introduction of Pacific salmon to provide large predators and exciting sport fishing.

By 1970, as a result of these invasions, fishing pressure, and local contamination from excess nutrients and toxic chemicals, the native fish community in Lake Huron was at a low ebb. Commercial fishing statistics reflect this. From a high of about twenty-eight million pounds in 1900, the annual harvest of all species had fallen to about four million pounds by 1970.

From this low point, restoration efforts began in earnest. Commercial fishing was further regulated to reduce pressure on key species, sea lamprey control was instituted on a large scale, lake trout rehabilitation became a top priority, and massive campaigns to clean up polluted areas began in all the Great Lakes. Today, considerable progress has been made on these fronts, except for lake trout rehabilitation, which still languishes in the lakes below Superior.

What has resulted, in general, is a shift back toward nineteenth-century conditions. The change was seen first in Lake Superior. Lake trout reproduction there, aided by stocking, has resumed in many spawning areas. Dense schools of lake herring are again being seen, as smelt decline. The resilient whitefish has increased to numbers rivaling those early in the twentieth century.

In Lake Huron, the biggest recovery is that of whitefish. As described earlier, commercial fishermen in Canada report catches as good as any this century. Perhaps equally important, the bloater, a large, native, deepwater chub, has been gaining ground in relation to the two other principal prey species in the lake—rainbow smelt and alewife. The Great Lakes Science Center has been conducting fall surveys of the major prey fish stocks in Lake Huron since 1973, conducting bottom trawling near Harbor Beach, AuSable Point, Alpena, Hammond Bay, and De Tour Village, supplemented in recent years by offshore trawls at Six Fathom Bank and off Goderich, Ontario. Over these years, the relative biomass of bloaters among the three species rose from about 1 percent to over 60 percent in the early 1990s. In terms of actual abundance, the alewife has declined by about one-half since the mid-1970s, but the smelt has not declined in these surveys, contrary to what you might expect from the small stream spawning runs of recent years. Apparently, offshore spawning by smelt has maintained numbers while stream spawners have been selected out by the large harvest there. Among other prey species, deepwater sculpins, slimy sculpins, and ninespine sticklebacks appear to have decreased in recent years, while trout-perch are holding steady. There is little evidence that the lake herring has shown any significant recovery in Lake Huron.

One of the scientists studying these trends is Gary Curtis, whom I managed to separate from his computer long enough at the beginning of my Lake Huron year to give me a glimpse of the big picture. After getting a rundown on the major prey species, I asked him why he thought the alewife was slumping. "Alewife abundance," he said, "may be affected by environmental conditions as well as predation by salmon and other large fish. It's a marine species, not adapted well to the greater environmental extremes in the Great Lakes, especially cold. Conditions such as water temperatures during spawning and the rate of spring warm-up may have affected alewife reproduction and abundance." Gary is studying the long-term dynamics of alewives and may have a more definitive answer later. Other scientists are studying smelt and chubs.

Interactions among fish species and their environments are complex, so it's hard to understand what is going on down there, especially since direct observation is difficult. Consider the yellow perch, for instance. "In the '30s and early '40s, perch fishing was really good here," said Jack Falls, proprietor of a sport shop in Port Sanilac. "Perch fishing and pheasant hunting made Port Sanilac." In the late 1940s, when my in-laws brought their children up for a day, perch fishing was still good. "I thought I'd never finish cleaning those fish," my mother-in-law recalls. In the 1960s, however, the perch population crashed. Sometime in the 1970s, my father-in-law and I and four others on the *Miss Port Sanilac* caught one perch in half a day of fishing. Since then, perch fishing at Port Sanilac has been spotty, at best.

In Saginaw Bay, a major perch-fishing area that has been studied by the DNR, cycles in perch populations occur, but no one is sure of the causes. Peaks of abundance occurred from 1943 to 1955 and 1978 to 1989. Lows came in the late 1920s and early 1930s, from the 1960s through the mid-1970s, and again in the mid-1990s. Proposed explanations for these variations range from weather conditions, fishing pressure, and competition from exotic species to competition within the species itself depending on the density of perch.

Jim Baker wrote a paper about all this—"The Great Perch Puzzle"— for the many mystified perch fishermen. A cold, late spring, he explained, can depress reproduction and first-year survival because it delays the spring bloom of phytoplankton, which delays the population explosion of zooplankton, which feed on the phytoplankton. If the perch fry hatch at their normal time, in late April, there is little zooplankton for them to feed on and many die. If they hatch later, at the same time as the delayed increase of zooplankton, they may not grow enough by autumn to survive the winter.

Another possible explanation for poor perch reproduction, Jim wrote, is competition with exotic species such as white perch and zebra mussels. The white perch is another invader that entered the Great Lakes via the St. Lawrence Seaway. First discovered in Saginaw Bay in 1983, it became abundant in the late 1980s. Since its young compete with young yellow perch for the same food and living space, it may have been partly responsible for the decline of yellow perch during the fall of 1989 and the succeeding winter.

The zebra mussel competes with yellow perch in a less direct but perhaps equally effective way. Zebra mussels were first found in Saginaw Bay in 1990 and soon "proliferated in astronomical proportions." Each adult zebra mussel, of which there are now millions in the bay, can filter more than a quart of water every day, from which it takes phytoplankton. This reduces the food for zooplankton and thus zooplankton populations, reducing the food for young perch. The zebra mussel isn't totally bad for yellow perch, however, because straining out so much phytoplankton makes the water clearer, thus allowing more penetration of sunlight and encouraging the growth of aquatic vegetation. This in turn provides habitat for invertebrate perch food, and more habitat for perch.

Sport fishermen like to blame commercial fishermen for a lack of fish, but Baker ruled this out as a recent cause for perch declines. "There is compelling evidence that heavy exploitation by commercial fishermen has had a significant impact on Saginaw Bay perch abundance in the past, but that is not the case today." Commercial fishermen are not allowed to take perch under 8.5 inches and are restricted to trap nets. Their catch parallels the ups and downs of perch cycles and is much smaller than the sport catch. In 1993, for instance, sport fishermen in the bay took about 890,000 perch; commercial fishermen took 75,000 pounds (at one-half pound per fish this would be about 150,000 perch).

Hunters and fishermen also like to find nonhuman scapegoats for lack of game or fish: red foxes get blamed for low pheasant populations, and wolves for declines of caribou. Similarly, "the growing population of large walleyes in the bay has led many perch fishermen to blame the decline of their favorite species on predation by walleyes," Baker wrote, but "our research does not support this conclusion." The DNR studies showed that walleyes take only small numbers of perch, preferring fish with soft rays to the spiny-rayed yellow perch.

One other explanation for the yellow perch cycles has more scientific validity. This is the density-competition theory. In the simplest terms, it goes like this: favorable conditions produce very large year classes of perch. The increase in numbers of small perch heightens competition between individual fish for food. "Larger perch out-compete smaller perch and the smaller fish ultimately starve to death. . . . Many medium size fish will also die at the onset of sexual maturity because they can't find enough food to meet the increased energy demands upon their bodies as the production of sperm and eggs begins." The loss of small perch results in more food for the survivors, which grow faster. The population becomes smaller but consists of larger fish. This situation prevails until especially favorable conditions for another year class of the highly prolific perch come again, starting the cycle all over.

Whatever the reasons, the bay's perch populations fluctuate between small numbers of large fish and large numbers of small fish. Baker concludes his epistle to perch fishermen: "one of the only absolutes in this complex equation is that we can't have lots of perch and big perch at the same time!"

If the early 1970s marked the beginning of improvement in Lake Huron's fish community, it also was the time for serious attention to water quality, throughout the Great Lakes. The prime symbol of this need became Cleveland's flaming Cuyahoga River, which was so loaded with oil and debris that in June 1969 it caught fire. Lake Erie's massive algae blooms, and high levels of toxic chemicals in fish and water birds throughout the Great Lakes further highlighted the lakes' poor condition. Books and articles came out with titles like *The Late, Great Lakes,* sounding a wake-up call for the Great Lakes like Rachel Carson's earlier *Silent Spring* had done for the whole continent on the subject of environmental contamination.

Nothing short of a major, bi-national cleanup effort would reverse the lakes' deterioration, and this began with the 1972 Great Lakes Water Quality Agreement. The institutional framework for carrying out this agreement was already partially in place, thanks to the Boundary Waters Treaty of 1909, under which the International Joint Commission (IJC) was created to achieve cooperation between the United States and Canada on boundary water issues. The IJC, and particularly its Great Lakes Water

Quality Board, became the watchdog and advisor with respect to the 1972 agreement and its subsequent revisions. The IJC makes continuing assessments of the state of the Great Lakes and of the effectiveness of government programs to fulfill the purpose of the agreements, and it analyzes the reports and plans prepared under the agreement.

The 1972 agreement dealt primarily with reducing nutrient flow to Lakes Erie and Ontario. During the next six years the IJC's International Reference Group on Pollution from Land Use Activities (PLUARG), created under the agreement, produced more than 100 reports, which laid the groundwork for the greatly expanded 1978 Great Lakes Water Quality Agreement. The overarching goal of the 1978 agreement is "to restore and maintain the chemical, physical, and biological integrity of the Great Lakes Basin Ecosystem." As the goal implies, the agreement takes an "ecosystem approach," recognizing the need to address linkages among air, land, and water and the effects of human activities on these. It's a tall order.

Lake Huron is in much better shape than Erie and Ontario. In most of Lake Huron, limnological conditions have changed only slightly since the 1800s. This good water quality can be attributed to the lake's deep, oligotrophic character and its relatively small human population. The population density per square mile in its drainage basin in the late 1980s was only about 48, compared with 264 for Lake Michigan, 299 for Lake Ontario, and 416 for Lake Erie. Only Lake Superior had a lower population density (about 14) and a higher level of water quality.

This is not to say, however, that Lake Huron is free from excess nutrients and toxic chemicals, particularly near shore. Phosphorous from agricultural fertilizer and, until recently, from detergents, and nitrates and nitrites, primarily from agricultural runoff and atmospheric deposition, produce greater than normal algae blooms. As of 1987, 362 chemicals had been identified in waters of the Great Lakes basin. The IJC's Water Quality Board listed the following eleven as "Critical Pollutants": dioxin; furan; benzopyrene; DDT and its breakdown products, including DDE; dieldrin; hexachlorobenzene; alkylated lead; mirex; mercury; polychlorinated biphenyls (PCBs); and toxaphene. Many of these enter the lake from the atmosphere as well as the land.

Most of these chemicals bioaccumulate in fish, wildlife, and humans, becoming more concentrated as they move up the food chain. Fish consumption advisories, applicable especially to pregnant women and nursing mothers, have been issued for the Great Lakes and many of their tributaries. On the Michigan side of Lake Huron, the 1995 advisory issued by the Michigan Department of Public Health called for no consumption, by anyone, of lake trout over twenty-six inches caught south of Tawas Point, and of carp and channel catfish from Saginaw Bay. (Commercial sales of the last two species were not affected because the U.S. Department of Agriculture, which regulates the allowable level of toxic chemicals in fish sold, did not ban sale of Saginaw Bay carp and channel catfish.) PCBs and dioxins were the principal chemicals of concern in these fish. The long-term health effects of the toxic chemicals, individually and in combination, are poorly understood, and present fish advisories may underestimate the risks.

Fish-eating birds, being high up the food chain, absorb high levels of toxic chemicals, with sometimes fatal effects on embryos and occasionally on adults. The effects of specific chemicals are difficult to pin down, but the link between DDT and eggshell thinning was conclusively demonstrated. DDE, a breakdown product of DDT, interferes with the transfer of calcium carbonate to the eggshells, causing thin shells. The weight of the incubating bird breaks the shell. Cormorants are particularly affected because they incubate their eggs by wrapping the webs of their feet around them—in effect, standing on them. As a result of DDT ingestion from the mid-1950s to 1970s, the double-crested cormorant population in the Great Lakes plummeted. In 1972, researchers found that 95 percent of the cormorant eggs in the Lake Huron colonies had broken or disappeared by the end of the incubation period. Other colonial waterbirds on the Great Lakes, particularly terns and herring gulls, suffered losses for the same reason. Along the shores, fish-eating bald eagles and ospreys nearly disappeared, as few young survived to replace their parents. The nadir for these raptors was reached in the 1960s and early 1970s.

There is strong evidence that PCBs, dioxin, and probably other chemicals cause deformities in several kinds of waterbirds. Crossed bills, which prevent feeding and therefore cause death, were frequently seen in double-crested cormorants. Other birth defects affecting waterbirds included club feet, shortened appendages, missing eyes or brains, major organs outside the body, and abnormal accumulations of fluid in tissue.

At the forefront of studies on this problem has been the Ludwig family. It all began with Dr. Fred Ludwig of Port Huron. He began banding birds in 1927, when in high school. In 1929 he banded at his first waterbird colony—on Sulphur Island south of Alpena. During the years up to World War II he extended his work to other islands. After the war and up to the present, he continued the banding, with the help of his wife, his father, his two sons Jim and Ted, and their children. Altogether, they have banded more than 625,000 birds, including land as well as water birds. In his late eighties, "Dr. Fred" was still going to the northern reaches of Lake Huron for five or six weeks each summer with family members in his thirty-six-foot Grand Banks trawler to band at waterbird colonies. The afternoon I visited him, he had to interrupt our conversation to extricate and band a young song sparrow caught in the mist net he still operated in his back yard. "I think I practiced medicine so I could play with my hobbies," he said. (His hobbies include, besides birds and bird-banding, orchard-growing, stamp collecting, painting, and music.)

Dr. Fred's son Jim became an ecologist and, with Joe Hickey of Madison, Wisconsin, was one of the first to demonstrate the effects of DDT on wildlife—Hickey with robins and Jim Ludwig through a laboratory experiment with herring gulls. The Ludwigs' concern about other chemicals arose during their banding of water birds in the 1970s. "We started seeing deformities in the birds—cormorants, herring gulls, Caspian terns, eagles—with crossed bills, club feet," said Dr. Fred. "In fact, we identified fourteen major types of deformities in birds." With support first from the Michigan Department of Natural Resources and later the Dow Chemical Company, they greatly expanded their studies. "In order to get all the data, we had three boats working and we were hitting as many as seventy-five islands every year. We hired a lot of college kids to help do the field work. In some colonies we checked eggs that had not hatched and found that as much as 32 percent had deformed embryos. That's due to the effects of PCBs and dioxin in the fish. . . . [Our studies showed that] the PCBs and dioxin interfere with the growth hormones in the thyroid gland. The male birds—herring gulls and Caspian terns—become feminized and don't breed properly.

"The chemical and paper industries are the ones that give trouble. The bleaching process with chlorine produces the PCBs and dioxin. The paper company at the Spanish River up in the North Channel has a lot of runoff from their operation, and one year—1984 I think—in the Caspian tern colony on Cousin's Island, which is six or eight miles from the Spanish River, most of those birds had arrested development [of the embryos] at about fourteen to sixteen days. . . . They didn't fledge a single bird out of that colony that year."

As a physician, Dr. Fred is also worried about the long-term effects on humans of toxic chemicals in the Great Lakes. "If we're lucky, it will take five generations to get rid of the PCBs. I don't think people should eat fish from the Great Lakes." Even the drinking water, which has much lower levels of PCBs and other chemicals than fish do, may be contributing to the problem. "Checking the death records for the state of Michigan," he says, "all the counties that abut the Great Lakes have higher cancer death rates than the counties within the center of the state. St. Clair County [at the south end of Lake Huron] is one of the worst."

I think most scientists would agree that the effects of PCBs, dioxin, DDT/DDE, and other chemicals on wildlife and humans are probably even more complex, if not less serious, than stated by Dr. Ludwig. On a more pleasant note, the banning or restriction of DDT, dieldrin, mirex, PCBs, and toxaphene in the U.S. and Canada have led to lower levels of these chemicals in the Great Lakes and in wildlife. For example, the PCB concentration in herring gull eggs on Chantry Island in Lake Huron dropped from over 80 ppm in 1974 to about 15 ppm in 1983, although the level in lake trout and rainbow smelt from Lake Huron did not decline.

Populations of birds affected by the above chemicals have also improved. Double-crested cormorants, one of the most sensitive species, have increased enormously. The number of cormorant nests on the Canadian side of Lake Huron rose from about 300 in 1979 to about 17,000 in 1993. Fred Ludwig believed there were about 35,000 in 1996 in the entire lake. Between at least 1940 and 1972, no osprey nests were known from the east side of Georgian Bay. In 1992–93, there were sixty-two occupied nests within five kilometers of the shore there. On the entire lake, it is estimated that up to 200 pairs of ospreys are now nesting. The St. Marys River area has a high concentration, but there are very few ospreys on Michigan's Lower Peninsula shore, probably because of a lack of nesting trees and of large expanses of shallow water. (Saginaw Bay might support more ospreys if artificial nesting platforms were provided, a measure that was very effective on Georgian Bay.)

Conversely, bald eagle nesting has rebounded well on the Michigan side but poorly on the Ontario side. In the mid-1970s, only two occupied bald eagle nests were known on the Michigan shore (Sugar Island in the St. Marys River). By the mid-1980s, when Michigan's Breeding Bird Atlas survey was conducted, eight shoreline townships (each thirty-six square miles or less) had one or more pairs of nesting eagles. Doug Reeves, DNR District Wildlife Biologist at Bay City, in 1995 said there were at least nine nests within thirty miles of Saginaw Bay—most within five miles—and that they were seeing increases almost yearly. However, Ontario's Breeding Bird Atlas survey, conducted from 1981 through 1985, found only one square (thirty-six square miles—on St. Joseph Island) with nesting bald eagles. By 1996, at least two other active nests were known, one on Manitoulin Island and one north of Meaford, on southern Georgian Bay.

It is strange that bald eagles have been slow to recover on Georgian Bay while the osprey recovery there has been rapid.

Although bioaccumulation of chemicals has led to problems at the top of the food chain, the water quality in Lake Huron, as mentioned earlier, is generally considered good. But there are a few areas where it is not good. The fairly substantial rivers flowing into the southern end of the lake on the Canadian side drain large agricultural areas and carry fertilizer chemicals and pesticides. Certain embayments with industrial activity have experienced even greater impacts. These have been identified as Areas of Concern (AOC) by the IJC's Water Quality Board. Forty-two such areas were recognized in the Great Lakes basin in the early 1980s. Lake Huron had five: Saginaw River and Bay on the Michigan side; Collingwood Harbour and Penetang Bay to Sturgeon Bay in southern Georgian Bay; Spanish River on the North Channel; and St. Marys River at and below Sault Ste. Marie. For each AOC, a Remedial Action Plan (RAP) is required. Studies at Collingwood Harbour showed that remedial actions had significantly improved sewage effluent quality, and in 1994 this became the first AOC on the Great Lakes to be delisted. The other four on Lake Huron and its tributaries need more work.

The Penetang Bay to Sturgeon Bay AOC, locally called, more simply, "Severn Sound," suffers primarily from nutrient enrichment that produces excessive algae growth. This makes the water murky, unpleasant and unsafe for swimming and boating, odorous, and bad-tasting. Decaying algae use up the dissolved oxygen needed by aquatic plants and fish. The primary cause of these algae blooms is phosphorous, which enters the sound from municipal sewage and agricultural runoff. Local governments and shoreline property owners are attacking the problem through improved sewage treatment facilities and land management practices that reduce runoff and create better shoreline habitat for fish and wildlife.

The Spanish River AOC, which extends from the town of Espanola fifty-two kilometers downstream to the river mouth at Spanish, was degraded especially by paper mill effluents at Espanola and atmospheric deposition of heavy metals from the mining, milling, and smelting at Sudbury, to the northeast. Muskellunge were extirpated from the river, and redhorse sucker, channel catfish, and the already rare lake sturgeon were much reduced in abundance. Contaminants from both sources have now been reduced, and options for restoring fish species are under study.

The St. Marys River transports high quality water from Lake Superior into Lake Huron, but industrial and municipal wastes discharged at Sault Ste. Marie have contaminated the sediments. Clean-up efforts have improved the situation, enough that aquatic life, unfortunately including sea lampreys, seems to have benefitted, but the river remains an AOC.

Saginaw Bay is a much bigger area and a much bigger problem than the other Areas of Concern around the lake. It receives effluent and runoff from Lake Huron's largest urban region and from a watershed of 8,709 square miles with one million people. With its shallowness and eutrophication—increase of nutrients and consequent decrease of dissolved oxygen needed by aquatic organisms—it has been called a small Lake Erie.

In the early 1900s, Saginaw Bay was a mesotrophic to oligotrophic body of water supporting a diverse plankton population typical of such waters and large numbers of lake herring, lake whitefish, chubs, walleye, sauger (now possibly extinct in Michigan waters), pike, yellow perch, lake trout, and sturgeon. The bottom fauna, too, was diverse, including an abundance of burrowing mayfly nymphs, an important food for fish. The clarity of the water encouraged the growth of submerged aquatic plants and associated invertebrates, which attracted thousands of diving ducks in spring and fall.

But with increased urban and industrial growth in the 1930s and 1940s, and increased use of chemical fertilizers and pesticides on farmland, the flow of phosporous and other nutrients to the bay caused explosive growth of blue-green algae, and heavy metals contaminated bottom sediments. Soil erosion increased the turbidity of the water and smothered fish-spawning beds and eggs with sediment. Development and use of toxic chemicals such as DDT and PCBs added to the increasing pollution. And invasion by exotic species such as the smelt, alewife, white perch, zebra mussel, and spiny water flea (*Bythotrephes cederstroemi*) further upset the earlier, more natural, ecology of the bay. The benthic (bottom) fauna became dominated by pollution-tolerant worms and flies, such as midges, and mayflies disappeared. The zooplankton population shifted to small forms less favorable to good fish growth and survival. As a result of such changes, abetted by excessive commercial harvests, lake herring vanished from the catch and lake trout, lake whitefish, and walleye harvests drastically declined. Fish that are tolerant of turbid water, such as catfish and the introduced carp, increased.

All these conditions put restrictions on human use and activities in the bay and its tributaries, such as swimming, boating, and channel dredging, which disturbs toxic material in bottom sediments. The quality of drinking water was affected, and some fish became hazardous to eat because of toxic chemicals in their tissues.

The Saginaw River flowing into Saginaw Bay, in the distance. Polluted runoff from the urbanized, 8,709-square-mile watershed has made the bay and river Lake Huron's largest Area of Concern. Many projects are underway to clean it up.

Such were the problems that had to be addressed in the Remedial Action Plan for Saginaw Bay and the Saginaw River. Government agencies, citizen groups, and others with concern for the bay cooperated in producing the first plan. With additional funding from the Saginaw Bay National Watershed Initiative, they included measures on the entire watershed that would improve conditions both there and in the bay and Saginaw River. The current objectives of the RAP are to "(1) reduce toxic material levels in fish tissue to the point where public health fish consumption advisories are no longer needed for any fish species in the AOC, (2) reduce toxic material levels in the AOC to those of Michigan's water quality standards, and (3) reduce eutrophication in Saginaw Bay to a level where the bay will support a balanced mesotrophic biological community."

148

The RAP has now been revised and updated and significant progress has been made. The region's people have been made aware of the problems and measures they can take; needed research is underway; sewage treatment facilities have been improved at nearly two dozen municipalities and industrial plants; the city of Saginaw is expending $90 million to build retention basins to handle its combined sewer overflow problem; contaminated bottom sediments in certain "hotspots" in the Saginaw River are scheduled for cleanup; and numerous projects have been undertaken to control stormwater and nutrient runoff and soil erosion, stabilize streambanks, reduce pesticide use, and generally minimize harmful material entering the bay. Of the thirty-seven priority actions listed, all had been at least partially implemented by the end of 1991.

Have conditions in the bay improved? Yes, to a limited extent. A 1977 Michigan ban on phosphorus in detergents, coupled with improved sewage treatment facilities, reduced phosphorus loadings from these facilities by about 87 percent between 1974 and 1992. However, about 80 to 90 percent of the phosphorus now entering the bay comes from non-point sources, and another 6 percent from the atmosphere—sources that are difficult to control. Some reduction in total phosphorus concentrations in Saginaw Bay has been achieved, but concentrations remain above the targeted level. As of 1997, the limited monitoring of water quality in the bay had not yet confirmed any other improvements.

With such a large watershed and so many sources of pollutants, including the atmosphere, major improvement of water quality in Saginaw Bay may take a long time. The effects of zebra mussels—now poorly understood—may play a big role in the process, for good or ill. At any rate, the scale of remediation efforts, if continued, bodes well for the future of the bay.

Looking at all of Lake Huron, one can see that a return to the pristine conditions and marvelous fish abundance around the year 1600 is impossible. Too many human impacts have occurred and too many exotic species have invaded the ecosystem. But a healthy shift toward those earlier conditions, beyond what has already happened, seems within reach. It is a matter of encouraging the native "parts," especially the lake trout; controlling, where possible, the unwanted invaders, especially the sea lamprey; keeping new invaders out, primarily through management of ballast in ocean-going ships; further reducing the inputs of nutrients to the lake; and eliminating, if possible, the inputs of toxic substances. It's a challenge to the whole Great Lakes community, and to the will of two nations.

# CHAPTER 12

# JUNE SHORES

M ost lake watchers, like me, watch the lake from the shore most of the time, with only occasional forays onto its surface or into its invigorating edges. And much of my watching had been from one place—our cottage at Port Sanilac. I decided it was time to look more closely at Lake Huron's shores, whose life is so intimately bound up with the lake, and to look at more places beyond my home beach.

This required selectivity. Lake Huron's 3,827 miles of shoreline are mostly sandy in the south and mostly rocky in the north, but beyond that gross generalization one can find within a few miles, in either the north or south, sand beaches, pebbly shore, rocky shore, and marshes, depending on the coastal configuration, offshore lake deposits, prevailing winds, exposure of shoreline bedrock, and other conditions.

So I set out one morning early in June to study a sample of shore environments, with their plant, animal, and human life. First stop was Wildfowl Bay, where marshes fringe the mainland and some offshore islands, as they do around many other parts of shallow Saginaw Bay. Myles Willard accompanied me this day, paddling bow in my blue canoe and sharing his forty years' experience of these waters.

We first skirted a few cattail stands near shore. This year's slender leaves projected two or three feet above the water among the brown stalks from the year before. "Marsh wren's nest," Myles announced. We poked into the cattails to inspect it. The globular nest with the entrance hole on the side was fastened to new shoots under a sheltering fan of dead leaves. As we pulled away, the owner complained, or registered relief, with his chattering, bubbling song.

"There's a lot of muck around the lee side of these cattail stands," Myles said. "You can get stuck up to your waist in it. When I went duck hunting in the marshes I carried my gun in one hand and a paddle in the other. It was awkward, but I needed the paddle to dig around my feet if I got stuck."

I quizzed him about the many forms of life these marshes hold, and he named a few. "There are some prairie plants, like big bluestem and cordgrass, which is now scarce in Michigan, and in some places around the bay you can find the prairie white-fringed orchid, which is rare. Turtles? We get painted, Blanding's, snapping, and perhaps rarely some soft-shelled turtles. Frogs? Leopard, green, chorus, cricket frogs, spring peeper. Bull frogs are scarce. Mammals? Plenty of muskrats. In the fall it's easier to canoe in the cattails because you can follow the channels they've cut. Mink are common inland but scarce near the shore. Biologists think they may have been affected by the chemicals in fish." (Saginaw Bay, as mentioned earlier, is recovering from serious contamination.) "Snakes? Well, there are watersnakes, and people say those islands out there are full of Massasauga rattlesnakes. I looked real hard one time but never found any."

Now we headed out across a mile of open water toward Middle Grounds Island, the closest of a cluster of islands with extensive marshes around them. The day was sunny but windy, and, as seems usual when you're canoeing, the wind was blowing straight at us. Paddling and poling through the small waves over two- to three-foot-deep water, we eventually reached some broad marshes, a mosaic mostly of cattails and tall grasses and sedges.

It was another world out there, seemingly remote from human influence. Following edges and channels, we scared up a great mess of drake mallards, either bachelors or males now done with their mating duties and living a life of ease while the unseen females reared the young. With them was a scattering of wood ducks, teal, and a pair of pintails.

Myles wanted to find out if there were king rails out here, a rare species in Michigan, and he had brought taped rail calls for this purpose. We landed and he played the king's peculiar grunting call. Rails responded, but they were Virginias and soras. Myles selected the Virginia rail section of the tape, placed the recorder at the edge of the grassy marsh, and got back in the canoe. A Virginia answered and, very annoyed, came to see what male was intruding on his territory. When he emerged from the grass and approached the black tape recorder, I was stunned by the magnificence of the bird. The field guides usually show the species as buffy below with a reddish bill. This one, stretching to its full height—almost a foot—and turning its head this way and that to see where its competitor could be, was a rich dark chestnut below with a bright red bill. It glowed with fresh spring color. Finding no intruder, the rail ducked back into the grasses. Myles retrieved his recorder, and we shoved off for other parts of the marsh.

Pursuing a peculiar sound, we pushed into a stand of cattails. In the process, we scared spawning carp, which stirred up muddy clouds in their escape, some thumping against the bottom of the canoe. They are big fish, running to two feet or more, and are generally despised in North America as alien disturbers and usurpers of bottom habitats that rightfully belong to native species. Their size and abundance makes them the target of bow fishermen, especially in the spawning season, when they noisily splash in shallow water. A few days earlier, in the mainland marsh edges at our launching site, I had watched two men stalking them, firing arrows with line attached. Unfortunately, the carp thus retrieved usually end up as smelly carcasses along the shore. Though there is a Jewish market for them in big cities, most North Americans don't eat carp, as Eurasians do. I was to see this rather unnoble sport at other places on my June journey. The peculiar sound that had drawn us to this section of marsh, we concluded, was a Virginia rail call not described in the books.

It was an idyllic afternoon—peaceful, with black terns occasionally bouncing by in their aerial hunt for insects, Forster's terns carrying fish to nestlings somewhere beyond Middle Grounds Island, great blue herons ponderously flapping away from us, marsh wrens serenading, red-winged blackbirds and swamp sparrows flitting from one part of the marsh to another. And on our return crossing, the wind was at our back.

By now you may have discerned that I am more of an animal person than plant person. If I was to know Lake Huron's shores, however, I would have to pay more attention to their plants, which anchor sand dunes and somehow manage to live on and among the rocks. Later I would have the help of botanists, but at first I relied on books. Studying the dune plants at Port Crescent State Park, I felt again the delight of learning the names of things. An anonymous plant becomes a specific kind of individual, distinct from all other species. I've been properly introduced, and henceforth I can greet this species as an old friend.

The beach here was fifty feet wide and bare of plants where the water washed up. Beyond that the sand sloped up to dunes around twenty feet

Beachgrass anchors the sand on beaches and dunes around Lake Huron.
(Credit: Myles Willard)

high. The front of the dunes bore only beachgrass, a widespread plant that
grows on Atlantic Ocean dunes from Newfoundland to North Carolina
as well as around the Great Lakes. It is a key dune-builder, its rhizomes
extending outward underground and its stems upward as sand collects
around it. On top of the dunes I found chokecherries, balsam poplars,
and low shrubby sand cherries, with their delicate white flowers, another
dune plant that adjusts to burial by sand.

The back side of the dunes—a more sheltered environment—bore
many more plants, among them willow shrubs, more sand cherries, red-
osier dogwood, different species of grasses, starry false Solomon's seal, with
its burst of tiny white flowers, the thin bluish-white leaves of wormwood,
and a cheerful little yellow-flowered plant with fine-toothed leaflets that
turned out to be silverweed. All these I was to see many times on sandy
shores of Lake Huron. Topping off these few minutes of happy discovery

was another find—a spotted sandpiper fluttering off a nest holding four tan, dark-spotted eggs cupped down in the sand.

On my circumnavigation of the lake I paused again at Bois Blanc Island, which I visited on a whim. Known locally as Bob-Lo Island, it lies off Cheboygan, south of the much more famous but much smaller Mackinac Island. Summer residents were returning to their cottages. I helped a woman from Cadillac load innumerable boxes of supplies onto the small ferry. On the way across, she told me she and her husband, both teachers, had owned their cottage on Bois Blanc for seven years. The island's pull on them was year-round, but teaching duties made winter trips difficult. Still, "we came over on snowmobiles three times last winter, when the ice was strong," she said, "but only once the winter before, when the ice was not as good. The winter before that we walked over. It's a long way."

Bois Blanc Island has extended stretches of whitish pebble beaches, which I assumed were derived from the limestone bedrock, some sand beaches, and spots of marsh in coves. Almost entirely forested, its trees exhibit a pattern common to the northern shores of Lake Huron—white cedar, balsam fir, white spruce, and paper birch near the cool water, changing gradually inland to aspens and northern hardwoods—sugar maple, beech, yellow birch, red oak, with scattered white pine, red pine, and hemlock. The center of the island has lovely open stands of sugar maple on well-drained soil, a feature exploited by real estate developers (half of the island is privately owned, half is state forest). Cottage plots stay well-treed, however, and everybody lives either in the woods or along the shore.

In summer the island has 2,000 residents but in winter only about fifty. I talked to one of the latter at her Boathouse Restaurant. "I like it here in winter," she said. "It's so peaceful—until the ice gets strong and the snowmobilers come over." She rattled off all the birds that she knew nested on the island, and a few mammals. "But we don't have bears, skunks, or porcupines."

This got me thinking about mammals on islands. Unlike birds, of course, most mammals can't fly. That means they have to swim, float on something, or walk across ice. To become established on an island, a species has to find suitable habitat and reproduce successfully. The result, generally, is that the number of species, within any category of organisms, depends on the size of an island—with more room for individuals of a given species and more variety of habitats on the larger islands—and its distance from the mainland, the source of supply. If a species becomes extinct on an island, it can recolonize more easily if the island is large and the mainland is near.

Another factor with mammals is seasonality. Some hibernate during the winter, eliminating the option of crossing on ice. For a bear to get to Bois Blanc Island, it would have to swim at least three and a half miles, the closest distance from the mainland. Bears do swim short distances to islands, but apparently not often three and a half miles, and it would take a pair or a pregnant female to establish a population. Skunks spend much of the winter in dens and are not notable swimmers. Porcupines are not very adventuresome, and forage close to their shelter sites. All three species, however—black bear, striped skunk, and porcupine—have become established on Manitoulin Island and Drummond Island, farther north. Drummond Island is larger than Bois Blanc and is only one mile from De Tour Village, a mainland town. Manitoulin is much larger than either and is linked to Lake Huron's North Shore by two short bridges.

Pursuing the matter further, I consulted range maps in *Mammals of the Great Lakes Region,* by Allen Kurta. I found that forty-nine species of mammals live on the Ontario mainland north of Manitoulin, forty-nine on the Upper Peninsula of Michigan across from Drummond Island, and fifty on the northern Lower Peninsula of Michigan, opposite Bois Blanc. Manitoulin has forty-four species of mammals, Drummond thirty-one, and Bois Blanc sixteen plus six probable bats. (All the other totals include bats, too.) For further comparison, the Charity Islands in Saginaw Bay are about one-eightieth the size of Bois Blanc and lie seven miles from the Michigan mainland. Only seven mammal species have managed to become established there. In these examples the size and distance principle holds quite well.

The town of Gore Bay on Manitoulin Island looked fresh and green when I arrived the second week of June. After a late spring, the new grass fairly glowed, apple trees and lavender- and white-flowered lilacs were blooming, and most of the sailboats now floated serenely in the marina. When I motored into the Janet Head Campground I felt I was coming home. I staked my little blue tent facing the North Channel and the next morning, once again, loons awakened me. Only the campground manager was different. The young man of former visits had been replaced by an older man, a stocky, white-bearded friend of the owners. He had retired from the corporate world and now followed an entirely different life style, traveling in a Volkswagen camper, wintering in Vancouver, Nevada, or Costa Rica, and picking up spare cash from occasional executive headhunting or, for a while, a gourmet food business. His wife, the third, was thirty years younger than he and not long out of university. Their three dogs, a mastiff, a bloodhound, and a dachshund, somehow fitted into their moveable homestead. He seemed to be enjoying the new life, though sometimes he worried about money. He was genial and helpful, supplying me with long metal spikes to anchor my tent in the rocky soil.

My focal point on Manitoulin was the Misery Bay Provincial Nature Reserve, which lies on the south shore under cool winds off of Lake Huron. As described earlier, Manitoulin Island is a giant slab of limestone tilted gently toward the southwest. Two types of limestone form the surface rock: older, Ordovician limestone along northern parts of the island, and Silurian dolomite, a harder rock, containing a high proportion of magnesium carbonate, that overlies the Ordovician layer on the southern three-fourths of the island. This dolomite is exposed on thirty acres or more of the Misery Bay reserve and provides a unique habitat called "alvar." Boreal forest, fens, and a peat bog also occur here, along with a small sandy beach and sand ridge. These varied habitats, on about 2,000 acres of protected land, make home for over 400 species of plants. All come under the cooling influence of Lake Huron, an influence that diminishes rapidly farther inland, where deciduous forests are the norm.

Judith Jones, a local botanist, gave me a one-day tour of parts of this floristic richness. Judith is like some other biologists I met on this trip in that she ekes out a living doing several things. In her case it's teaching at a community college and conducting botanical studies as a consultant. She had come to Manitoulin seven years earlier, when she married an Ojibwe from the island whom she had met while guiding a canoe trip in northern Ontario. He was now working at a fish plant. "This is a great place to live," she said, "but it's hard to make a living."

Before starting our exploration, she explained the history of the sanctuary. "Its name," she said, "is thought to come from a chance comment of early settlers. One year there was a drought and there was no grass for the cattle, so some farmers came to this bay to cut marsh grass for them, but the mosquitoes and black flies were very bad. A man came along in a boat and asked them the name of this bay. 'Misery Bay,' they said. Later they learned that he was a surveyor and had put that name on the map.

"Misery Bay," she continued, "is the only nature reserve on Manitoulin Island. Most of the land was sold at a minimal price by Calvin and Eunice Sifferd to the Nature Conservancy of Canada, which sold it to the Ontario government at half the market value. But the province had no money to operate the reserve, so a private group called Friends of Misery Bay was formed to plan and assist with management of the area. Our motto is 'Misery Loves Company,' and we've got about 100 people in the group now. We've done a management plan for the park and we conduct monthly nature events here to get people interested and involved."

Our first stop was a section of alvar, much of which looked bare as a parking lot. Closer inspection, however, revealed a complex and varied assortment of plant life growing on the dolomite pavement. Lichens and mosses had gained a foothold in some places, making dark islands on smooth or pock-marked rock and lines along crevices. Growing in crevices were grasses, such as northern dropseed, tufted hairgrass, and little bluestem; members of the sedge family, especially a spikerush and two with no common name (*Carex scirpoidea* and *Carex viridula*); and small herbaceous plants—field mouse-ear chickweed, field wormwood, Indian paintbrush, with its two-toned yellow and orange bracts, and wild columbine, a plant adapted to many situations. Most conspicuous of all at this season, the yellow flowers of Manitoulin gold made rows down the cracks and bright scattered spots elsewhere. This last one is restricted to a few Great Lakes alvars and has its center of abundance on the western half of Manitoulin. Among the woody plants we found many shrubby cinquefoils, creeping juniper, which does creep, vinelike, over the ground, and my new friend from the dunes at Port Crescent State Park, sand cherry, blooming prettily here as well.

The rock itself is light-colored, but a miniature community of producers, consumers, and decomposers consisting of algae, bacteria, and fungi make the surface darker. Occasionally we saw loose slabs of light rock. These, Judith said, had been overturned by bears foraging for insects and grubs, exposing their light, uncolonized undersides.

Wherever depressions in the rock had allowed substantial soil to form, clumps of white cedar had grown up. In winter many deer congregate along the south shore of Manitoulin, partly for cover under the dense cedars, and partly for the browse they provide. We could see a distinct browse line on the white cedars around the alvars we investigated.

Anything that can live on alvar has to be admired. Often flooded in spring, alvars become very dry and hot in summer. In winter the limestone pavement heats rapidly when the sun shines, melting the snow. Judith told me of speaking with an eighty-year-old man who, as a boy, had helped move logs to the south shore in winter for pickup by barge when the ice melted. His job had been to shovel snow onto the spots where the pavement had melted the snow so the sleigh could go over.

On much of the south shore of the island, the dolomite pavement extends well out into the water, and that is the case here. "A friend told me people used to drive their cars into the water to wash them," Judith said. On the shoreline here, in cracks and small pockets of soil, we found silverweed, bird's-eye primrose, Baltic rush, shore or bog violet, ninebark, and the attractive hoary willow, a shrub with fuzzy, silvery leaves.

We concluded our trek at the head of Misery Bay itself, where the lake, in its regression over the past 4,000 years, had left behind conditions for the formation of marshes and fens, and inland from these, a peat bog. Each of these vegetation types was separated from the next by an intervening arc of tamaracks and other trees. As we walked along the shore toward the head of the bay, the ground beneath us became wetter and wetter. Sedges, rushes, and grasses took over, with scattered willow and alder shrubs. Judith pointed out bog-bean and the carnivorous pitcher-plant, with its drooping purple flowers and pitcher-shaped leaves, which have reflexed bristles inside and usually water at the bottom, both of which entrap insects that the plant then absorbs. This strategy enables the pitcher-plant, which grows in low-nutrient environments, to obtain imported nutrients. As we sloshed about, we were serenaded by the winnowing of a snipe overhead, a typical bird of the fens and marshes.

The presence of pitcher-plants indicated that we were moving from a marsh environment into a fen. The distinction is not clear-cut, however, and one would be hard-pressed to draw a boundary. Morton and Venn, in *The Flora of Manitoulin Island,* say that marshes "differ from swamps, bogs and fens in being well-aerated and nutrient-rich so that dead plant remains decay instead of accumulating as peat. . . . Marshes are dominated by grasses, sedges and rushes." Fens, the authors say, receive some dissolved nutrients and oxygen from an inflow of water, but some peat accumulates because aeration is still inadequate. Fens are usually dominated by sedges.

Fens are usually more acid than marshes (although the marly fens of Manitoulin and the Bruce Peninsula are alkaline), and peat bogs are more acid than fens. Peat bogs, as the name implies, accumulate quantities of peat and are characterized by a floating mat of vegetation underpinned by sphagnum moss. Judith and I didn't make it into the peat bog. She said it had stunted black spruce trees and the heath plants cranberry, leather-leaf, and bog-rosemary growing abundantly on the sphagnum.

Many of the plants we had seen in the reserve, such as the Baltic rush and the bird's-eye primrose, prefer the shores around the Great Lakes in this part of their range. Manitoulin's flora includes at least sixty such species, according to Morton and Venn. A few plants are found *only* on the shores of the Great Lakes. Of these we had seen Manitoulin gold, Kalm's St. John's-wort, and Hill's thistle (the latter among reindeer moss at the edge of an alvar). Outside the reserve, on sand dunes, we had found the thin bluish leaves of Pitcher's thistle and the bluish-white leaves of Great Lakes wheatgrass. We were in the wrong place for the dwarf lake iris, a diminutive plant with a lovely blue flower that grows elsewhere on Manitoulin's south shore. And we hunted in vain for Houghton's goldenrod, known from a few locations at the east end of Manitoulin. The hunt, I always think, is half the fun. Besides, you need to leave a few things to search for next time.

A few other plants we had seen, such as the sedge *Carex scirpoidea* and bog-bean, are primarily Arctic in their distribution. Plants in this category are thought to be relics from the ice age, maintained here by cool air from Lake Huron during the growing season.

One morning before leaving Manitoulin, I walked the shore at the Janet Head Campground. This environment, on the north edge of the island, is very different from the low-lying south shore. High and steep, with dense forest, Janet Head slopes down to a narrow shingly beach composed of rocks from the Ordovician layers exposed on the northern shore. Large and small slabs of limestone and grey shale lay underfoot. Alerted by the campground manager to the fossils in the limestone, I paused frequently for a look. I could see hundreds of shell outlines in the rock, some scallop-like and others that looked like corals or conical cephalopods, dating from the tropical seas that inundated much of North America during the Ordovician period 440 to 520 million years ago.

Few plants had managed to gain a foothold among the slabs and shingles. One of the most successful was white sweet-clover, an alien species that Morton and Venn describe as "an abundant weed of roadsides, waste places and shores." More attractive was a plant new to me, with reddish five-petaled flowers and deeply toothed leaflets. My flower identification guide, Walter Hoagman's *Great Lakes Coastal Plants,* led me to the red windflower, also known more prosaically as cut-leaved anemone. This is primarily a western plant that has a separate part of its range on the Great Lakes.

Slowly I picked my way over and around the trees that had tumbled down the wet, eroding slopes. Carefully watching where I put my feet, I saw spiders scurrying under the rocks and dragonflies flitting off. Two finds intrigued me: the wings of a ring-billed gull and the fairly fresh leg of a deer with the flesh gnawed off. I tried to imagine what had happened. Perhaps at night a great horned owl had snatched the gull from its roosting place on an offshore rock and brought it here for eating. And perhaps the deer, half-starved during the hard winter just past, had been driven by coyotes down the slope and killed. Maybe then one coyote had dragged a leg down here to the shore for undisturbed gnawing. The pairs of crayfish claws I saw on the rocks could more easily be explained—by the numerous tracks of raccoons in patches of mud.

At the farthest reach of my walk, I paused again and turned toward the North Channel. Just offshore, three loons clustered together were watching me, as if curious. For several minutes they hung around, then drifted out and began diving. Way out, a flock of mergansers took off, the sound of their wings smacking the water loud in the stillness and echoing off Janet Head. I started back toward camp and the next phase of my journey.

When you travel from Manitoulin Island to Killarney Provincial Park at the north end of Georgian Bay, you leave the limestone on the La Cloche Peninsula and enter the Canadian Shield. You're going back geologically hundreds of millions of years, to the Precambrian era, when rocks of the Canadian Shield were formed. These compose the bedrock all around the northern and eastern shores of Lake Huron, from Sault Ste. Marie to the southeast corner of Georgian Bay. At Killarney you see pink granite, part of a wide band that makes picturesque, pine-crowned rock islands along Georgian Bay and extends all the way to Labrador. North of the granite at Killarney, white quartzite forms parallel ridges forested with pine and red oak, the quartzite showing through like patches of snow.

Killarney Provincial Park is fifty-seven kilometers down a side road from Highway 69, the main route around Georgian Bay. You're in forests all the way, except for the openings of a few lakes and rivers. Ten kilometers farther the road ends at the small town of Killarney, a place reached only by plane or boat until 1962, when the road was built. Having made camp at the park, I set out for a look at shores where Lake Huron laps up against the ancient granite.

The lighthouse east of Killarney is a wonderful place to contemplate Georgian Bay. Perched on rounded pink granite fifty feet above the water, you can look west to the narrow channel that leads in past George Island to the town. Far to the south you see small islands that seem to float on the bay—a few of its "30,000." As I ate lunch, a middle-aged couple wearing white hats in a canoe painted like birch bark paddled by two hundred yards out, into the wind, as leisurely as if they were strolling around the block. A white float plane flew in from the southeast and landed at the mouth of the Killarney Channel. Two ring-billed gulls dropped onto my rock to see if I had any leftovers.

This is also a good place to admire plant life on the rocks. For a few feet above the water the rock is bare, scoured by waves and winter ice. Above that, though, miniature gardens of many colors and textures speckle the smooth rock. The lichens, I thought, were the best. Light grey, grey-green, dark gray, orange, and in a few places yellow, they splotch the rock as if someone had dropped spots of multi-colored ink. Moss grows in moist depressions and cracks, and grasses grow from the moss. In some crevices the short fronds of polypody fern poke out, and from others the lacy leaves of yarrow.

Killarney Provincial Park spans 48,500 hectares of forests, lakes, and low mountain ridges. It offers numerous inland canoe routes for people seeking a semi-wilderness experience. These tempted me, but I wanted more the waters of my Lake Huron. The park borders on Collins Inlet, a long narrow passage between the mainland and Philip Edward Island, and here, saying a fond farewell to the cloud of mosquitoes on shore, I launched my canoe one sunny morning.

The islands and most of the shore of Collins Inlet all are made of the region's ubiquitous pink granite, which slopes smoothly into the water or drops down in cliffs. I found, however, that there was more life back in the coves, where small marshes have gotten established in the shallow, quiet water. Each cove revealed something different. In the first I passed a small beaver lodge with fresh-cut branches on top. Was it owned by a young beaver pair just starting out, or by older beavers who had just moved from a cut-out area?

In the next cove I found a small sandy beach and got out for a stretch. Immediately I noticed deer tracks and two butterflies, one an orange and brown Compton's tortoise-shell and the other a black one I didn't know. Focusing my binoculars on it, I suddenly entered another world, at a different scale from that of normal human vision, a world I wasn't aware of when I stepped onto the beach. There were numerous tiger beetles with brown, light-barred wings, scurrying here and there to pick up bits of animal matter I couldn't see. Magnified eight times by the binoculars, a spider scared me as it emerged from the shoreline detritus. I thought what a frightening world that must be for a non-predatory insect, assuming that insects experience something akin to fear.

At the head of the next cove I followed a narrow brown stream to a beaver dam, on the way startling a large snapping turtle into the water from its sunbath. Eating lunch, I watched water boatmen skimming on the surface around my canoe. Their shadows extended below them, making them look like the heads of moving sticks. Over the beavers' marshy pond two red-shouldered hawks circled and then disappeared southward.

Up in the last cove I entered, a muskrat was carrying fresh-cut cattail stalks. It dove in front of a shoreline beaver lodge, suggesting that the muskrat, and not beavers, now lived there. Past the beaver lodge I paddled up another brown, winding stream. On such a stream I always expect something exciting around the next bend—today a moose maybe. Alas, no moose, but I did come upon a great blue heron poised to stab at a fish. I think it saw me but waited to make its strike anyway (unsuccessfully) before flying slowly away.

Great blue herons are a frequent sight in this Canadian Shield country where there are so many lakes and rivers, besides the great lake itself. I often wonder how such a large, slow-flying bird can be so successful, even in close proximity to human settlement. Elsewhere I have seen them in surprising places, far from the open wetlands where one usually sees them. One winter day in Virginia I discovered a great blue heron huddled beside a snow-covered culvert in a small brush-filled ditch, and in a New Jersey forest I found one beside a trickling rivulet. At first I mistook it for a wild turkey. In Maryland I once saw a dozen in a corn field.

Part of the great blue's success must be attributable to its broad food habits. Besides fish, it catches frogs, snakes, mice, insects, and sometimes even birds—almost any kind of animal food it can swallow. Knowing this, I was nevertheless surprised when, crossing Collins Inlet to the south side, I saw a great blue take off from a small island with a wriggling watersnake dangling from its beak. The heron flew to a marsh and was still trying to subdue the snake when I lost it to view.

The merlin, a small falcon, inhabits wooded areas across much of northern North America but is described as "very local" in the southern part of its range, which includes the shores of northern Lake Huron. It is fairly common in coniferous forests on the south shore of Manitoulin Island, however, and today I was delighted to discover one on an island where I stopped for a rest. I had happened upon the bird's nest site, which it gave away by hanging around and directing high-pitched cries at me. It didn't take long to spot the stick nest in the top of a shoreline white pine.

Elated with this discovery, I headed back up the inlet, now into the wind. Along the way I paused to enjoy Caspian terns as they dove from high above into the water after fish. Gull-sized, with a blood-red bill and a prehistoric squawk, they seem to me to have more character than other members of the tern clan, most of which are smaller and daintier. The

Caspians started me musing about the chain of predatory activity going on out here today. The men I had seen fishing from boats hoped to land a big fish—pike or bass. The pike or bass hoped to catch a smaller fish, as did the Caspian terns. And the smaller fish were hunting tiny ones, such as I had seen in the coves. Once I had spotted a turkey vulture cruising along the shore, looking for any fish that had washed up dead. It's nice how nature has a job and a place for everyone.

The social center at Killarney—at least for visitors—is down at the marina docks, where Bert Herbert has his fish and chips operation. Dispensed from an old white and red school bus attached to a frame fish-processing building, the fish and chips attract scores of boaters who put in here and other visitors who drive in. Bert knows many of them. He ended a conversation with one boat owner to come talk with me.

Then seventy-three, weather-beaten but healthy-looking, Bert was still fishing. "I began when I was ten years old," he said, "helping my father during school vacations. We fished pound nets between Manitoulin and Horse Island with a twenty-four-foot boat. In 1953 I went on my own, fishing with gill nets. The lake trout were going down but you could catch five tons of whitefish in a day in the early 1950s. In the mid-50s a lot of fishermen got out when the whitefish went down too. There were eleven license holders in Killarney. I'm the only one who stayed in. I caught perch, pickerel, a few whitefish."

Bert and his wife had five sons and three daughters. One son drowned going through the ice on his snowmobile. "I almost sold everything then," Bert said. Another son persuaded him to start the fish and chips business with the old school bus, "Mister Perch." "It was the best thing I ever did." Today he has fifteen employees working here, including fishermen. Many of them are his children or grandchildren. Bert still goes out on the *Warren L. II*, with two sons and a grandson helping him. They were fishing three or four miles out, setting 3,000 yards of gill net for whitefish, which had come back. At the end of our talk he said, "You can't tell it all in thirty minutes." Behind those few words I sensed years of struggle, hard work, occasional heartbreak, storms, laughter, and now enduring success as he presided over his dockside complex, known and loved by all.

Our talk ended partly because of an emergency. Alerted by radio, a young man—probably another grandson—roared off in an outboard to pick up people in trouble out by the lighthouse. A few minutes later he roared back and with the help of others dragged or carried an older woman, a younger, very distraught woman, and a small girl to a waiting ambulance, which took them to the town's health clinic, where a call for further medical treatment could be made if necessary. It turned out that they had been overcome by leaking carbon monoxide in a tightly enclosed new boat and the man driving had radioed for help. He was picked up on the second run. Fortunately, I learned later, administration of oxygen brought them all back to normal.

I hadn't planned on visiting Killbear Provincial Park, down on Parry Sound, but a staff member at Killarney Provincial Park told me about an interesting study going on there, so I went. Killarney is near the northern boundary of some of the northern hardwoods, like sugar maple, but Killbear is in the heart of them. Entering Killbear park, which encompasses a 1,100-hectare peninsula, you immediately are shaded by a lovely forest of sugar maple and beech. The park also has scattered stands of hemlock, which in winter attract some 300 deer from outside the park for shelter and nearby browse. Wolves from farther north follow them in.

However, my main interest here was not forests, deer, or wolves. It was Massasauga rattlesnakes. The eastern Massasauga is found from New York, Pennsylvania, and southern Ontario to eastern Iowa and Missouri, but over most of its range it is separated into small, local populations because of habitat destruction and human persecution. When such little pockets die out, there is no source for recolonization, and the species is gradually declining. Its largest continuous range now is on the eastern side of Georgian Bay.

Chris Parent, a master's degree student at Carleton University, had been studying the Massasauga at Killbear since 1992. When I talked to him, in 1996, he was researching a thesis whose main objective was to determine whether human activity affected the snake's behavior, something that was important for park planning. So far it appeared that the snakes ignored human activity (but unfortunately, when they find these retiring little snakes humans don't ignore them). Chris was also studying the demographics and genetics of the local population. He had implanted transmitters in a number of snakes and could thus map their travels and home ranges. Data on each snake were recorded in a computer.

The Massasaugas at Killbear usually hibernate at the base of a large tree with loose soil around it, but sometimes they choose vegetated depressions in rock outcrops or burrow down among bulrushes and cattails. During the summer males may travel in an area up to two kilometers wide, usually hunting in wet areas or at the periphery of rock outcrops. They don't seem to stop long in forests, just pass through them. The pregnant females stay near their hibernation site, almost always choosing a large rock outcrop nearby for the gestation and birthing period. Non-gravid females travel farther, but not as far as the males.

One morning I set out with Rob Willson and Amy Jakubowski, Chris's assistants, to record the whereabouts of some of the subjects. Stepping carefully and noting the strength of beeps from the receiving antenna, Rob located Artemis (Goddess of the Moon) lying among plants at the edge of a clearing in birch forest. This non-gravid female had traveled some 1,600 feet from her hibernation site in a wetland. She had stretched out her less than two-foot length to maximize absorption of sunlight, Rob explained. "Much of a snake's life is spent seeking the right temperature range. Thirty degrees Celsius is about optimum for most of them." Amy then recorded the temperature on the ground and at one meter above the ground. Artemis might stay here a long time, just waiting for a mouse or vole to come along. Massasaugas can go for two weeks to two months without food.

Next we visited a large rock outcrop in a forest opening, right on a popular trail. Most people would never see or suspect snakes here, and without our equipment, and markers showing previous locations, we might have missed them too. Gray, with dark spots, Massasaugas blend exceedingly well into their background. As it was, we quickly found Gwen coiled in front of a rock she could crawl under if alarmed. Gwen had hibernated just 160 feet away under a group of hemlocks. The researchers thought she was pregnant but had not seen her with a male the August before. Rob then located another female. This one they knew was pregnant—she had been ultra-sounded in a nearby hospital and about ten young had been revealed.

We searched further and found two more. The first Rob gently lifted into a bag with his snake stick. I spotted the second one, a very small young snake, coiled on dead leaves among juniper bushes and rocks. I felt elated, like a successful treasure-hunter. Rob donned heavy gloves and picked up this little one. It struck once, then lay quietly in the cupped gloves. This one also went into a bag.

Back in the lab, Rob let out the larger one onto a table. He guided its head into a plastic tube so the rest of it could be handled with bare hands. He pointed out the small bulge where a microchip had been implanted. Later the information on this chip could be read and stored in the computer. Then the small one was let out of the bag. Each young snake is photographed and can be reidentified by the pattern of marks on its back, which is different for each individual. Rob found this one in the photograph book. It had a spot for the third mark and the seventh was saddle-shaped. It had been born the year before, first caught on August 25 of that year, and recaptured in May of this year before we caught it again. The computer record showed that it had hibernated with its mother—Skimpy. Later its tail would be painted whatever color was selected for June—probably green. "We don't microchip the young ones," Rob explained.

This work, I learned, gives personal satisfaction as well as scientific knowledge. "We put the new knowledge into the interpretive programs here," Chris said, "and we can see new attitudes of visitors developing. Twenty years ago the snakes were invariably killed, but not now. They take an interest in the snakes when I point one out and tell them about its habits." Signs on the park roads say, "Please brake for snakes."

Killbear has its navigation light on a rocky point, too, although the rock there, according to the park management plan, is mafic paragneiss rather than the pink granite that prevails in most of the region. It is dark gray, with thin layers sloping up from the water at a forty-five-degree angle and eroded crevices between the layers. This had allowed many shrubs to become established, especially ninebark, sweet gale, sumac, ground juniper, and, once again, sand cherry. Here, too, gray, gray-green, and orange crustose lichens spotted the rocks, and mosses, grasses, and sedges sprang from cracks, as did a few pussytoes, yarrows, and yellow hawkweeds. I concluded from my small sample of shoreline rocks on the Canadian Shield that what mattered to the plants was more the structure, rather than the composition, of the rocks, since on the Shield all were acid, as opposed to the alkaline limestones on Manitoulin.

At nearby Snug Harbour, Bryan Perks was helping customers at the marina, which he managed along with his restaurant upstairs. Like Bert Herbert at Killarney, he had children and grandchildren around, and he knew nearly everyone who came in. Unlike Bert, he looked shaggy and haggard, although only around fifty. Perhaps some of that was due to twelve hard years on salt water in the Merchant Marine out of Newfoundland and another year in Alaska. Bryan had been a fisherman during various periods until 1983, when he sold his license and gear to the government, but he still fished with Glen Parr, the one remaining license-holder at Snug Harbour. Right now they were fishing for chubs in 300 to 400 feet of water. "The whitefish market is overloaded," Bryan said, "but chubs are selling for $2.20 [Canadian] a pound." They often had to contend with fog, but with a global positioning system device and radar this was no longer a problem. "We can come within ten feet of our net spar in the fog."

Bryan is a fourth-generation commercial fisherman, but Rusty Raney, at Tobermory on the Bruce Peninsula, is first generation. "I was the first in my family," he said as with seventy-eight-year-old hands he deftly tied new net onto the lines in his net shed. "I didn't inherit anything. Had to build it all up myself." That was why he now felt bitter. A recent court ruling had affirmed the treaty rights of Native commercial fishermen around the Bruce Peninsula, and the provincial government was seeking to buy out non-Native fishermen. "I don't know why I'm doing this [making new net]. You spend your whole life building the business up and then they take it away from you. But you've got to be ready in case we can keep fishing."

At the moment he still was, or his boat, *Dyker Lass,* was, operated by a hired crew. They, too, were fishing for chubs. Beside the net shed Rusty's son Wayne was smoking chubs in a tall rectangular box with white smoke pouring out the sides. He would sell them down at his fish store on the docks in Little Tub Harbour.

Tobermory's harbor is a busy place these days in summer. Power boats, sailboats, glass-bottom tour boats for viewing underwater wrecks, and divers' boats—some of them converted fishing tugs—go in and out, replacements for the many fishing boats of earlier days.

I took one of the glass-bottom boats, the *Sea View III,* out to Flowerpot Island, one of several islands in Five Fathom National Park. It was a very foggy Saturday morning and I was the only paying passenger. Two others—Michael Evans and Hercules Fortis—were park naturalists who were required to go, to lead a scheduled walk, so I got a personal tour. Flowerpot eventually appeared out of the fog as we approached its dock, and with my two guides I began the exploration. Named for two rock pillars that remain standing along the steep shore, and bathed with cool moist air from Georgian Bay, the island is a lush wild garden. Limestone cliffs and boulders in the shade of the dense forest are festooned with mosses, lichens, and ferns. Michael and Hercules pointed out the diminutive wall-rue, green spleenwort, maidenhair spleenwort, and the taller holly fern, four of the nineteen species of ferns found on the island.

They also showed me orchids, for which the Bruce Peninsula and its islands are famous. Of the peninsula's forty-four species of orchids, at least twenty-three have made their way out to little Flowerpot, only one mile long and two miles from the mainland. We saw one calypso, the fleshy saprophytic striped coral-root, helleborine, heart-leaved twayblade, Alaska orchid, and the leaves of round-leaved orchid, not yet blooming. Fortunately, no deer live here to strip the undergrowth of orchids and other plant riches.

Limestone cliffs rise high on the east side of the Bruce Peninsula. From here to Manitoulin and Drummond Islands, limestone is exposed on most of the shores. Granite rims the north shore of the North Channel and the northeastern shores of Georgian Bay. From the Pennsylvanian rock of central Michigan to the Precambrian Canadian Shield, layers at the surface become progressively older. (Credit: Myles Willard)

The plants on islands of Five Fathom National Park nicely illustrate the principle that the number of species diminishes with decreasing island size and increasing distance from the mainland. J. K. Morton and Joan Venn (*The Flora of the Tobermory Islands*) studied the floras of these twenty-four islands and recorded species totals on each ranging from eight to 375. Cove Island, by far the largest and within two miles of the mainland, had the 375 species. Flowerpot, a similar distance removed but much smaller, supported 363 species; its diversity could be attributed in large part to a greater variety of habitats than Cove has. On Bears Rump, half

169

the size of Flowerpot and three miles out, they found 196 species. And on Half Moon, a small, narrow, low-lying island about six miles from the mainland, they found only 135. Tiny White Shingle, far out in the mouth of Georgian Bay and awash during periods of high lake levels, could grow only eight species—brought in by waves and nesting gulls—during years of lower levels.

At Flowerpot's lighthouse, which had a keeper until 1989, we read a tragic story on a plaque. In August 1986, the lighthouse keeper's daughter and her fiancé had been on their way to be married here, on a deck overlooking the water, when their plane disappeared over Lake Erie. What bitter irony for a lighthouse keeper, who devotes his life to guiding travelers across dangerous waters.

"Joe Johnson is the best field naturalist I know," Dennis Rupert had said one day down in Sarnia. "He's probably walked more square feet of the Bruce Peninsula than anyone else. And he has an unusual sensitivity to and rapport with living things. He can imitate barred owls perfectly—both male and female." So I arranged to spend my last day on the Bruce with Joe. Sitting in my Isuzu Trooper in Wiarton early that morning, he gave me a little background on himself and the local flora. He had grown up in Nova Scotia and taught math and biology there. This didn't suit him, however (Rupert had said he was sort of shy and had trouble keeping discipline). After working for International Nickel at Thompson, Manitoba, Joe moved to Alberta and later to Long Point, Ontario. In 1971 he went to Wiarton, where he stayed and gradually became the resident chief naturalist, as it were, of the Bruce Peninsula. He had seen all the species of orchids (forty-four) and nearly all the ferns (of which there are around fifty, the exact number depending on the taxonomy) on the peninsula—an unrivaled achievement—and now was working on a flora of the Bruce Peninsula area, which has close to 1,300 species of vascular plants. He had inspected in the field all but about fifty of these, too. He's also a whiz on birds, conduct-ing field surveys and adding his expertise on innumerable Christmas bird counts.

Joe is certainly not shy now, and freely imparts his fifty or so years of knowledge about the natural world. This day we concentrated on fens and sand dunes. At the Oliphant Fen Joe and others had constructed a semi-circular boardwalk with interpretive plaques. We didn't need the plaques, however, as Joe explained everything himself. "Fens seem to occur where there is seepage from the landward side and protection offshore, like the Fishing Islands for five miles along here, or in a sheltered cove. This is a marl fen. You can see the whitish calcium carbonate deposits on the bottom and on the algae."

As a worried snipe called incessantly from the top of a telephone pole, Joe pointed out the dominant plants growing in the inches-deep water: twig rush, three-square bulrush, and the provincially rare Indian-plantain, which reaches its greatest abundance in this five-mile stretch of shore. On bits of drier ground grew clumps of shrubby cinquefoil, sweet gale, and stunted white cedar. Always on the lookout for the less obvious, Joe spotted two tiny insectivorous plants—linear-leaved sundew and some butterworts, with their purple flowers—along with the conspicuous pitcher-plants. A solitary showy lady's slipper was bloooming at the edge of the fen. Surely the most beautiful of North American orchids with its rose mouth and white sepals and petals, showy lady's slippers were now blooming along many of the Bruce's wet roadsides. Several times I had seen cars pulled over and intent photographers capturing this exquisite beauty on film. "Rose pogonia and grass pink [two other orchids] will also bloom soon in the fens," Joe said, and later we saw in passing the tall flowering spike of a white bog orchid.

Across the road from the boardwalk the fen extended out to the open water. "There is more hard-stemmed bulrush as you progress toward the shore, and less vegetation generally," Joe commented. "Ducks sometimes find enough cover to nest in places like that, however, and spotted sandpipers often nest on the drier sites in it."

As we left this area, I thought how uniform and monotonous the fens looked from afar, and how varied they were when you looked up close. The fens are home to many unusual and rare plants, and Joe, with other conservationists, continues to work for their protection.

At Sauble Beach, still bare of bathers in late June, we explored some of the less trampled sand dunes. Here I was glad to learn from my guide how to separate the two principal grasses of the foredunes: marram grass (or beachgrass) and the provincially rare sand reed grass, which at first glance look very much alike. "Marram grass has sharp-edged leaves and can cut your hand. Sand reed grass has abundant hairs on the leaf sheaves. I can spot that right away." And so could I, when I knew what to look for. Behind the foredunes, in an area where bank swallows busily flew in and out of their nesting holes in vertical dune faces, many shrubs had gotten established, especially shrubby cinquefoil, sand-dune willow, Kalm's St. John's-wort, and sand cherry. "In August I pick the berries from sand cherries to make jelly," Joe said. "The bathers always ask me what I'm doing."

171

Far back of today's shore, well beyond the sound of surf, we walked a bit of the Nipissing dunes, now some 5,000 years old. Joe had traced these dunes for miles and now showed me one of the more accessible samples. Rising steeply thirty or forty feet, the dunes were covered with forest. They looked ghostly in the shade. Tall sugar maples, with a sprinkling of basswood, white ash, beech, black cherry, and smaller trees, grew here now—the types of trees found on most inland sections of the Bruce. In their shadow we found a cluster of green orchids and scattered marginal shield-ferns. Joe dug his hand through the humus and showed me the white specks below it—sand. I could almost hear the surf rolling up here 5,000 years ago and see the beachgrass blowing in the wind. I wondered what humans and animals came down to these shores then to see what Lake Nipissing offered.

The story of successive beach ridges, from Nipissing time down to the present, built as the lake dropped (because of deepening of the St. Clair River outlet and greater rebound of the earth in the north), is revealed even better at Pinery Provincial Park, near the southern end of Lake Huron. By following the Cedar Trail extension from the shore inland, one can see the change of plant life as the dunes become older. On the hot, humid day I walked this trail—June 29—people were swarming the beach and venturing into the water. Summer (and Canada Day weekend) had arrived. Few walked the trail, however, and I had plenty of solitude to contemplate nature and time.

On the dune ridge fronting the beach, grasses, bearberry, and yellow puccoon were most visible, with willow shrubs on the back side. On the next dune ridge, ground juniper, red pine, chokecherry, red cedar, and white pine had joined the mixture, patchily, with much open ground remaining. On the third ridge, a few black oaks and dwarf chinquapin oaks appeared, and beyond that was a confused system of dunes with oaks finally in charge but with many red and white pines among them. The canopy here was nearly closed. Two thousand years, as it were, had passed as I walked. From this age back to the Nipissing dunes, radiocarbon-dated at 4,800 years, the forest on dunes was closed and continued to be oaks—red, black, and white, the latter the last to appear—with the two pine species as subordinates. I mentally thanked the scientists, such as J. H. Sparling and Robert Morrison, who had studied this succession in detail and worked out the relations between time and plants.

By the time you get down to Pinery park you're in predominantly deciduous forest (in spite of the name). Gone are the spruces and firs seen many places on the Bruce Peninsula. You're in what the Canadians classify as the Carolinian zone—the "southland" of Canada, which extends eastward along the north sides of Lakes Erie and Ontario past Toronto. You've left the Great Lakes–St. Lawrence zone, a mixture of northern hardwoods and boreal conifers, which, as we've seen, borders the northern three-fourths of Lake Huron and in Michigan occurs north of Saginaw Bay. At Pinery you find such "southerners" as black oak, white oak, red cedar, tulip-tree, and summer grape. Among birds are the red-bellied woodpecker and cerulean warbler.

The admixture of species with southerly distributions extends to all categories of organisms, including insects. The day after I left Pinery, a butterfly count was held here. Modeled on Christmas bird counts, in which birds are counted on one day within a fifteen-mile-diameter circle around Christmas time, butterfly counts are now conducted at many places in North America. Pinery Provincial Park is rich in butterflies not only because of the latitude but also because it contains rare habitats such as oak savanna, with open space and flowering plants on which certain butterflies depend. The counters would be praying for a sunny day and the finding of rarities such as the mottled dusky wing, dusted skipper, tawny emperor, and the less rare but more beautiful giant swallowtail.

When I arrived back at the cottage, I looked at our sandy beach with new eyes. I had a new appreciation of the balsam poplars, beachgrass, and riverbank grapes that grow there. I could see them now in their geographic distribution and relation to the beach contours.

I realized, too, that in the nesting season we no longer seemed to have a bird that I had seen so frequently on other Huron shores and formerly here—the spotted sandpiper. I suppose the summer activity along our stretch has grown too great. The sandpipers can't find undisturbed places to feed and nest.

I'm not worried about spotted sandpipers, however. There are still lots of shorelines suitable for them. I (and the rest of the conservation community) *am* worried about the piping plover, a small, pale shorebird, which, though never common, once nested on many Great Lakes beaches and now is perhaps entirely gone from Lake Huron. Its problem is that it requires the wide sandy beaches that humans now flock to. Some hope remains that piping plovers still breed on a few Huron islands with such beaches where people are scarce or absent.

When I got home I also was reminded that the shore is ever-changing. Shortly after I returned, strong northerly winds blew for two days. When they subsided I discovered that the waves had carried away most of our beach, leaving a small cliff at the edge of our low dune. Some of that sand probably was added to the beach just north of the harbor, where the long-shore currents have been depositing sand ever since the harbor breakwalls were constructed, in 1951. Over that short time, the beach there has widened well over 100 yards. The lake gives, and it takes away.

Back in the mid-1980s, the Great Lakes mostly took away. Levels reached their highest since records were first kept in the late nineteenth century. Especially on Lake Michigan, cottages began tumbling into the water as waves ate cliffs away. People began yelling for the government to do something, like dredging the St. Clair River deeper, to let more water out. The lakes subsequently lowered on their own and now are back at more "normal" levels, so you don't hear people complaining much anymore. But who knows? We might be in for an even bigger rise one of these years.

If the lake rises again, beyond the normal seasonal cycle, it will disturb more than people. It will, for instance, submerge the nesting places of many colonial waterbirds, another subject I investigated in my travels.

# CHAPTER 13

# COLONIAL WATERBIRDS

The fortunes of Great Lakes colonial waterbirds—gulls, terns, herons, and cormorants—are constantly changing. A host of conditions affects them, especially the food supply, competition for nesting sites, weather, and lake levels. On the Great Lakes, these birds nest most frequently on small islands, where they are relatively safe from predators and human disturbance. But they are not always safe from the lakes themselves. Many of the nesting islands are low-lying, and a rise of one or two feet in water levels can drastically shrink the area available for nesting or overwash the entire island.

White Shingle, a little new moon of an island way out in the mouth of Georgian Bay, starkly illustrates this element in the life of waterbirds. As described by J. K. Morton and Joan Venn in the mid-1980s, when levels were very high, White Shingle "is a gravel bank on a submerged limestone reef. In recent years . . . it has been awash in rough weather when waves break across it and winter ice is pushed over it." Impossible for nesting then, it had been home to thirty-five pairs of herring gulls in 1980.

Nesting sites are thus at a premium, and the birds choose some that are less than ideal. At Bois Blanc Island there is a long thin bar where gulls and terns nest just offshore from the Boathouse Restaurant. One summer evening I was sitting in the restaurant watching the activity out there. The ring-billed gulls stood, sat, and preened on the grassy end of the bar; unseen others probably sat on eggs. The herring gulls, much

175

fewer and more widely spaced, watched their grey fluffball young as they pecked around on the more shrubby end. Once in awhile, all the common terns, startled by something, rose into the air in a bunch, then gradually settled down. All looked rather peaceful until two shotgun blasts rang out next door to the restaurant. All of the birds—several hundred—flew up, screaming. Like the snowstorm in a glass ball, they swirled around for some time before returning to the ground. The restaurant proprietress yelled at the boys and ran over there to scold them. Returning she huffed, "They said they just wanted to see the birds fly." As if it might possibly excuse them, she noted they were nineteen and twenty years old.

Shotgun blasts are not the only thing that disturbs this colony. The occasional bald eagle that flies over is something that such waterbirds have lived with for millennia, but not so the power boats and jet skis that roar by only a few yards offshore from the nesting island. I wondered how the birds could endure this, and if they would.

Some colonial waterbirds are adaptable, however, and have taken to nesting on buildings and spoil islands. A few of the gulls that nest at the Bruce Nuclear Power Development on southern Lake Huron have used the rooftops there, and common terns nest in numbers on spoil islands in the St. Marys River. The Diked Disposal Island at the head of Saginaw Bay, built from material dredged from the channel into the Saginaw River, has attracted cormorants, great egrets, black-crowned night herons, herring and ring-billed gulls, and common and Caspian terns, plus the first confirmed nesting of the cattle egret in Michigan.

Gulls and terns also establish colonies at places along the mainland shore where they feel safe. One such place was the breakwater at U.S. Steel's harbor near Rogers City, Michigan. As the company shipped out limestone from its huge quarry nearby, ring-billed gulls, herring gulls, and common and Caspian terns raised their young every year, protected by the company's trespass prohibition. Harrison ("Bud") Tordoff at the University of Michigan had told me he took his ornithology students there every spring, with the company's permission. So now, many years later, I went for a look, first talking with Bill Grigg, a Rogers City birder and executive of Michigan Limestone Operations, which now owns the property. Things had changed.

"About five to eight years ago," Bill said, "a number of people at the plant were infected with histoplasmosis. The virus was traced to the great amount of gull droppings. There were about 5,000 ring-billed gulls, 500 herring gulls, and a few common and Caspian terns nesting there. The company spread a layer of clay to bury the droppings, then put up a grid of wires about six feet above the ground. Gulls don't like to go under them. That essentially stopped the nesting."

When I drove out to the visitors' parking lot, I could see gulls flying and resting around the edges of the rocky breakwater, but no sign of nesting. Besides the wires, there was now a resident red fox out there. This colony was history.

According to censuses conducted between 1976 and 1980, Lake Huron had more total nesting gulls, terns, and cormorants than any of the other Great Lakes. Cormorant numbers have subsequently exploded, on Lake Huron especially, so Lake Huron's number-one ranking remains. The lake holds that position probably because of its thousands of islands, most of which lie in the North Channel and Georgian Bay, and many of which meet the requirements of colonial waterbirds.

Chantry Island, a mile out from Southampton, Ontario, just south of the Bruce Peninsula, is both densely populated with waterbirds and probably is the most diverse in species of such nesting islands in Lake Huron. Most colonies consist of one or two species, some have three or, more rarely, four. Six colonial species nest on Chantry, and probably a seventh, not to mention ten species of waterfowl. For these and other reasons, a Canadian wildlife official with the Ministry of the Environment described Chantry Island as "Ontario's most important Migratory Bird Sanctuary south of James Bay."

And these are the reasons I decided to visit Chantry. Getting there was half the fun (read, all of the headache). Martin Parker, town clerk of nearby Port Elgin and widely acknowledged regional chief birdwatcher, had received permission from the Canadian Wildlife Service to take me out there. But when, at 5:00 P.M., we went to the marina where he expected to rent a boat, it was closed. The marina across the Saugeen River had no boats for rent. "I'll try the mayor of Port Elgin," Martin said. "He's a friend of mine." The mayor, who lived on the Lake Huron shore, would lend us his small aluminum boat, but it had no motor. A quick dash to United Marine Sales and Service, where Martin had another friend, would yield a twenty horsepower motor, provided the vertical distance at the boat's transom was not too long. Back to the mayor's for measurement (OK) and return for motor and gas. By the time we had hauled the boat, motor, and gas over the rocks to the water, it was 7:00 P.M.

The effort was worth it, many times over. I had been in waterbird colonies before, but none of this size or variety. As we approached the pebble beach at the southwest end, hundreds of herring gulls resting on the water became agitated and dark grey young ones swam away, their

177

heads flattened to the water as if hiding. By the time we had beached the boat, many of the gulls were in the air, screaming. I had forgotten the overwhelming cacophony of a disturbed gull colony. And the smells—of fish, excrement, and here of some noisome weed. Overhead, black, snaky-necked cormorants flew off their nests in a willow tree. We walked up the beach, passing widely spaced herring gull nests—small cups of plant material placed among the stones. Most nests were empty now (it was June 27), but a few had one olive brown, dark-blotched egg, probably infertile and abandoned. A couple of nests had three eggs, the usual complement. "Could be late nesters or renesters," Martin said. Dozens of light grey, speckled young herring gulls and older dark grey ones scrambled over the rocks into the water.

We passed the ruins of the former lighthouse keeper's house and the tall, white lighthouse, one of the six "imperial towers" built in Ontario in the 1850s and now, automated, still functioning. Turning from the beach, we picked our way over the dead branches of trees felled by high water during the mid-1980s and through dense stands of stinging nettle to the ash trees beyond. Standing on stick nests up in the trees, fuzzy-headed young great blue herons, great egrets, and double-crested cormorants gawked at us, the young cormorants regurgitating fish when we came near. A few fledged black-crowned night herons, having left their nests, watched us from tree tops. The bare ground beneath the trees was white-washed with guano, which had killed the herbaceous plants but not the trees themselves.

A few yards farther we came upon the first group of ring-billed gulls. Arriving later in the spring than the herring gulls, the ring-bills had been forced to use nesting areas among the trees and tall grass behind the beach, which they probably would have preferred, Martin thought. They had built their skimpy nests close together on a bare circle no more than fifty to seventy-five feet across, where their droppings had killed the vegetation. As we approached, all the ring-bills rose into the air and flew around in a tight little blizzard, screaming in tones higher-pitched than those of the herring gulls but fortunately not diving at us, as some of the herring gulls had. All their half-grown young scurried off like a grey flood, under dead branches and into the tall grass. A few nests here still held an egg—colored like the herring gull's but smaller. Scattered about lay dead gulls—mostly young but one or two adults. "There's a red fox out here this year," Martin explained. "I think that fox is going to have a tough time when all the young are fledged. There's nothing else to eat, and it's a long swim back to the mainland."

We were to see many more of the fox's presumed victims, most of them uneaten.

One ring-billed gull area adjoined a group of cormorant nests placed on the ground—their preferred location. One of these nests held two bluish-white eggs and a third egg out of which a chick was hatching. Most nests held three young, one of which was larger than the others. Like hawks and owls, cormorants begin incubating as soon as the first egg is laid, and the chick hatched from it gets a head start. In times of food scarcity, it will hog the fish brought by the parents. In that situation the others probably will die, but at least the first born will survive—a brutal but effective adaptation.

Walking through the marshy tall grass that covers the west side of the forty-two-acre island, we found a fourth ring-billed gull nesting area. "This wasn't here last year or this April," Martin said. It was a sign of the growing ring-billed gull population all over the Great Lakes. On this bare patch we saw many eggs and very small young; the parents were apparently latecomers as well as newcomers.

Near here a pair of great black-backed gulls flew about. "I saw them in this same area in April," Martin said. "They must be nesting." This was another sign of an expanding population, although on a much smaller scale. The great black-backed, a bird primarily of the Atlantic coast, did not nest on the Great Lakes before 1954. Now it has three or more small "colonies" (usually only one pair) on Lake Huron and a few others on Lake Ontario.

Pausing first to scan the many gulls and ducks on the little embayments along the marshy west side of the island, we pushed through the grass and back to our boat. We had caused only a temporary disturbance in the colony, a disturbance justified, I think, by its research purpose and one that did no harm. As we motored back across the smooth evening water, the red sun setting, the birds on Chantry Island went about their normal business, raising another generation.

Two of the species we'd observed on Chantry—the ring-billed gull and double-crested cormorant—have increased amazingly on the Great Lakes. Quite scarce as a nester in the early 1900s, the ring-billed gull population on the lakes rose to about 400,000 pairs in the late 1970s and approached one million pairs in the 1990s. In spite of being smaller and less aggressive than the herring gull, whose numbers have remained fairly stable in the Great Lakes since the 1930s, the ring-bill has certain advantages over the herring gull. It feeds on a broader range of items, from worms and insects to fish, eggs, mice, and all manner of garbage; it

Rising numbers of ring-billed gulls crowd waterbird colonies around Lake Huron. (Credit: Myles Willard)

matures earlier (at two or three years versus four or five for herring gulls); and is generally more adaptable to human activities, following the plow for grubs and nesting on buildings, spoil banks, or other constructions if good natural sites aren't available. In Washington, D.C., within its winter range, I've noticed over the past thirty to forty years that ring-billed gulls have learned to scavenge throughout the city, dropping into small downtown parks to eat the lunch leavings of office workers or wait for a handout. This is now a widespread habit of the species. "McDonald's gull," some people call it.

While the ring-billed gull expansion on the Great Lakes has occurred over more than sixty-five years, the cormorant population explosion has taken only twenty. This dramatic rise contrasts stunningly with the earlier history of double-crested cormorants on the Great Lakes. Although they had nested at Lake of the Woods, farther west, for hundreds of years, cormorants were not known to nest on the Great Lakes until 1913, when nesting was suspected on Lake Superior. From here they spread farther eastward, appearing on Lake Huron in the early 1930s and on lakes Erie and Ontario in the late 1930s. Feeding on huge populations of the introduced rainbow smelt and alewife, and finding plenty of islands suitable for nesting, cormorants might have reached their present levels in the 1960s or 1970s but for two things: human persecution and toxic contaminants.

By the 1940s cormorants had increased to the point that sport and commercial fishermen, who thought cormorants reduced the species they sought, began shooting cormorants and destroying their nests, eggs, and young. Public pressure convinced government agencies to start control programs in the late 1940s. Both sanctioned and unsanctioned controls largely ended by 1960. A report by Environment Canada concluded that these efforts probably slowed but did not reverse the cormorant population growth.

Much more severe was the effect of toxic chemicals—particularly DDT and PCBs—which reached high levels in the Great Lakes from the 1950s to early 1970s. DDE, a breakdown product of DDT, caused eggshell thinning and consequent breakage from the weight of brooding birds. There is strong evidence that PCBs caused deformities such as crossed bills. By the early 1970s, hardly any cormorants could be found nesting in the Great Lakes. During the 1970s, however, restrictions on these chemicals led to their decline in the lakes and in waterbird eggs and tissues, and the cormorant began its astounding recovery. The number of nesting pairs on the Great Lakes rose from only 125 in 1973 to more than 38,000 by 1993. In 1996, Lake Huron alone was thought to have more than 30,000 pairs.

What caused this amazing increase? Besides improved water quality and the abundance of prey fish, some researchers point to the many fish farms in the southern United States, where wintering cormorants gorge. They return to the Great Lakes in prime breeding condition.

The prevalence of cormorants these days has fishermen again arguing for their control. They say the cormorants are catching large numbers of sport and commercial fish—enough to hurt human fishing. They contend that cormorants are consuming a large part of the young salmon and trout stocked annually, that they reduce the prey species the large fish feed on, and that they deplete local supplies of pan fish, such as perch and bass.

What do the scientists say? Dozens of studies during this century show that the cormorant is an opportunistic feeder, catching whatever small- to medium-sized fish (normally up to about thirteen inches) are available. Alewives and smelt form much of their diet because they are so abundant. Studies in Lake Ontario have shown that less than 2 percent of the prey found in cormorant pellets is lake trout or salmon, and that annual consumption of prey fish by cormorants is about 0.5 percent of the total prey fish population, as opposed to 13.4 percent taken by sport fish.

The contention that cormorants reduce pan fish, such as perch and smallmouth bass, near their nesting colonies may have more validity. People haven't been catching as many of these fish since the cormorants at nearby colonies increased, and scuba divers no longer see large schools of perch in some of these areas. To gather more evidence on this question, the Ontario Ministry of Natural Resources and the Michigan Department of Natural Resources in 1994 began a study of the feeding habits of cormorants in Lake Huron. The study results showed that 77 percent of the fish consumed by adult cormorants and 95 percent of the fish fed to nestlings were forage fish, such as rainbow smelt, alewife, sticklebacks, slimy sculpins, shiners, sunfishes including rock bass, white suckers, and crayfish. Large numbers of perch were taken only during the spring spawning—about a two-week period. Smallmouth bass did not figure prominently in the diet.

Nature may eventually take care of the question of whether there are too many cormorants. After rising 35 percent a year from 1973 to 1991, cormorant numbers began to level off. In 1994 the cormorant population of Lake Ontario decreased by 6 percent, and in 1992 Newcastle Disease Virus killed up to 30 percent of the young in several colonies. Stocks of the smaller prey fish have been decreasing in recent years. So disease, food shortage, perhaps a lack of new nesting habitat may stabilize the cormorant population. Nature abhors a vacuum, but she also abhors—in fact prohibits—unlimited growth.

The heron species on Lake Huron have shown no major increase or decrease in recent decades. The great blue heron, with thirty or more colonies around the lake, is the most common. Black-crowned night herons, with about twenty coastal colonies now around the lake, showed some decline during the worst pesticide-affected years but appear to have recovered. Michigan, however, still lists the black-crowned night heron as a species of special concern.

Great egrets, the stately white herons that wander widely in late summer, were not known to nest on Lake Erie until the 1950s. In recent years they have continued to move northward. By the mid-1980s, nesting was confirmed at two locations in Saginaw Bay and one at the south end of Georgian Bay. Great egrets later began nesting at Chantry Island. Still uncommon, the great egret may or may not become a long-term breeder on Lake Huron. Its smaller relative, the cattle egret, was found nesting at a heron colony in Saginaw Bay in 1985. An African and Asian species that became established in South America in the 1930s and then spread rapidly northward, the cattle egret now appears annually around Lake Huron, even sometimes as far north as Manitoulin Island, but has gained only a tenuous toehold as a breeder. It is most often seen in fields, or in pastures with livestock, where it hunts insects, and seems an adaptable bird that could make itself at home on the many farmlands around the lake. What impact this might have on the other colonial herons is unknown.

Common and Caspian terns, the two other principal colonial waterbirds on Lake Huron, are perhaps the most sensitive to changing conditions. They usually nest on sandy or gravelly parts of islands, with or without a thin cover of vegetation. These are often the lowest-lying areas and the first to be flooded during storms or periods with high lake levels. On some islands, the terns are being crowded out by the expanding numbers of ring-billed gulls, which arrive earlier in the spring and expropriate tern nesting habitat. Caspian terns are also under stress from toxic chemicals, especially PCBs, that are carried in their prey fish. In spite of the stresses, Caspian tern nest counts reached their highest level by the late 1980s (about 5,300 on the upper Great Lakes; more than 2,000 of these on Lake Huron). Common terns have been declining, however, in the Great Lakes generally and in Lake Huron. The number of nests in Canadian Lake Huron, where the majority of colonies are located, dropped from a high of 3,627 in 1960–72 to 2,107 in 1980. A two-thirds decline in the number of nests was recorded on the Michigan Great Lakes between 1960 and 1985.

When a popular bird such as this graceful "sea-swallow" is threatened, concerned people usually try to help it. In 1986 William Scharf, one of the principal researchers of Great Lakes colonial waterbirds, cleared brush on small islands in the St. Marys River to make more bare ground for common terns. This resulted in a 79 percent increase in nesting on these islands. Thousands of nest boxes put up by people all over eastern North America brought back the eastern bluebird from a worrisome low level. Common terns, however, are harder to help. Brush grows back quickly.

The interactions among colonial waterbirds are many and complex, with ever-changing effects on individual species. There is both coexistence and competition, as well as predation. There are also changes in the environment brought about by the birds themselves. Nesting space, as we have seen, is a key factor. This can be affected by an increase of one species. It is also affected by arrival times of the various species; the early bird gets the space, so to speak. On Chantry Island, this sequence is approximately as follows: herring gull, great blue heron, black-crowned night heron/ring-billed gull, great egret/double-crested cormorant, common tern/Caspian tern.

The tree-nesting species—herons and cormorants—to some extent sort themselves out. Great blue herons tend to nest highest up, great egrets lower or in smaller trees, and black-crowned night herons in shrubs or small trees. Cormorants are the most flexible, nesting both in trees and on the ground. Plant succession affects the bird species mix as small trees shade out shrubs. Black-crowned night herons, for instance, might decrease as some of their nesting habitat grows too tall or dies.

The birds themselves—particularly cormorants, great blue herons, and great egrets—kill some foliage and trees with their whitewash. This occurs most frequently in the northern parts of the Great Lakes, where trees are shorter-lived and less deeply rooted, and thus more susceptible to damage from feces. Cormorants and great blue herons will nest in dead trees but night herons and great egrets, which usually don't, can eventually be deprived of sites by years of droppings. Dead trees break and fall more readily than live ones, so in the long run all the species lose out. It's a long process, however, and these birds have existed with it for hundreds of years if not millennia. They can rise and fall, or move, with the cycles of death and rebirth.

In a more direct way, too, the birds are not safe from each other. Herring gulls are a major predator on Caspian tern chicks and sometimes take eggs or small young from cormorant nests. None of the colonial birds, in fact, are entirely safe from the depredations of herring gulls. Herons, too, will eat young birds when they get the chance. Black-crowned night herons have an advantage here, since, as their name implies, they feed at night, when other birds are usually asleep. Night herons then have no trouble gorging themselves on defenseless ring-billed gull and common tern chicks, along with fish, frogs, and other prey. Danger lurks for young birds night and day.

On Chantry Island, all the processes of competition, predation, and environmental change continue, as they have for centuries. Since 1980, black-crowned night herons have declined and great egrets and cormorants have moved in, the cormorants rapidly. Cormorant nests were first noted in 1986, grew to 130 in 1989, and 402 in 1990. Some of the people in Southampton, whose lake view is dominated by the island, say it's become an eyesore because so many trees have died. "I'm out there sailing all the time and I can hardly stand what it's beginning to look like," said one outspoken resident. "It was a nice little island instead of a rockpile." Some people put all the blame for killing trees on the cormorants. Martin Parker maintained that the century-high-water lake levels of 1986 probably did more damage to the trees than the cormorants did. Some suggested going out with shovels and buckets of earth to plant trees. Parker recommended that people "leave it alone" and it will eventually come back on its own.

Chantry Island is thus a local example of a lake-wide issue: To what extent should humans meddle with the natural ecosystem? Plant trees or leave the island alone? Stock the lake with exotic game fish or encourage the native lake trout? I'm for lake trout and leaving Chantry Island alone.

# CHAPTER 14

# THE SUMMER PAUSE

S ummer on the lake is a time when the turning wheel of the seasons seems to pause. We know it really doesn't—subtle changes go on as always, and it is the birth and growing season for many plants and animals, in the water and around it. But we who vacation there pause, and we like to think nature is doing the same, holding us in a state of suspended, blissful lassitude.

While in this pleasant state, we can watch a show—of visual changes that cycle through all the colors and weather the summer lake is subject to. Sunrise can be a gentle pink that creeps across the sky before the fiery sun itself appears, or a blazing fury of orange and red and purple in the clouds. As the day progresses, with its varying sky and weather, the lake changes color. Brilliant blue, darkening to the horizon, may give way to bands of pale green and purple, or dull to a solid grey-blue. Sunset, of course, is on the landward side for us in the Thumb. It has its moments of beauty but not quite the drama of sunrise over water.

On rare summer nights, nature gets tired of being nice and shows us her wildest power. The wind comes up, bending the beach's poplar trees half over, the waves build to a crashing roar, and lightning streaks down to the water as thunder cracks overhead. We lose our peaceful state and feel a little fear. But on the horizon a ship, with lights from bow to stern, progresses slowly northward as if immune, part of the show.

Eleanor, our oldest, on a windy day.

During the day, there are other shows. Gulls and terns work up and down the shore, the gulls picking food from the beach or water, the terns diving headfirst after fish. The gulls, I assume, are non-breeding birds as the nearest colony is more than fifty miles away in Saginaw Bay, and they congregate offshore or by the harbor at night. I don't know where the few terns are coming from. They appear and disappear. Many of them are small common terns, but now and then a gull-sized Caspian tern comes by, its blood-red bill pointed straight down and its rasping, improbable squawk startling our ears.

On weekends the fishermen are always out there, trolling for salmon and trout. In mid-summer they are a mile or more from shore, seeking the colder water where the fish go. The sailors move among them, giving those of us on land the pleasing sight of a wind-filled red or white sail. Mama and Papa Worth always liked to sit on our upper deck to watch the

Port Huron to Mackinac racers go by, though the wind has to be right to bring them near shore. And the ships. Papa always interrupted a meal to announce a passing lake boat—anything from a tug to a thousand-footer, three to five miles out in the shipping lanes.

I have my own gradient of likes or dislikes for different kinds of boats. First come the working boats—the freighters and commercial fishing tugs—closely followed by sailboats, which make no noise and are beautiful, in tune with nature. Canoes and kayaks would be up there with sailboats, but I've seldom seen either in our part of the lake. Sneakboats and other duck-hunting craft have a certain appeal connected with their specialization, history, and nature-oriented purpose. Sportfishing boats are OK, though the activity is more pleasing than the boats themselves. In the negative half of my gradient come first, non-fishing powerboats, which are noisy, sometimes ostentatious, and serve no useful purpose as far as I can see, unless they are used to transport people to someplace worth going to. At the bottom of my scale is the abominable jet ski—pure irritation to those who have to listen to it, sounding like an angry bee, killing the peace of a summer afternoon on the beach. At the cottage we see all of these except fishing tugs and duck-hunting boats, and for the most part they add something enjoyable to the Huron scene.

Our family scene at the cottage is four-generational. Mama Worth (now a great-grandmother) tends her plants when not cooking or swimming. She seems to have the same view of gardening that she does of providing food: more is always better. Therefore the garden becomes a haphazard riot of flowers, and trees are planted without much thought for the room they'll eventually take. We will have a forest in the yard one day—a beautiful one of conifers, birches, and sugar maples.

Papa Worth, being incapacitated the last few years of his life and hard of hearing, naturally turned the television up above the comfort level for everybody else. Before we got cable, we could receive a Canadian station, poorly. Papa and I would watch Canadian football through a haze of television snow. Once a hard-working highway engineer, Papa now supervised from his chair, handing out jobs and checking on their progress. Woe to any member of the younger generations who did not work!

The lake, of course, has always been our focus, whether looking at it or going into it. Mama Worth is the avid swimmer among us, going in twice a day if possible and, in the recent past, swimming up to a half mile. Now, in her late eighties, her range has shortened but not her love of swimming. After coming up from Florida in June, she checks the water almost daily until it rises above sixty degrees or so, then plunges in. This happy day usually does not arrive until around the Fourth of July, because the cold water from Lake Superior flows straight down our shore. After that first plunge, almost no condition keeps her from her daily swims.

The rest of us are more chicken about water temperatures. My rule is, if the water is cold enough to hurt your feet, it's too cold for swimming. Once in, our feet tell us a few things about the lake bottom. Just at the edge, there's a band of pebbles that hurts tender city feet. After that it's mostly a gradual slope with a sandy bottom, except for a few scattered round boulders. Fortunately, those near shore have not become encrusted with zebra mussels, I suppose because the boulders are subject to wave action and winter ice scouring.

Most years, one of these boulders rises above the surface. This is the one the children named the Whale Rock long ago. Since the summer lake level has fluctuated about five feet over the past thirty years, the Whale Rock rises well above the surface some years and lies well below it in others. When visible, it became a destination for our three girls and me—something you could sit upon, like a gull, when you got there. It was more of a challenge for the children, because they were too short to stand on the bottom if they got tired en route.

When not playing in the waves or digging in the sand, we might walk along the beach, seeing what we could find. Usually there wasn't much of a zoological nature, other than clam shells, pointed snails, or an occasional dead fish (except when we had the big alewife die-off in the late 1960s). But the pebbles were interesting for their many colors and patterns. We searched especially for Petoskey stones, which contain geometrically arranged, fossil corals in which the calcium has been replaced by quartz.

As the years passed, the girls became more interested in the town than the beach, because the town was where the boys were. Unfortunately for our girls, however, Port Sanilac is a small town and therefore has few boys. When our girls, now in their twenties and thirties, come now their focus is family, not the lake. Their parents and grandmother are about the only swimmers, and I have become more of a dipper than a swimmer. Strange how the water gets colder as you grow older.

While we become lazier at the cottage in summer, the town becomes its busiest. Retirees and weekenders return from their winter and working homes, doubling the population. Boat owners come up from all over southeastern Michigan to take their sail or power boats out of the harbor and onto the lake. Anglers without boats line the harbor breakwalls. And even some ordinary tourists find their way here along the edge of the Thumb, although we aren't on the route to the major vacation areas farther north. This influx allows Port Sanilac's various shops and restaurants to open up or expand their hours in summer.

Like most of the small towns around Lake Huron, Port Sanilac has thought up ways to attract visitors during that window of opportunity between Memorial Day and Labor Day. We have our Blessing of the Fleet, just like Detroit does. The Fourth of July parade brings out old fire engines and hopeful local politicians. Art in the Park attracts painters, photographers, crafters, and their patrons. In late July, the Summer Festival offers an intriguing medley of activities, from spaghetti-eating, pie-eating, and Best Dressed and Ugliest Dog contests to bands, the aero-spin ride, community beer tent, and Native American pow-wow. All summer the Barn Theater puts on plays, disturbing the resident barn swallows no end but pleasing audiences. Local entrepreneurs are promoting a really big attraction—the Shipwreck Museum—but funding for it has been slow coming in. What will we be in ten or twenty years? Not much different, I hope, as do many or most of the townspeople.

Over the years, I have taken an interest in cottage names. Most people at Port Sanilac haven't named their place, maybe because they live there enough of the year that it's a home rather than a vacation hideaway. For several years, we had a sign out that read "Libby's Cove," in reference to Mama Worth and the fact that she was the one who wanted a cottage where she could swim. But we're not on a cove, just a straight beach. The name was suggested by a Libby's Cove the Worths saw in Maine. Eventually the sign disappeared in the jumble of our garage, and now we have no name.

As I drive along Lake Huron's shores, I note the cottage names, wondering what lies behind their choice. I have developed three categories: the standard, expectable names such as Camelot, Our Tranquilizer, Rainbow's End; the humorous or clever—Nanchucket, Scotch on the Rocks, Northern Composure, Shore Is Fine, Idle Ours, Shangri-Lodge, G. U. Pastit; and the downright puzzling—Corsini's Finntalia, The Broken Pelican.

I have tried to test a hypothesis: Canadian cottage names have fundamental differences from American names, reflecting differences in national character. But all I could conclude was that Canadians make more reference to their ancestry, especially Scottish, and perhaps use more play on words and literary reference. On both sides of the lake, cottage names seem to come in clusters. Perhaps naming by one cottager inspires or challenges the neighbors.

Whatever the name or no-name, the cottage represents a haven, a place where the cares of the working life are set aside, a place for dreaming, perhaps made more so by the seemingly boundless waters of Lake Huron.

CHAPTER 15

# SMALL BOATS, LONG JOURNEYS

No one longs for summer more than Lake Huron's sailors. At Port Sanilac, a few put their boats in the water as early as April, soon after ice-out, and by mid-May sails are a common sight on the horizon. On weekends from May through September, the Bark Shanty Sail Club runs races around short courses offshore or on longer courses up and down the shore. Handling a sailboat in all winds and weathers is a slowly acquired skill, but one that is advanced well by racing. As one member said, "Racing is good; it accelerates the learning curve."

That skill is most called upon when one ventures out of sight of land, where there's no shelter if a storm comes up. Even in good weather, the experience of being far out on the bosom of Lake Huron, although exhilarating, can also be a bit unnerving. Dick Schaffner, a former educator and now a real estate agent in Port Sanilac, used to sail his twenty-seven-foot Tanzer, *Friendship,* all over the lake. "The first time sailing across was kind of scary," he said. "We were out of sight of land for about four hours. Another time my wife and I sailed to Grand Bend [forty miles across in Ontario] to go to a woollen mill. Coming back [a six-hour sail] we got into a thunderstorm. Lightning was crackling all around and it got dark. You could see different storms coming from the west and try to avoid them, but there was no chance. Afterward I asked my wife what she was thinking about during the storm. She said, "I was afraid we'd sink and I'd lose my woollens."

Today's sailors are the latest in a long line of small-boat venturers on Lake Huron. (Credit: Myles Willard)

Georgian Bay and the North Channel, with their many islands, are especially loved by Lake Huron's sailors for their scenery and sense of remoteness. "Everybody wants to go to the North Channel," Schaffner said. "You don't have to go to a commercial harbor, you can anchor in a bay. No tv or newspaper or phone." That's the appeal of sailing, I guess— the separation from ordinary life on land, the visceral connection with wind and water, the quiet communion with nature.

Today's sailors are just the latest in a long line of venturers on Lake Huron in small boats. For many centuries, Indians of the region traveled the lake in dugouts and birchbark canoes. The dugout, usually made from a white pine log, was too heavy for portaging. On journeys that required portaging, the lighter, more versatile birchbark canoe became the craft of choice.

When French explorers and Jesuit missionaries came into the Huron country in the seventeenth century from Montreal or Quebec, through rivers and lakes to the big lake, they relied on natives and their birchbarks for transportation. The trip from Quebec to the Jesuit mission Sainte Marie aux Hurons, at the south end of Georgian Bay, took up to thirty days and required some fifty portages. For Europeans it was not a pleasant journey. The priest Jean de Brebeuf warned, "You must expect to be three or four weeks on the way, to have as companions persons you have never seen before; to be cramped in a bark Canoe in an uncomfortable position . . . in danger fifty times a day of being upset or being dashed upon the rocks."

The heyday of this mode of transportation in historic times was the period from 1763 to 1840, when the British, having wrested Canada from the French, developed the fur trade to its highest level. This was the high time, too, of the voyageurs—French Canadians, Indians, and half-breeds who manned the canoes between Montreal and the Rocky Mountains, carrying trade goods for the Indians westward in exchange for the furs, mainly beaver, that they carried back eastward. The main route followed the north shore of Lake Huron on the way into Lake Superior.

Alexander Henry was one of the first Englishmen to travel this route. As a young man, Henry left New Jersey and accompanied the expedition of General Amherst against Montreal in 1760. He then stayed in Canada to seek his fortune. Thinking it might lie in the fur trade, he set out in 1761 from Montreal to Michilimackinac at the Straits of Mackinac to obtain furs. Fortunately for us, he made notes and in 1809 published an account of this trip and the sometimes hair-raising episodes that followed.

The journey began on August 3 nine miles above Montreal at the head of the Lachine rapids. The *canots de maître* (Montreal canoes), thirty-six feet long and six feet wide, were loaded with trade goods, provisions, guns, and other gear—a total of three tons in each canoe. At Saint-Anne's eight gallons of rum were loaded into each canoe and the voyageurs went to confession. Thus purified, they partook of the rum, got drunk, and started fighting. When things calmed down, the canoes shoved off. It was a colorful spectacle—the voyageurs with their red sashes and red caps; the canoes painted red, black, and green; in each canoe six men in pairs digging in with short paddles, one man standing in the bow and one in the stern with a long paddle; the men stroking in unison to the beat of a song.

The route lay up the Ottawa River and then the Mattawa, whose banks, Henry wrote, "are almost two continuous rocks, with scarcely earth enough for the burial of a dead body. . . . Mosquitoes, and a minute species of black fly, abound on this river, the latter of which are still more troublesome than the former." He had some awareness of post-glacial history, perhaps handed down by the Indians. "At the height of a hundred feet above the river, I commonly found pebbles, worn into a round form, like those upon the beach below. Everywhere, the water appears to have subsided from its ancient levels; and imagination may anticipate an era, at which even the [offshore] banks of Newfoundland will be left bare."

After making eleven portages on the Mattawa they came to Trout Lake, then crossed a series of granite ridges, by portages, ponds, and creeks, to Lake Nipissing. From here it was downstream to Lake Huron, and Henry's canoemen at this point may have followed the custom of throwing away their poles, with loud huzzas at the prospect of easier travel ahead.

Easier, but more dangerous. Going upstream, they had poled, pulled, or portaged up or around the rapids. Now, going down the French River, they would run most of the rapids. This took a great deal of skill as their canoes, with their birchbark skins, could easily be punctured. In the smaller rapids they followed the smooth V of water down to and through the standing waves at the foot. In the deeper, more turbulent rapids, they had to skirt the standing waves while avoiding rocks. Wooden crosses on the banks marked the graves of those before them who had been unsuccessful.

Damage to the canoes was inevitable. Someone would sponge out the water leaking in, and at camp a roll of birchbark would be hauled out, a piece sewed on with spruce rootlets, and seams covered with pine or spruce gum. Near the mouth of the French River, they camped on

196

a meadow—still present today in this rocky terrain—and made more repairs before the next leg of their journey, which would take them down the westernmost channel of the French River (which has four mouths) and into Lake Huron.

"What remained," Henry wrote, "was to cross the billows of Lake Huron, which lay stretched across our horizon, like an ocean." They entered it on August 31, "the waves running high, from the south, and breaking over numerous rocks. At first, I thought the prospect alarming; but the canoes rode on the water with the ease of a sea-bird and my apprehensions ceased."

There would, however, be plenty of moments for apprehension in the days and months ahead because, as Paul Fountain wrote in the middle 1800s: "These lakes (Huron and Superior) . . . are subject to sudden squalls. . . . Unless therefore you have time to reach the land, an upset is inevitable. Consequently it is necessary to creep around the shore; but when a bay . . . is come to, the crew, naturally, to save time and labour like to strike straight across from headland to headland. As some of the traverses are not less than twenty miles broad, it is necessary to study the weather and to be an accurate judge of . . . probabilities. . . . For the waves of Huron and Superior are not inferior in size and power to those of the ocean, if indeed, they are not more to be dreaded."

Canoe travel, even in moderate waves, required caution. Heading into a wave, the voyageurs stopped paddling so the bow would not plunge below the crest of the next wave. And often a head wind sent them ashore. To progress in this circumstance would be very slow, and damage to the canoes could occur. (I understood this well one day on an arm of McGregor Bay. Canoeing down the arm with the wind was easy, but coming back against it I had to quarter from the shelter of one island to another to make any headway at all. It took me two hours to go one mile.)

Henry's party passed the exposed Point Grondine, where the surging swell moans among the big rocks, and traveled among many small islands, "bare or scantily covered with scrub pine-trees," which protected them from the open lake. They probably then followed Collins Inlet, a narrow channel between the mainland and Philip Edward Island. At the west end of the inlet they again faced open water. Here, if there was a strong headwind or bad weather, the voyageurs often took an inland route, through lakes, rivers, and portages—now part of Killarney Provincial Park—to Baie Fine on McGregor Bay. Henry's party continued straight from Collins Inlet across McGregor Bay to Great La Cloche Island, named for a basalt erratic (glacially transported rock) which, when struck, sounded like a bell.

The Indians at a village here told Henry that the Indians at Michilimackinac, being still loyal to the French, would kill him. The village Indians said they therefore "had a right to a share of the pillage" and demanded a keg of rum, which they would take if not given. "I judged it prudent to comply," Henry concluded.

It was too late to turn around as they hadn't enough food for the return journey. Campion, Henry's assistant, said he should put on the dress of a voyageur to escape detection as an Englishman. "To this end, I laid aside my English clothes, and covered myself only with a cloth, passed about the middle; a shirt, hanging loose; a molton, or blanket coat; and a large, red, milled worsted cap. The next thing was to smear my face and hands, with dirt and grease; and, this done, I took the place of one of my men, and, when Indians approached, used the paddle, with as much skill as I possessed. I had the satisfaction to find, that my disguise enabled me to pass several canoes, without attracting the smallest notice."

After traversing a tiny channel that separates Great La Cloche Island from the mainland (where a historical marker on Highway 6 now describes the "Route of the Voyageurs"), the way led through a maze of islands near the north shore of the North Channel, with the length of Manitoulin Island off to the south. They stopped at the mouth of the Mississagi River, where the Indians gave them sturgeon, then proceeded past Thessalon, southward through the strait at Point des Detours (near present-day De Tour Village), past Isle aux Outardes (Goose Island) and Michilimackinac Island (the "Great Turtle"—Mackinac Island today), to the fort at Michilimackinac on the Straits of Mackinac.

Henry spent two years here and at Sault Ste. Marie—a time of great danger as well as interest. He described fishing through the ice with wooden decoy fish for lake trout at the Sault, and the Indians netting whitefish in the St. Marys River rapids. The Indians at Michilimackinac nearly did kill him. In 1763 they caught the garrison by surprise and, leaving the French Canadian residents unharmed, massacred fifty of the seventy British soldiers. Henry was saved only by the intervention of a chief, who took him captive to replace his own brother, who had been killed by the British during the French and Indian War.

Henry's return journey to civilization came about because the Indians at Michilimackinac feared that Sir William Johnson at Niagara would come with an army and the Six Nations to attack them unless they made friends with him. Accordingly, a sixteen-Indian deputation, plus Henry, was organized to make the trip, but first, before an undertaking of such magnitude, the Great Turtle had to be consulted. In a nighttime ceremony conducted in a giant wigwam and orchestrated by a shaman, the Great Turtle was asked about the English at Fort Niagara. The spirit replied that Sir William Johnson would "fill their canoes with presents" and all would return in safety. Thus assured, the party set off.

The journey was nearly halted by Henry's ignorance of the spirit world. At Point Grondine, where they put ashore because of strong winds, Henry encountered a rattlesnake that he described as four to five feet long (probably a timber rattlesnake as the Massasauga is much smaller). He was going to shoot it but the Indians stopped him. To appease the snake they blew pipe smoke toward the "grandfather" who, it appeared, "really received it with pleasure." The Indians followed it, asking the snake to take care of their families during their absence, "and to be pleased to open the heart of Sir William Johnson, so that he might *show them charity*, and fill their canoe with rum." A chief requested that the snake take no notice of the Englishman's insult.

This was the first time this species had been seen so far to the north and west of the French River, and the Indians thought the snake had been sent to turn them back. Henry persuaded them to continue, but the next morning on the lake strong winds threatened to swamp them. Two dogs, each with its front legs tied together, were thrown overboard as a sacrifice to the god-rattlesnake. A man sitting next to Henry suggested they sacrifice him to the spirit too, but luckily the wind abated.

They proceeded down Georgian Bay, crossed inland by way of Lake Simcoe to Lake Ontario, and were received favorably at Fort Niagara, where Henry was released. In later years he traded in the Lake Superior region and made a trip to the Great Plains, taking many more notes on the Indian tribes.

After the War of 1812, conditions on the upper Great Lakes were very unsettled. The area was still essentially British in loyalties, and the international boundary had not yet been totally delineated. Backed by U.S. Secretary of War John C. Calhoun, Michigan territorial governor Lewis Cass organized an expedition to explore the southern shore of Lake Superior and the upper reaches of the Mississippi River, with an eye to future American settlement. The main objective was information about the land and its potential.

The principal members of the expedition were Cass; Maj. Robert Forsyth; James Doty; Capt. David Douglass, topographer; Charles Trowbridge, assistant topographer; Alexander Chase; Dr. Alexander Wolcott;

and Henry Schoolcraft. Schoolcraft, then twenty-seven, had learned the glass industry as a youth and later had traveled to the lead regions of Missouri. He was appointed to serve as geologist and minerologist. After the expedition he published the day-by-day journal he had kept. That narrative and the notes of Doty and Trowbridge give us a picture of the Michigan shore of Lake Huron at that time, as well as the difficulties of canoe travel on the lake.

The expedition set out from Detroit on May 24, 1820, in a three-canoe flotilla. Voyageurs manned one, Indians under an Ottawa chief another, and seven soldiers the third. In all, there were somewhere between thirty-eight and forty-three men (the accounts differed). In the enthusiasm of departure, the Canadians challenged the Indians to a boat race. Strong headwinds, which "blew waves breaking over our canoe and gave us a severe drenching," soon dampened the enthusiasm, however, and sent the party ashore at Gross Pointe.

Two days later, they launched again, with pleasurable "anticipation of the novel and interesting scenes we were to encounter." They were met by more waves as they crossed Lake St. Clair. "The most of us were unused to canoes," Doty wrote, "and the traverse was very unpleasant. . . . We were shivering with cold when we landed" on the St. Clair River. Going up the river the next day, Schoolcraft noted Indian canoes and nine vessels at anchor, with merchandise, military stores, and troops for Michilimackinac, Green Bay, and Chicago. The Canadian shore, compared with the settlements on the American side, was "generally in the state of nature." Constantly they observed "ducks, plovers, and snipe." Pulling into Fort Gratiot, one-half mile below the entrance into Lake Huron, Trowbridge recorded that they "landed amidst the roar of cannon which, contrasted with the animated songs of our Frenchmen, had a pleasing effect."

On May 28 they made thirty-five miles, following the American shore, which was covered chiefly with white pine, poplar, birch, and hemlock. (The white pine, for lumber, and the hemlock, for tanbark, would later be heavily exploited.) They camped on a beach near present-day Port Sanilac. Next day the weather showed them the fickleness of Lake Huron. Paddling one to two miles offshore, they passed the White Rock, "known to all canoe and boat travelers of the region." In the afternoon the wind shifted so they could hoist sails, but around four o'clock a storm came up. As they ran for shore, the landing was "dangerous from the number of detached stones projecting above the water, or merely hid beneath it." (Such stones today threaten the many motorboats putting out from these shores.) Trowbridge, too, was apprehensive: "the construction of these vessels, so frail yet so generally and so widely used . . . is such, that without the most extreme caution, the traveller is every hour in danger of losing his canoe, baggage and perhaps his life." With a gale blowing, a vessel had anchored a half-mile offshore. Here the land was "skirted with bull-rushes, quake grass . . . and other aquatic plants."

After being detained for two days by headwinds, they started off at 6:00 A.M. on June 1, only to be forced to land after three miles. At three o'clock they embarked again and with sails up made twenty-five miles to Saginaw Bay. Schoolcraft described the sand dunes, covered with pines and aspen, near present Port Austin, and commented that this is "one of the safest shores for boat and canoe navigation. The frailty of these vessels is not here threatened by those hidden blocks of granite and other primary stones, which we have found so very annoying along the coast between Fort Gratiot and Point aux Barques." He foresaw the future prosperity of the Saginaw River area, then inhabited by bands of Chippewa and Ottawa, who enjoyed fine hunting grounds and an abundance of fish. "[W]e are led to suppose that [the area] presents uncommon incitements to enterprising and industrious farmers and mechanics."

The following day the calm weather allowed them to make the twenty-mile crossing of Saginaw Bay. Shoving off from Oak Point, they stopped briefly at Shawangunk (Charity Island) to make notes on the forests and geology, then completed the often-dangerous traverse. They continued on to the mouth of the Au Sable River, making a good fifty-six miles that day. At the river, they smoked the pipe of peace with the local band of Chippewa, shook hands all around, and gave them tobacco and whiskey, after which the Indians departed for their village.

The next day, June 3, they made forty-eight miles to Little Sturgeon Bay, southwest of Middle Island. At Thunder Bay, Schoolcraft concluded that, contrary to a widely held belief, "the highly electrified state of the atmosphere at this Bay seems to have no foundation in truth." He found the broken rock along the shore from Thunder Bay to Little Sturgeon Island to be "a compact limestone, abounding in petrified remains."

June 4 was a frustrating day, with short advances between storms. Trowbridge wrote that "we were much troubled with the musquitoes, now very numerous. . . . The evening was somewhat cold, and we found our Buffaloe skins and Blankets very comfortable." June 5 was not much better. While the voyageurs and soldiers paddled the canoes alongshore the rest went on foot. They camped at the end of a portage across a sandy peninsula at Presque Isle. Here the Indian paddlers brought in "a brown rabbit, a water turtle, and some pigeons." Schoolcraft lamented that there had been little time to hunt on the journey, though they had seen many tracks of deer and bear. Ducks had been scared off well out of shooting range by the sound of the paddles.

On June 6 they reached their first destination—Mackinac Island—after contending with high waves at Bois Blanc Island, an island, Trowbridge wrote, where, "as the land is not thought valuable there have as yet been no settlements made upon it." Mackinac Island was another story. For Schoolcraft, "Nothing can present a more picturesque or refreshing spectacle to the traveller, wearied with the lifeless monotony of a canoe voyage through Lake Huron, than the first sight of the island of Michili-mackinac" with its lofty bluffs capped with two fortresses on which the American standard was conspicuously displayed.

Reflecting on his journey to this point, Schoolcraft seemed disappointed. The scenery had not been varied enough to keep up interest, the natural history less interesting than expected (partly because of lack of time ashore). Only the geology, especially the fossil-ridden limestone, had really excited him. He reckoned the straight-line distance at 300 miles but the actual route following indentations of the shore 400 miles. The weather, according to his measurements, had been cooler than normal—an average of fifty-one degrees.

On June 13, reprovisioned, the party set out from Mackinac Island with four canoes and a twelve-oared barge carrying twenty-two soldiers (the Indians at the Sault were thought to be hostile). Young Doty, just twenty, was worried about the twelve-mile crossing to Goose Island. This traverse "is considered dangerous from the waves and wind being generally very high—the wind has a sweep of 200 miles on the lake [from the southeast]." They made it successfully, however, and camped up the St. Marys River opposite Drummond Island (then British), from which drifted that night the sound of music from a British garrison. Trowbridge apparently had a more romantic turn of mind than Schoolcraft did, for he jotted in his journal, "The islands in the mouth of this River are almost innumerable, and their elevated situation and beautiful foliage, contrasted with the clear and extended expanse of water, afford to the contemplative traveller a source of infinite gratification."

The expedition reached Sault Ste. Marie on June 14, but not without difficulty. At one rapid on the west side of Neebish Island they damaged three canoes on large limestone rocks and had to stop for repairs. At a second rapid, Doty recorded that they were temporarily stymied. "For ten minutes our canoe, with all of the men at the oars and paddles did not stir three feet either way." Their guide had directed them to the wrong side of Neebish Island. On the east side they would have found deeper water. (Both sides are now ship channels, deepened where necessary by blasting.)

At Sault Ste. Marie the Indians were found to be unhostile, and eventually the expedition continued westward through Lake Superior to the upper Mississippi country. Schoolcraft later became Indian agent for twenty years at Sault Ste. Marie and Mackinac Island and wrote extensively about the tribes he dealt with, helped not a little by his wife, a granddaughter of a great Chippewa chief and daughter of an English trader and Indian "princess."

Schoolcraft's careful though humorless description of his Lake Huron journey contrasts, like cold water against hot, with that of a later traveler, the ebullient Mrs. Anna Jameson. Mrs. Jameson had already gained considerable fame as a writer of biography and travel literature when, in December 1836, she left England to join her husband, who was the attorney general of Upper Canada (now Ontario), at York (now Toronto). The purpose of her trip was to reach a separation agreement with him, so it is not surprising that she left him for much of the next year to travel on Lake Huron. What *is* surprising—in fact unprecedented—is the nature of that travel, accomplished by a woman described as fair, small, and delicately featured.

The trip began conventionally enough with a steamboat journey from Chatham to Detroit and then another to Mackinac Island, where she met and stayed with the Schoolcrafts. Her spirits by then were soaring. On a canoe trip over to nearby "Woody" Island, while the men went ashore, she and a young Irish lady floated about, singing Irish melodies and Italian serenades.

Later, at Sault Ste. Marie, she became even more adventurous. She wanted to descend the rapids of the St. Marys River, which reminded her "of an exquisitely beautiful woman in a fit of rage." With an Indian steering and herself sitting in the bottom of a ten-foot fishing canoe that was "light and elegant and buoyant as a bird on the waters," they shot down the three-quarter-mile-long rapids in seven minutes. She felt no fear, just "giddy, breathless, delicious excitement." Her friends said she was the first European female to make this tumultuous run.

The next leg of her journey took her from the Sault to Manitoulin Island, in a flat-bottomed bateau that was rowed and sailed by four "half-breed" (French-Indian) voyageurs. Accompanying her on August 6 were the MacMurrys (a missionary couple), their baby son, and two Indian girls. The voyageurs were Masta (a great talker), Le Blanc (the best singer and leader of songs), Pierrot ("a most comical fellow"), and the steersman and captain, Content. That first night they camped on an island in a tent, Mrs. MacMurry in the middle with her baby on her bosom, Mr. MacMurry on one side of her, Mrs. Jameson on the other, and the two Indian girls at their feet. Anna's bones ached as she turned from side to side on the rocky ground. Just before dawn a thunderstorm struck, the lake "swelling and roaring."

Her spirits flagged momentarily that day, as the wind came up and the waves rose high. They "scudded with an almost fearful rapidity before the wind. In crossing a wide, open expanse of about twenty miles, we became all at once very silent, then very grave, then very pathetic, and at last extremely sick." Still, she could be eloquent about the island-studded scenery of the North Channel: "We passed successive groups of islands, countless in number, various in form, little fairy Edens."

A day later they reached Great La Cloche Island, where the North West Company station provided "the only signs of civilised society during our voyage." She mentions the rock that sounds like a bell when struck but didn't try it. Moving on, they camped on an island "clothed in many places with a species of gray lichen, nearly a foot deep." This time she put lichens under the sleeping mats for padding. The cooking fire spread to a fallen trunk and then to the tree it was leaning against. The men cleared the area around the burning trees so the fire wouldn't spread farther, and they ate dinner. The scene, Anna thought, was "wildly magnificent" as she contemplated the waves, rocks, trees, and figures and faces of the men in the brilliant firelight.

At Manitoulin Island, they learned from men on a black schooner that "William the Fourth was dead and that Queen Victoria ruled in his place." At this spot on the eastern end of the island the annual government distribution of presents to the Indians had just taken place. As the party came into a little bay, the shores were "covered with wigwams and lodges, thick as they could stand amid intermingled trees. . . . Some hundred canoes were darting hither and thither . . . and a beautiful schooner lay against the green bank." That evening she was invited to the council meeting, where Mr. Jarvis, the chief superintendent of Indian affairs from Toronto spoke to his "children," and some Indians, with wild cries, put on a war dance for Mrs. Jameson's benefit. Her party camped among the multitude—some 3,700 Indians from several tribes—and she felt safe.

At Manitoulin she joined the superintendent's party, which was heading back to Toronto. There were two canoes, each twenty-five feet long and four feet wide. In her canoe traveled Mr. Jarvis, the "governor's son, 14 or 15," "old Solomon the interpreter," and seven voyageurs. She sat on the bottom on her roll of blankets and night-gear, with a pillow at her back. "I had near me my cloak, umbrella, and parasol; my note-books and sketch books [she sketched and watercolored on the way], and a little compact basket always by my side, containing eau de Cologne, and all those necessary luxuries which might be wanted in a moment." Altogether there were twenty-one men and herself.

The trip down Georgian Bay, through the innumerable islands, seemed one of near-constant joy to her. "This day we had a most delightful run among hundreds of islands; sometimes darting through narrow rocky channels . . . and then emerging, we glided through vast fields of white water-lilies; it was perpetual variety, perpetual beauty, perpetual delight and enchantment, from hour to hour. The men sang their gay French songs, the other canoe joining in the chorus." She loves "the purity, the coldness, the transparency of the water."

Interestingly for someone more attuned to cultural matters, she describes aspects of the vegetation that were not carefully and scientifically studied until the turn of the nineteenth century or later: plant succession and island biogeography. She notes, for instance, the process of "preparatory vegetation . . . each successive growth preparing the soil for that which is to follow. There was first the naked rock washed by the spray . . . then you saw the rock covered with some moss or lichens; then in the clefts and seams, some long grass, a few wild flowers and strawberries; then a few juniper and rose bushes; then the dwarf pine hardly rising two or three feet, and lastly trees and shrubs of large growth: and the nearer to the mainland, the richer of course the vegetation, for the seeds are wafted thence by the winds, or carried by the birds, and so dispersed from island to island."

She enjoyed the ducks, pigeons, and bass that enlivened the menu but frowned at certain excesses of the men's hunting instinct. They chased and shot a mink and then a mother duck, leaving the ducklings to fend for themselves. The voyageurs would imitate the soft call of gulls and when they came close shot them. "The voyageurs eat these gulls," she wrote with revulsion, "in spite of their fishy taste, with great satisfaction."

Not even rain could dampen her overriding enthusiasm. Under a dark, wet sky "the scenery was even more beautiful than ever." That night, their last on Georgian Bay, Mr. Jarvis brought her some hot Madeira, and the voyageurs, as spirited as Mrs. Jameson, "sheltered under the canoes and sang and laughed" during a great part of the night.

They landed at Penetanguishene and lodged at an inn. She anticipated throwing herself on the little bed with its white cotton curtains. "But nine nights passed in the open air, or on rocks, and on boards, had spoiled me for the comforts of civilisation, and to sleep *on a bed* was impossible; I was smothered . . . altogether wretched and fevered; —I sighed for my rock on Lake Huron."

The party then took the usual route through Lake Simcoe to Toronto. Anna Jameson gained a satisfactory separation from her husband, went back to England in September 1837, and devoted most of her remaining twenty-three years to studying and writing about art history.

These accounts are only three of the many written about travel on Lake Huron in the seventeenth, eighteenth, and nineteenth centuries. But they illustrate well the human responses to the lake—a sense of adventure, fear, scientific interest, delight in the scenery—that will continue down the centuries ahead.

# CHAPTER 16

# FALL COMES DOWN THE LAKE

T he coming of fall is quieter even than the arrival of spring, as if
nature is reluctant to let go of the blessings of summer. On the lake,
summer and fall seemed to mix together for a long time before I could
say that summer had truly gone.

Signs of fall appeared first on the land. Small flocks of sanderlings,
sometimes accompanied by other members of the shorebird tribe, ran
up and down before the beach waves in July and August, seeming to
say, "Believe it or not, frost will be coming." As is their habit, they
had abandoned their Arctic breeding grounds after little more than a
month of nesting and were feeding and fattening their way south at a very
leisurely pace.

Our sandy beach sees only a tiny fragment of the shorebird waves that
pass this way. What most of the sandpipers and plovers seek are broad
mud flats where they can probe for invertebrates. Such flats are exposed
in abundance around Saginaw Bay when lake levels are low or the wind
is right, but in 1995 we didn't have those conditions. In late August
and early September golden plovers and buff-breasted sandpipers come
through, and they seek plowed fields and turf farms. The buff-breasted is
scarce, so Myles Willard, my brother-in-law Tony, and I were delighted
on August 29 to spot one of these dainty little birds picking at the turf
way out on the smooth green expanse of Beck's Sod Farm, in the northern
part of my county.

If shorebirds don't really say "fall" to us, surely tree color does. The poplar leaves had begun turning yellow during August, perhaps from dryness as much as anything else, and on August 31 they were beginning to float down onto our driveway. At the back end of our long narrow lot, touches of red had appeared on the chokecherries. But the sugar maples and willows and birches remained green and the days warm.

For humans, Labor Day weekend traditionally signals the end of summer, and Port Sanilac is no exception. One sees family reunions and yard sales along the country roads and more people than usual on the beach. The merchants sadly contemplate the slower days to come and the students the daily discipline of school.

Out on the water, there was one last frenzy of buzzing jet-skis and in counterpoint the quiet grace of sailboats. Many boats trolled for salmon and trout, farther out than usual at this time of year because of the hot summer. Soon, though, the cooling water would send the fish shoreward, where chinook salmon would make pathetic attempts to spawn in the harbor or up streams scarcely deep enough to carry them.

Cooling air was beginning now to suck heat from the surface water, launching the major transformation of the fall turnover. As the surface water cooled it would become heavier and sink, starting the mixing that would end only with the nearly uniform winter temperatures from top to bottom.

The night before Labor Day was cool and, I thought, might have triggered some landbird migration, so on that holiday I visited two lakeside parks to check. Warblers were scarce, but flocks of robins, blue jays, and flickers were on the move. Surely fall would be well on the way at the north end of the lake. On September 7 I headed up there to see.

A big high pressure system coming down from Canada produced two cold nights at the state forest campground on the Munuscong River, near its entrance into the St. Marys River. On the second morning I emerged from the sleeping platform installed in my Isuzu Trooper to find a flock of warblers feeding where sunlight hit the birches and balsam firs. Now in fall the warblers' colors were more muted, in keeping, one might say, with the less joyful nature of the southward flight contrasted with the eager northward flight in spring. Across the river, a merlin perched on a high dead branch, its head swiveling back and forth as it watched for such small birds, but apparently not seeing these. Somewhere beyond the forest on the other side of the Munuscong, sandhill cranes loudly "crrrucked," a wild, throaty call that suggested a gathering. They would not migrate for another month or more, but maybe they were starting to think about it.

At Sault Ste. Marie, the salmon had decided it was fall and were heading for their release sites or hatching grounds. Boats trolling for them choked the St. Marys River, and a line of boats were tied up all along the outflow from under the Edison power plant, where salmon converge. The railing along the river here was solid with anglers casting lures. They were catching mostly pink salmon but occasionally a chinook, a bystander informed me. "I saw one chinook as long as my arm," he said. Dozens more fishermen waded the St. Marys rapids farther upstream. The scene seemed a modern version of the flotillas of canoes that carried Indians and white men dipnetting whitefish in the rapids during the last century.

On Manitoulin Island I checked into the Janet Head Campground and secured my tent with rocks as well as tent pegs against a strong north wind, which was blowing high waves onto the shore. That evening a small boat pushed out of Gore Bay into those waves, its captain apparently determined to catch salmon that were now heading toward the island's streams. After dark a man in the campground was cleaning a large salmon at the edge of the water.

Down at the Purvises' Burnt Island fish station, the main quarry, as usual, was whitefish. The fishing had been good, maybe too good. "We'll probably reach our quota on whitefish in October," Irene said. Unless they could rent somebody else's quota, they wouldn't be able to keep fishing to the end of their normal season—just before Christmas. "Most of our whitefish market is Jewish," Irene said, "and the prices go up before their holidays. If we have to quit early we'll miss Hanukkah, besides losing the business with our regular buyers in the late fall."

At noon one day, I drove down to Misery Bay, on the south shore. The sugar maples en route had a yellowish tinge on their green, and here and there a small patch of red. At the bay I met a group from the Sudbury Ornithological Society who, like me, were looking for signs of the fall bird migration. Doreen Bailey was among them. Jubilantly, she announced, "I made it up to 210 species yesterday. Got a peregrine falcon and a Connecticut warbler at the Mississagi Lighthouse." As we ate lunch, a merlin and a sharp-shinned hawk took turns chasing each other over our heads. Were they migrants or local nesters? No way to tell, but in either case they must soon be going south. Chris Bell, leader of the Sudbury group, said loons were gathering on Manitou Lake, in preparation for the southward journey.

After lunch, Roy Campbell, a local farmer, and I followed Doreen's brown pickup over to Frechette Bay (locally known as Mac's Bay) to see what else was gathering. Our first sighting, however, was singular. A large black bear ambled along the shore, turning its wide head in our direction from time to time and then disappearing into the fringing forest. At nearby Murphy Harbour we did see a gathering. On and around the rocks dotting the water at the head of this bay sat dozens of ring-billed gulls and some 200 immature common mergansers. In a month or two, they or their confreres would be fishing in my end of the lake.

As I packed my tent to leave Manitoulin, a red-necked grebe floated offshore. In the coming weeks, red-necked grebes—long-necked, loonlike birds—would gather in the bays on the north and south sides of the island. In North America, this species nests in a band extending from northern Ontario and the western Lake Superior region to Alaska and winters mainly on the Atlantic and Pacific coasts. Birds heading for the Atlantic seem to go mostly through the northern parts of the upper Great Lakes, collecting temporarily in certain areas. I have seen them around Isle Royale in Lake Superior in the fall, and thousands pass Whitefish Point, in eastern Lake Superior, in late summer and fall. Manitoulin Island must be on their preferred route as well, and some linger here into early winter, as others do in southern Georgian Bay. Farther east, many stop on Lake Ontario, where they also gather during the return trip in spring. From the cliffs east of Toronto, I marveled at their masses one raw April day years ago. Other than at such places, the red-necked grebe is scarce, and most birders consider it a red-letter day when one is sighted.

Back at the cottage, I settled in to watch the progress of fall. By September 18 our red maple near the lake was spotted with red, and at the back of our lot the sumacs were red and the chokecherries red and yellow. Perhaps pushed by a cold air mass coming slowly down from Canada, migrant birds filled our trees. Along with several kinds of warblers there were white-throated, white-crowned, and Lincoln's sparrows; ruby-crowned kinglets, flickers, chickadees, blue jays, Swainson's thrushes, a red-breasted nuthatch, and a brown creeper—the latter the first I had seen at the cottage. Over the next few days, many of these birds remained, joined by two tiny winter wrens, who announced their presence with sharp "jip-jip" calls from under the arborvitaes.

By the morning of September 22, with the temperature in the mid-forties, most of these birds had gone. Writing at my desk in Papa's parlor, I heard a thud on the bay window beside me. Going outside, I found a brown creeper lying dead on the concrete walkway. I picked up the tiny body, which seemed weightless—just a bit of brown, white-flecked air I thought—and laid it among the petunias. I felt especially sad because I thought I knew it. It probably had been the one probing the bark on our trees for several days, building energy for a night flight down to Ohio, and now my transparent window had killed it. That evening, in an evening mood, I remembered that my ashes would one day join the minuscule substance of that creeper in the garden. Large and small in life, we would be the same in death.

The next morning the temperature had dropped into the thirties and wisps of "frost smoke" rose from the lake. On our beach a herring gull was picking at a dead catfish, now just a head and tail held together by skin. Farther down, 200 gulls rested in the usual spot on the sand near the harbor. It was Saturday, and many boats were trolling, not far offshore now, with eight sailboats scattered among them. Four boatloads of fishermen were anchored in the small harbor, while three dozen anglers cast their lures from the breakwalls, hoping to antagonize a salmon or brown trout into striking. I asked a man in his thirties how it was going. "No luck," he said, "I'd even like to see somebody else catch something—just for a little excitement. Right now I'd rather be in the cattails, duck hunting." Farther out on the flat north breakwall, three sanderlings and a white-throated sparrow were picking insects off the small plants growing in crevices. A warbler flew in from the lake and headed for the safety of trees. Higher, thirty Canada geese flew south, honking.

As noon approached, fishermen began leaving the breakwalls and I headed back up the beach. Just then a merlin sped by and disappeared among the trees by the harbor. Soon the dark little falcon returned, clutching a small bird. It landed on top of a tree stub near Liens Creek and began plucking its prey. It preferred to face into the brisk northwest wind, but as I approached it turned around to face me, still feeding. I got quite close before it flew, its brown back proclaiming it a female or juvenile. A bird of northern forests in summer and open country farther south in winter, it was perhaps on its way to the Gulf Coast, where small birds abound. There was even a slight chance it was the merlin I had seen at the Muscongus River, or the merlin that had chased a sharp-shin at Misery Bay on Manitoulin. In any case, it was a sign of fall, of the great escape from hard times to come in the north.

About this time, I acknowledged the beginning of fall in domestic ways. I switched from whiskey and ginger ale, my traditional pre-dinner summer drink at the cottage, to Scotch and soda, which somehow seems more bracing and complementary to a fire in the stove. I lit the first fire in the wood stove since spring and, to ensure continued fires, called Paul Messing. Paul drives a truck for the county road commission, but he picks up extra cash selling firewood. He buys the remains left from timber cutting and saws them into fireplace length. A day after I called, Paul arrived with two cords of maple and ash, cut into fourteen-inch logs to fit our small stove. In November he would take two or three weeks off to go trapping along streams and drainage ditches. "Last year I caught three dozen mink and more than 300 muskrats," he said as he pitched logs beside our garage. "Got $3.25 for muskrats, $13.60 for my female minks, but I put the males in the freezer to try to get a better price later. Made $1,800." More logs went sailing off the truck. "I love this time of year, but before you know it, the snow's flying."

The snow wasn't flying yet, though. Quite the contrary. Warm air returned and with it on certain days came a hatch of insects. Flocks of gulls picked them off the water and caught them in the air. During the last few days of September the temperature rose into the seventies and, much to my annoyance, the buzz of a jet-ski was heard.

I had to leave the cottage for two and a half weeks in October. Papa Worth, my father-in-law, had died in Florida. October 3, the day before I left, was sombre and wild:

"The rains came today. First significant rain I've seen since August. Waves crashing in on an east wind. . . . 6:30 P.M. To Paisano's at the harbor for dinner. Luminous, wet-looking black and white clouds billowing out over the lake. There's an evening glow on the boats in their slips. White waves are flung high above the breakwalls. On the south breakwall, at the end where it's sheltered by the north wall, two die-hards are still fishing. . . . 8:30 P.M. Started a fire to cheer me up on this dreary evening."

When I returned from Florida in late October, many of the trees inland were bare, but many others still bore color: yellow and orange on birches and aspens, red on sumac and some sugar maples. The willows, early to green in spring and late to change in fall, just had tinges of yellow. At the cottage, our red maple was bare, as were the grape vines on our low dunes, but the willows and most of our sugar maples were still green. The lake's stored warmth was delaying the progress of fall in a narrow band along the shore. (On the Lake Michigan side of the state the prevailing west winds create a wider band where seasons lag.) Depending on where you looked, you might think it was summer, fall, or winter.

Down at Mary's Diner one Saturday morning, the talk had turned to fall things. Four men—two old, two middle-aged, wearing blue and white baseball caps that said "Exchange State Bank"—made a few dollar bets on that day's college football games, arguing about the point spread. They speculated about the outcome of the first World Series game, about to be played by Atlanta and Cleveland, and then moved on to nonseasonal

A paper birch sheds its leaves as fall progresses on the lake. (Credit: Myles Willard)

topics, such as a local fire: "Why did they need seven firemen to put out such a small fire? Some of them were just watching."

Mike Hanson was by now well into his fall mode, checking on hunters and stalking people who tried to snag salmon at night coming up streams and into the harbor. "If they get caught," he said, "it costs them $10 per pound plus court costs—about $200 for a fourteen-pound fish. The penalty ought to be making those people eat the fish—they're starting to go rotten when they spawn. The fishermen leave a mess on a person's property. It's getting better though. The Port Sanilac police [all three of them] are helping me at the harbor."

A few days after this conversation the local Baptist pastor came to clean our dining room rug, which had suffered the results of numerous infant meals during the summer. I asked him how much time he spends with his church. "As much as I can," he replied, "but I drive a school bus and do carpentry besides cleaning rugs. That's what a country pastor has to do these days to make a living. It does get me into a lot of people's homes, though, and I can tell them about the Lord."

Like many men in the Thumb, he still finds time to hunt and fish. He had been pheasant hunting that morning (missed) and hoped to go bow hunting for deer that afternoon. He had a buck staked out. One time, he said, he caught a salmon for his father-in-law with his hands. "I threw a rock to chase it into shallow riffles and then caught it. You can't spear them or net them, but the rules don't say anything about catching them with your hands."

So far there had been no fall equivalent of the spring streams of ducks, gulls, loons, and cormorants going north, just occasional waterbird migrants. But on November 1 there was a change:

"8:30 A.M. 49 degrees, overcast, southeast wind blowing in grey-brown waves. Cold air mass moving down from Canada into Plains states—expected to affect us in a couple of days. First significant movement of waterfowl I've seen at the cottage. Buffleheads, mergansers, perhaps other ducks moving south. All ring-bills and herring gulls seen were flying southward." Our sugar maples now reflected the late fall date, ranging from yellow patches among the green, to totally orange, to bare.

The next day, bugs were flying again, and Bonaparte's gulls were chasing them, but colder weather, and the waterbirds it pushed southward, soon returned:

"November 4. 7:15 A.M. 29 degrees, frost on ground. Looks like the petunias and geraniums have finally had it.

"November 5. Sunday, 7:30 A.M. 27 degrees, chilly SW wind. Followed a feeding frenzy of mergansers and gulls north up the shore as they chased bait fish. Stream up near the next point had a thin film of ice on it.

"November 6. 7:30 A.M. 29 degrees. A cold, blue, sunny morning. Petunias and geraniums have definitely had it.

"November 9. 7:30 A.M. 23 degrees. Light snow forecast for this afternoon.

"November 11. About 1:00 a heavy line of rain comes through with SW wind, which then shifts to NW. Powerful with high gusts, it blows me all over the highway driving back from Sarnia. Temperature drops, rain turns to snow—enough to dust the ground. In the Port Sanilac harbor, waves crashing over the north breakwall. Some ducks and a loon taking shelter there.

"November 12. 7:30 A.M. 27 degrees. Lake calmer, but brown from the pounding last night. Many gulls, mostly ring-billed, flying south—the heaviest gull flight I've seen yet. . . . 4:00–5:30 P.M. An interesting walk to the harbor. Grey clouds, 32 degrees, but no wind, so fairly pleasant. Waves last night left low mounds of pebbles on the beach. Liens Creek running strong but I can jump across. In the harbor: buffleheads, red-breasted mergansers, two common mergansers, a redhead, goldeneye, hooded merganser, and a small goose on the south breakwall that turned out to be an immature blue-phase snow goose. [It stayed in the harbor for two weeks.] Muskrat swims out from the phragmites and cattails in the south corner. On the rocks at the inner edge of the harbor an immature cormorant is standing asleep. A red-breasted merganser with a broken wing—shot I suppose—leaves the rocks and swims under the docks at my approach. Six people fishing along inner edge of the harbor. Two sailboats—*Saralysia* and *Queen of Hearts*—and the *Miss Port Sanilac* still in the water.

"November 13. 4:00–5:30 P.M. 34 degrees, snow flakes idly drifting down. Walked to the harbor. Liens Creek partially skimmed with ice. Three brown hooded mergansers back in there, their Afro hair-dos raised straight up in alarm. Pretty much the same assortment of ducks in the harbor as yesterday. . . . The *Miss Port Sanilac* was cruising along the lake horizon when I arrived, and later she was near the sling lift with a bunch of white plastic buoys on her deck. Bill Lyons was on board working. Said they had just taken up the racing buoys. Then they'll 'pull' the *Miss Port Sanilac* for the winter. Icicles beginning to form on the breakwalls."

With waterfowl now much in evidence, I decided it was time to check out the hunting scene at Fish Point State Wildlife Area, on the south shore of Saginaw Bay, one of the best of several such wildlife areas around the bay. On the way, I stopped at some of the waterfowl gathering places along the shore of the Thumb. Harbor Beach had a sprinkling of ducks. A man was watching them with binoculars from his car. Said he was retired but his wife was still working—as a Presbyterian minister there. Whiskey Harbor, partly frozen, was empty of birds, as was Eagle Bay—what I could see of it through the snow showers. Port Austin harbor sheltered a few ducks and Wildfowl Bay, most of it iced over, still held a small number of tundra swans, Canada geese, and ducks. At Bay Port, from the Bay Port Fish Company dock, all I could see was one Canada goose, ice halfway to Sand Point, and two guys on stools ice fishing. So far, a poverty of waterfowl.

As I approached Fish Point across flat, wide-open farm fields, a blizzard of snow buntings sounded a new theme—abundance. Farther along, thousands of mallards and geese rose from corn stubble, and at the wildlife area itself Arnie Carr, the former manager now doing part-time duty here from his regional office, said there were about 5,000 ducks. I was late for the peak, however. They had had many more in October, and about 4,000 swans the first week of November. The blackboard in the office showed that 6,085 ducks, 823 geese, and one pheasant had been taken so far this fall. The goose season had been closed as of November 12 to protect the subspecies that predominates here in migration—the lesser interior Canada goose. This subspecies, which nests in the James Bay region, formerly numbered 100,000 but now is down to 75,000, for reasons unknown (in contrast with the giant Canada goose, which has rebounded in Michigan and other parts of the Northeast to the point of becoming a nuisance on golf courses and other public places; an early hunting season for this subspecies has been established to reduce its numbers).

The Fish Point wildlife area, some five square miles in extent, is a complex of fields, marsh, and refuge ponds extending almost to the shore of Saginaw Bay. In the spring the managers make sure the diked areas hold enough water for the breeding ducks—mostly mallards, blue-winged teal, and wood ducks. They plant corn, buckwheat, and sorghum on the cropland, and sometimes plant barley. During the summer they cultivate the crops and, late in the season, plant winter wheat as a cover crop. The geese start feeding on the wheat and ducks on the buckwheat and barley. In late August the duck populations start building up, as wanderers and migrants join the local breeders. The fields are flooded in the fall and many more ducks come in. These flooded fields are then partitioned into hunting blocks for daily parties of hunters, who load their gear into canoes or other shallow-draft boats and pull them to their assigned section. Here they set out their decoys, hide in the cornstalks, and await the first unwary ducks.

In the middle of the wildlife area rises a twenty-foot-high observation platform to accommodate bird- and hunter-watchers like me. With scope and binoculars in hand I ascend the platform around 4:00 P.M. on this gray afternoon as snowflakes drift down. November has been colder than normal and now many of the fields hold ice instead of water. On the patches of open water strings of decoys float, and with binoculars I can discern brown-clad men at the edges amid the brown cornstalks.

To the north the refuge ponds, where hunting is not allowed, half hidden by trees and bushes, are black with ducks and geese. One manager had told me they usually stay there during the day and fly out at dusk to feed in surrounding farm fields, but Arnie Carr said they often go out to feed on days of bad weather like today. The hunters try to intercept them coming and going from the refuge area.

216

This afternoon most of the flights are incoming. Flying high, groups of mallards and honking Canadas come in from the farm fields to the south to join their fellows in the refuge. Any that stray lower are enticed with a chorus of quacks and gabbles from the cornstalks, and now and then I hear the pop of a shotgun. Once I see a man walk through the cornstalks and retrieve a fallen duck.

Around 4:30 two great horned owls start calling from the fringe of shore trees to the west—a deep "hoo-hoo, hoo-hoo." One, perhaps the male, has a deeper call than the other. As darkness falls the hoots come more frequently. It occurs to me that they must have easy pickings among the sleeping or wounded ducks.

In the dusk, hunters begin returning to their pickup trucks, pulling a boatload of decoys or cracking through ice with every few steps. I am no doubt as cold as they are as I descend from the platform to my car. Probably 999 out of every 1,000 ducks have survived the evening. Most will avoid hunters, horned owls, and other hazards to reach their winter quarters in some other marsh to the south.

Duck hunters often face much worse weather than that of this day, and sometimes have the misfortune to be out on the water when monster storms arrive. The storm that hit Lake Huron on November 9, 1913, drowned many duckhunters as well as sailors on ships that sank. Myles Willard had a more fortunate but unusual experience on November 10, 1975. He and a companion were duck hunting at Berger Bay, near Fish Point. The south wind was so strong it had blown the water far out into the bay and they were walking on mud. Myles saw a frog jump and get blown backwards. The wind bent the trajectory of their lead shot when they fired at ducks overhead, and when Myles's friend managed to hit one it was blown so far to the north that he couldn't retrieve it. Myles finally sat down on the mud and waited until a duck flew low toward him. He fired when it was way upwind and it landed almost at his feet. Walking back against the gale, he picked up a bagful of fish—seven kinds—stranded on the mud, for dinners later on. That night, on Lake Superior, lashed all day by that same wind, the 729-foot *Edmund Fitzgerald* nose-dived to the bottom.

Duck hunting these days lacks the aura it held around the turn of the century, when there were more waterfowl, and more private duck-hunting clubs. William B. Mershon happily recorded for posterity those days on Saginaw Bay, in *Recollections of My Fifty Years Hunting and Fishing,* published in 1923. He began hunting with his father around 1865 in the Saginaw River marshes in primitive craft. "The Duck boats then in use were canoes made from a single white pine log and were very ticklish affairs to ride in. They used to say that one had to have his hair parted in the middle to keep them balanced."

In 1896, after he had become a successful lumberman, Mershon and five other men organized the Tobico Hunt Club on property they owned—the Tobico Marsh on Saginaw Bay, near Bay City. In all the years up to the disbanding of the club in 1957, only two other men became members. For most of the club's history, hunting was allowed only two days a week, from September 15 to November 10. Two frame cottages provided quarters for the members and another housed the caretaker and his family. Hired men, including the caretaker, poled members through the marsh in narrow duck boats, for shooting directly from the boat or from one of their platform "blinds" in the cattails. Mershon recalled these days with fond, maybe universal duck-hunters' nostalgia:

"October has come. We are out earlier now, for the redheads are here, pintail and widgeon too and mayhap a green winged teal and blue bill or scaup. So we must try for the morning flight over decoys. . . . We go to a blind prepared some days before that the ducks have had time to become used to. If the wind is brisk and the place well chosen we may have good sport. . . .

"By mid-forenoon the duck movement lags. The day is warm; a smoky haze hangs over the marsh and to where the forest edge shows maples with leaves reddening. Your face tickles from cobwebs that the air is carrying in wondrous threads; they hang on cattail and rush. The [wild] rice has ripened and fallen. Now it is easy to push a boat through it, so let us leave the blind and try to jump mallards and black ducks from its beds or the bog holes along the margin. . . .

"We punt in the direction so the ducks will get up on the right hand side. This makes the shooting swing easier. No noise now. Don't shoot if the kill is to fall in some place where it can not be retrieved. . . . We hear the noon train pass in the distance. It is lunch time and we may as well rest for two or three hours, so back to the blind, get out the lunch bucket, a smoke, and then a snooze. . . . By and by Herman [the caretaker] touches me and whispers, 'there are some redheads in the decoys.' I take a peek. Sure enough there are half a dozen that have come in unnoticed. . . . I stand up to give them a chance. Bewildered they do not fly. I shake my gun at them and yell and Herman throws an empty shell. This starts them and I get the shot of both barrels on the wing. I hear a companion shooting now and then at the far end of the marsh and then a flock of bluebills come from his direction. Maybe

I have a shot, maybe I do not, but it is a great day to be alive and out of doors.

"My companion comes in soon after I reach the boathouse. Our ducks are hung in a cool place. . . . Dinner, cigars. The evening is chilly so a fire of white birch in the fireplace is cheering. A game of old sledge or seven up and by nine-thirty in bed.

"November is here. Cold and raw, a veritable duck day. A little ice formed around the shore rushes during the night. The wind is from the northwest and blowing great guns. . . . Canvasbacks were here yesterday. Geese have been passing south for a week. The herring gulls are flapping over the open water of the marsh . . . greenwings are a plenty and great greenhead mallards from the far north are here. . . . All of this means the end is near. How differently the marsh affects you today than when the opening day was here.

"Picking up decoys now is no fun and what a temptation it is to leave them out until the next day in hopes it will not be so cold on the fingers. . . . How the dead grasses bend and billow in the wind. One thinks the marsh on such a day a lonesome place; sort of a haunted house. A grand expanse, no longer a place of dreamy quiet, yet we are full of happiness and satisfaction, for the cause of this absence of quiet is the north wind that makes a real duck day."

William Mershon might be happy to know that his beloved Tobico Marsh is now a public refuge, the wish of Guy Garber and Frank Andersen, the hunt club's last members. Today thousands, rather than a handful, can enjoy the marsh and the waterfowl that still drop in as fall descends.

The south end of Lake Huron gradually narrows to its exit through the St. Clair River. Many migratory waterbirds cut overland before reaching this point but many others funnel through here, especially during periods of strong north winds associated with cold fronts. Northwest winds blow birds toward the Canadian side, northeasters toward the American side. Sometimes there are great numbers and great rarities. Birdwatchers have found the ideal spot from which to enjoy the show—a parking lot at Point Edward, on the Canadian side by the entrance to the river, with a small grassy hill behind it. Here one gets a broad view of the lake and the open sky above. Here I hoped to see an exciting sample of the birds coming down the lake.

October 28 was not exciting. In spite of a strong northwest wind after a morning of rain, there wasn't much to see other than a few ducks, gulls, and loons, and two flocks of shorebirds that flew down the river.

Two scuba divers, who climbed down the seawall and drifted swiftly in the current toward the river, provided the only significant interest.

The next day was better. Perhaps brought by continuing northwest winds, waterfowl of many species floated offshore, getting up and flying a few hundred yards eastward every time the current carried them to the mouth of the river. Scaup, red-breasted mergansers, green-winged teal, ruddy ducks, buffleheads, and a few scoters, with many white-cheeked little horned grebes among them, rode the waves in front of me. Up the Canadian shore, off Cantara Park, a storm of gulls hovered over hundreds of fishing mergansers, trying to snatch some of the ducks' prey when they brought it up.

When the birdwatching gets slow here you can boat watch. Sometimes a Purdy gillnetter comes plowing back from the lake, its radar antenna revolving. Or a small tug comes alongside a freighter to pick up the pilot who has steered the large boat up the narrow river. This morning a sailboat motored out of the river mouth, set sail, and proceeded up the lake—definitely captained by an avid sailor, this late in the season. Across on the Michigan side two Coast Guardsmen in orange survival suits boarded a small orange pontoon boat and disappeared up the shore. In contrast with these last two boats, the two freighters that passed that morning looked huge. One was registered to a home port of Limassol, Cyprus, carrying what, going where, and picking up what, I wondered. Hard to tell where it actually came from or what its mission, considering the many possibilities.

Late in the morning Dennis Rupert appeared. A solid, deliberate sort of man, he set up his spotting scope in the chill wind and carefully scanned the water. After watching him for a few minutes, I became convinced that he saw everything within a mile's radius. One of the top birders in Ontario, Dennis lived in nearby Sarnia and was a dedicated watcher at this point for years. "In late October," he said, "I start coming here as often as I can, sometimes on the way to work, and at least for an hour or two on weekend days. Some days I've been here at eight o'clock and don't go home until five o'clock."

He regaled me with some of the rewards of this watching. "Starting the second week in November, we get big flocks of brant. On good stormy days there may be a hundred brant on the water, and pomarine and parasitic jaegers [pelagic birds seldom seen from land in the East]. The fall of 1993 we had nine jaegers at one time. Most of the jaegers are parasitics, but one time there was a long-tailed and two pomarines sitting on the water eating something.

"I've seen huge flocks of blackbirds, robins—whatever else is moving. In late November the snow buntings start to arrive and you can see long white strings of them out over the lake—thousands of them. . . . The landbirds go straight over to the Michigan side, sometimes right over your head. The waterbirds tend to go right along the edge of the water and down the river."

Days and weeks of watching produced surprising sights. "One time I saw a bald eagle coming down the American shoreline and two jaegers went after it and chased that eagle all the way across the end of the lake until it went south overland. Then they caught sight of a harrier and drove it back over the land. . . . I've seen short-eared owls coming down the lake, right down the middle of the shipping channel. They're strong fliers.

"The Lake Huron shoreline is a great place for snowy owls. They like to perch on a rock jetty at the marina [on the Canadian side]. One time we had two perching there ten yards apart. I think they sat there for two hours. Snowy owls are masters of the air. I've seen a snowy owl take a vole from a kestrel in the air. I wouldn't have believed it if I hadn't seen it."

My several days at Point Edward did not produce any such dramatic sightings, but this particular morning did end well. At Cantara Park, as we trained our spotting scopes on the waterbirds offshore, Dennis picked out two Pacific loons—a rare migrant on the Great Lakes that winters on the West Coast. Smaller and paler than winter common loons, and with other characters distinguishing them from red-throated loons, these birds swam near each other, unaware of their rarity but perhaps wondering where they were. You never know what will come down the lake among the masses of the expected.

CHAPTER **17**

# BIG BOATS, KILLER STORMS

B y December, most of the freighters and tankers coming down the lake are making their last runs. Ice will soon close the St. Marys River and make the St. Clair River difficult. Only a few ships will continue internal trips on the Great Lakes after the Soo Locks and the Welland Canal close in January.

Late fall and early winter are the most dangerous times of year on the lakes—the times when the worst storms hit, often accompanied by snow and ice. The clash of warm, humid air from the Gulf of Mexico with cold, dry air from the Arctic, along with heat still being released from the water, produces strong winds that can rise suddenly and change direction.

In spite of modern communication technology and improved weather forecasting, some storms take mariners by surprise. Captain Patrick Owens of Marysville, Michigan, vividly remembers the November 10, 1975, storm that sank the *Edmund Fitzgerald* in Lake Superior. "They missed that storm so bad. It was a southwest wind when it started. I was upbound on the *John Dykstra*. We came out of the [St. Clair] river down here and they had the winds going southeast. It wasn't that much because my skipper had the ballast all pumped out because he wanted to make time. I had to go down and wake him up when we got above Harbor Beach. I told him 'this wind is southwest at fifty and fifty-five miles per hour.' 'Oh no, it's supposed to be southeast,' he said. There we were, no ballast. When we come clear of this point [Pointe aux Barques—top of the Thumb] we

223

were pumping ballast and we had to head right practically into that wind. Between Presque Isle and De Tour, the highest winds that we monitored were eighty-four miles per hour. She really blew. As soon as we got into De Tour they had the [St. Marys] river closed."

Captain Morgan Howell was piloting the *Puhaus,* a Polish ship, up from Chicago that day. "When we got in the Straits it was blowing a gale—fifty or sixty miles an hour. It was wild. I didn't know the *Fitzgerald* had sunk. I was trying to get us down to Bay City with the cargo. Coming into Saginaw Bay there was still a violent gale. I had to go in there at full speed, dropped two anchors, run against the anchors with a lot of chain out. I cut her to half speed to make a landing, tied her up. I had a Polish captain who was hard to get along with. He hadn't spoken to me all the way from Chicago. When I docked the ship he came walking over to me and he said, 'Captain Morgan, you're half an hour late!' I was speechless. I could have punched him in the nose."

Captain Morgan, as he calls himself, began sailing on the Great Lakes in 1922, when he was eighteen. He started out as a deckhand on the *Corona,* a side-wheel passenger boat out of Toronto. "I met the girl I married on that ship," he said. "She was a good sailor—never got sick. I had her with me on trips here, there, almost everywhere. She went on trips with me that money couldn't buy. She's gone now."

Most of the Captain's career was spent on passenger ships on the Great Lakes. His first command, in 1948, was the *S.S. Put-in-Bay,* but his favorite was the *S.S. Aquarama,* whose silhouette now graces his front door in St. Clair. He also skippered cargo ships and tankers on the Great Lakes, Gulf of Mexico, and the Atlantic. During World War II he delivered ships to the Royal Navy—subchasers, minesweepers, and others. He was aboard the destroyer *Calgary* at the Normandy landing. "She was shot up like Swiss cheese. That's the wheel off her, right there," he said, pointing to a wheel with one spoke missing. "When I brought it back home, my wife took it to a carpenter and had a new spoke put on. When I saw that I was really upset. I didn't want a new spoke on. I wanted to leave it the way it came out of Normandy beachhead. She thought she was doing me a favor of course."

I asked him when he had retired. "I've never retired," he replied, but he admitted to having quit full-time sailing in his early eighties. When I talked to him he was ninety-two, short, wiry, with a voice much larger than his body. He did his exercises every morning, and was taking a course in Japanese at the St. Clair County Community College. His house beside the St. Clair River was full of nautical mementos—ship models, photographs of ships he had sailed on, a board displaying sailors' knots. A barometer—the best, he said—hung on the wall. Beside it a ship's clock chimed two bells as we talked. Out the window a St. Mary's Cement ship came into view, downbound through his back yard, it seemed. With his hand-held radio, Captain Morgan contacted the skipper, asked how many horsepower she had and a few other things. "I don't know this skipper," he said, "but a lot of them are my friends."

"I'm going to get on a Canadian ship next week and head for the Atlantic. We'll load up with iron ore after we get the wheat off at Baie-Comeau and head back for Chicago. I'm going along, you know, as advisory and for friendship, and just to make sure I don't forget the route—a refresher. I do it every so often."

Captain Owens has had a lot of experience with Lake Huron's fall tempests. "We loaded stone [limestone] out of Calcite at Rogers City, Presque Isle, and when I first started sailing we loaded out of Rockport, in behind Middle Island. In the fall of the year, Lake Huron is rough. You get a lot of southwest weather. So when we came down across the lake we used to steer right for Thunder Bay Island [off Alpena], then go right along the shore and into Saginaw Bay, so we could haul and come right straight across. See, with the wind coming from the southwest, you've got the lee of the shore; then, when you turn, you've got the sea coming over the quarter [instead of amidship].

"The regular course is way out. But in the fall of the year, if you run those courses like that you'll load up with ice. The worst months are the last part of October, November, and December. In November the water isn't that cold, but when it gets to be December you get a lot of ice. The worst is that fine spray, because as soon as that comes aboard it hits and it stays.

"With a northeast wind we went up the Canadian side from Port Huron. You get a lot of that in the spring of the year. Of course in the spring the first two or three trips you've got ice all over that lake. You never know when you're going to run into it—fields of it, some of them fifteen to twenty miles long. It depends on how the wind is blowing. If it's an easterly wind, it blows it all the way over to the American shore, and a westerly wind pushes it all the way back. . . . You can go through it, except down around Port Huron you can get a bottleneck with that northeast wind blowing the ice down. A lot of these ships don't have enough horsepower to get through. We got stuck quite a few times."

Fog is heaviest in late May and June, when warm air moves over cold water and moisture in the air cools and condenses. But fog isn't so much of a problem anymore, Owens said. "Every ship now has two radars. That's one thing. Another thing is there's a lot less ships. When I started sailing there were probably 600 American ships running up and down the lakes. There must have been thirty steamboat companies then. Now there's only ten, eleven, twelve companies."

Small boats are more of a problem, especially in the rivers, and most of all in the St. Clair River. "Nowadays with all these small boats and sailboats, you never know what they're going to do. The first thing—you don't know if they see you. The second thing—you don't know if they're going to go right, they're going to go straight, if they figure they own the river. If you get caught in a fog, in the radar you cannot tell the difference between a buoy and a small boat. You know where the buoys are because you have a chart. You know there are three buoys out there, but there might be four or five objects on the radar and you don't know which ones are the gol-darned buoys. You keep the fog horn going."

Throughout the year, a captain needs to rely on his own weather sense as well as the marine forecasts. Captain Morgan had said he learned a lot from the clouds, but Owens looked mostly at the barometer and the gulls. "When you see seagulls up high," he said, "you know you're going to get some weather. How them birds can tell, I don't know."

I asked his opinion of the different lakes. "I think the worst is the north end of Lake Huron. You get severe weather up there. If it blows out of the southeast, you're nailed up there. If it blows out of the northwest, you're nailed. On Lake Michigan, the worst wind is one that comes straight down from the north, because from northeast through southeast, and the same way from northwest through southwest, you can go along the shore. Lake Erie gets rough in a hurry, and it also quiets down in a hurry. Lake Superior? Well, besides being cold and long, it gets pretty miserable in the fall of the year, too. You get a lot of northwest wind, but most of the time you can go around the north shore. You lose about six or eight hours, but at least you get a comfortable ride."

Captain Owens's home, like Captain Morgan's, faces directly onto the St. Clair River. Sitting on his deck, watching sailboats going up to Port Huron for the start of the Port Huron-Mackinac race, he reminisced about his career on the water. Born and raised at Marine City on the St. Clair River, he followed the profession of his father and grandfather. "I got started in 1945, between the eleventh and twelfth grades. That was a summer job, on the *S.S. Adriatic*. I was a deck hand and deck watch. Those ships I was on then are all long gone. We sailed all over the four lakes. We didn't get down on Lake Ontario. Two days after I graduated

The *Middletown,* a 730-foot self-unloader, enters a stormy Lake Huron from Port Huron.

I was on the *S.S. James C. Wallace,* as a temporary watchman. I went wheeling—was promoted to a wheelsman—that same year." In the years after that Owens sailed on many ships. For twenty-four years he worked on Ford Company vessels, rising to temporary skipper and then, in 1985, to permanent skipper of the *S.S. Benson Ford.* Working for Ford was "the best job I ever had." He retired from full-time sailing in 1991, then, in his sixties, continued with temporary jobs, such as piloting tugs for Malcolm Marine. "But I don't care to be running around the lake in November anymore."

All the ships Morgan Howell and Patrick Owens sailed on survived during their watch. Many others, through the centuries, haven't. Estimates of the number of ships lost on the Great Lakes vary widely. A newspaper article from the 1970s stated that "over 15,000 commercial vessels have gone down in the Great Lakes." Jack Parker, in *Shipwrecks of Lake Huron,* writes, "As some marine historians claim, there have been more than 6,000 shipwrecks in our Great Lakes since man began recording these instances of tragedy." Whatever the true total, it is very large.

Lake Huron may be the most bottom-strewn graveyard of the five lakes. The unnamed historians to which Parker referred stated it is likely that 40 percent of the Great Lakes shipwrecks occurred in Lake Huron. In his book, Parker lists more than 1,100 Lake Huron shipwrecks recorded in "all known and available records," stretching from 1805 to 1980, plus the *Griffon* in 1679. The 1996 edition of *Know Your Ships* lists one as recent as September 1990—the *Jupiter,* which "exploded and burned at Bay City." Parker's mournful litany of causes goes on and on: "struck ice floe and sank," "capsized in Georgian Bay," "disappeared on upper Lake Huron," "foundered in lake storm off Goderich," "collision and sank," "lost without a trace," "scuttled near Sault Ste. Marie," "stranded and ashore at Forestville," "wrecked at 9 mile Pt.," "broke in two on rocks in fog."

Many of those sunken ships Parker listed have been found, but even more have not. No doubt the most exciting find would be the *Griffon.* The French explorer Rene-Robert Cavalier, Sieur de LaSalle built her at Buffalo and sailed up Lake Huron in 1679. Like many another ship since, the *Griffon* ran into a storm when she rounded Pointe aux Barques into the mouth of Saginaw Bay. The little ship weathered that one, in the lee of Charity Island, and made it to Green Bay, but she was not so fortunate on the return voyage. Captained by "Luke the Dane," a seven-foot pilot-navigator, with a crew of five, she set sail for Buffalo with a load of furs and disappeared somewhere in Lake Huron.

Two wrecks have unofficially been identified as the *Griffon,* but positive proof has been found for neither. One wreck, found in the late 1800s, lay on a shoal in the Mississagi Straits at the western end of Manitoulin Island, just north of the Mississagi Lighthouse. Records indicate that islanders and local Indians looted the wreck for pieces of iron, bolts, chains, and other relics that might have aided in the ship's positive identification. Old stories about the lighthouse told of five skeletons found in a shoreline cave near the wreck and a sixth found a short distance from the others. Unfortunately, a storm around 1980 moved the wreck off its ledge and into deep water. Diving attempts since then to find evidence of the ship's identity have been unsuccessful.

The other wreck, located by a commercial fisherman in this century, lay in a shallow cove at Russell Island, near Tobermory. Its few remains were removed to Tobermory for safekeeping. Parker's account of these wrecks concludes: "While both wrecks have been scientifically proven to be of ancient origin, and while scientists and wood experts stated that both could be as much as 300 years old, neither has been firmly identified as the missing *Griffon*."

Any area on the lake that combines heavy traffic and shoal waters produces more than its share of shipwrecks. Most fatal have been the island-strewn area near Tobermory, at the tip of the Bruce Peninsula; the waters around the Thumb; and the coast from Thunder Bay to Presque Isle. The Straits of Mackinac have seen many wrecks, too. All this tragic maritime history lying underwater, and its attraction for divers, prompted the state of Michigan to establish four bottomland preserves in Lake Huron—the Straits of Mackinac, Thunder Bay, Thumb Area (at the tip), and Sanilac Shores—and the Canadian government to create Fathom Five National Park. These preserves give protection to the artifacts remaining after owners or insurers of the sunken boats have abandoned reclamation attempts.

Tobermory calls itself the "Scuba Diving Capital of Canada," with good reason. Each year some 8,000 divers visit the twenty-three registered sites in Fathom Five National Park. On the Michigan side, similar numbers of divers go out to the shipwrecks near Alpena, and 4,000 or so visit the Straits of Mackinac and Port Sanilac, a growing center of diving.

Many of the wrecks the divers explore met their end in famous storms. While ships undoubtedly sank every year through the eighteenth, nineteenth, and early twentieth centuries, those that went down in the worst storms are the best remembered. And while every century and every lake probably have had equally terrible storms, those of the twentieth century, because most recent and best recorded, lie strongest in memory. Lake Superior had its November 30 "1905 Blow," Lake Erie its "Black Friday Storm" of October 20, 1916, and Lake Michigan the November 11, 1940, "Armistice Day Storm."

On Lake Huron, it was the "Great Storm of 1913." For five days—November 7 to 11—this storm spread havoc across the Great Lakes and ashore, from Wisconsin to Pennsylvania. Sweeping across the four uppermost lakes, it sank or wrecked twelve large vessels, seriously damaged twenty-five others, and drowned more than 250 men and women. On Lake Huron it took the biggest toll—eight ships and 180 or more lives. (Ship manifests sometimes did not list all passengers, so the exact total of lives lost is unknown.)

Two intense low-pressure systems—one crossing the Canadian provinces and one sweeping across the plains states—collided on Saturday,

Scuba divers prepare to enter the water at Tobermory.

November 8, over Lake Superior. Accompanied by driving snow, the gale force winds shifted during the night from southeast to southwest, then north. By Sunday, November 9, the storm had claimed two ships—the *Leafield* and *Henry B. Smith*—in Lake Superior and the 225-foot barge *Plymouth* in northern Lake Michigan.

On Lake Huron, captains thought the storm had blown out by Sunday morning and ventured south from the St. Marys River and north from Port Huron. Poor communications, ignored weather forecasts, the late-season desire for profit, and the weather-be-damned, I-can-handle-any-storm attitude of some captains combined to spell disaster. As the storm cell moved across Lake Huron it regained intensity and was joined by an unusual third system from the Caribbean, creating a monster with winds gusting up to ninety miles per hour swinging wildly from northwest around to east and then south and building waves said to exceed thirty-five feet. Ships were caught in a maelstrom with waves and wind coming from different directions.

Three ships sailing south never made it. The *James C. Carruthers,* bound for Midland in Georgian Bay with a load of grain, disappeared without a trace. The 416-foot *Hydrus,* carrying ore to Cleveland, also went down. And the 250-foot packet freighter *Wexford,* attempting to reach Goderich with a load of grain, was last seen thirty miles north of her destination. None of these ships has yet been found.

The storm also sank five northbound ships. The *Isaac M. Scott,* a 504-foot straight-deck freighter, made it past Thunder Bay before succumbing to the pounding waves. The others fell victim before passing Saginaw Bay. The rudder of the *John A. McGean,* a 432-foot bulk carrier, tore partially loose and broke off a propellor blade, leaving the ship helpless. She sank ten miles off Port Hope, near the tip of the Thumb. Thirteen miles north of Pointe aux Barques, the *Argus,* twin of the *Hydrus,* was caught in a deep trough, "crumbled," and went down—a horrible sight revealed to Captain Walter C. Iler on the *George C. Crawford* during a brief lull in the snowstorm. Trying to save his own ship, he could do nothing for the *Argus.*

The *Charles S. Price* and the *Regina,* also claimed off the Thumb by the storm, became linked in a peculiar legend. The *Regina,* a 249-foot package freighter, steamed out of the St. Clair River shortly before 7:00 A.M. Sunday, November 9. She was loaded with supplies for towns along the Canadian sides of Lake Huron and Lake Superior, including general merchandise, barbed wire, cheese, and quantities of champagne and Scotch that would comfort northern residents through the long winter. Steel sewer and gas pipes protruded above her rails. Just a few miles behind the *Regina,* the 504-foot *Price,* carrying coal, plowed along. Neither captain was worried as the wind was northwest, only about fifteen miles per hour. Late in the morning, however, the wind shifted around to northeast and increased to sixty miles an hour, a velocity it maintained for twelve hours. Captain Arthur May on the *H. B. Hawgood* was the last to see either ship upright. Struggling back toward the St. Clair River, he spotted the *Regina* near Harbor Beach, still headed slowly north, with "seas breaking over her," and later the *Price,* also headed north and "making bad weather of it." When the storm subsided, a "mystery ship," later identified as the *Price,* was found floating upside down about eight miles out from Port Huron. A week later, she sank. No one knew the fate of the *Regina.*

After the storm, wreckage, life boats, and bodies began washing ashore on the Canadian side from Southampton south to Kettle Point. Observers were mystified when they found the body of a sailor identified as John Groundwater, from the *Price,* with a *Regina* life jacket wrapped around him. Public and press imagination soon magnified this into numerous dramatic possibilities. Most popular were stories that the two ships had collided, some *Price* men scrambled aboard the *Regina* and when she was foundering took some of her life jackets, or that the *Regina* passed sailors from the *Price* in the water and tossed them life jackets. More plausible, however, is the following explanation: The only documented case of a *Price* sailor with a *Regina* life jacket was that of John Groundwater. People were taking anything of value from the bodies. When the local constable threatened fines or imprisonment for looting, people returned their loot to the bodies. The life jacket may have been taken from a *Regina* sailor and placed on or around (which placement was never clear) the body of John Groundwater.

Further mysteries remained, especially the exact locations of the ships sunk in the storm. If the wrecks could be found, their condition might tell more about what happened to them. Divers have been trying to answer these questions for decades, and some have been successful. The *Price's* location was known when she sank, in sixty-four feet of water. In 1971 scuba diver Kent Bellrichard found the wreck of the *Isaac M. Scott* nine miles northeast of Thunder Bay Island. Diver Dick Race discovered the *Argus* a year later north of Pointe aux Barques in 240 feet of water. And in 1985 diver/photographer Dave Trotter reached the *John A. McGean* off Port Hope in 175 feet of water. All the wrecks were lying upside down, indicating they had capsized.

The *Regina* is the latest of the 1913 victims to be discovered. Garry Biniecki, a police sergeant with the Sanilac County sheriff's department, had been told by a fisherman friend that his line had several times during 1984 and 1985 bumped an object out in the upbound shipping lane between Lexington and Port Sanilac. On July 1, 1986, Garry took Wayne Brusate and John Severance out for a search, using Wayne's side-scan sonar, which provides an image one-quarter mile wide on either side of a boat's path. To their delight, they located the wreck, dove to it, and were able to identify it. It lay in seventy-seven feet of water and, like the others, was upside down.

Garry has since made 400 or 500 dives on the *Regina* and has developed his own theories about what happened to the *Regina* and the *Price.* He found a gaping hole in the bottom of the *Regina* "that looks like it was made by the ship smashing down on a large boulder." He suggests that Captain McConkey may have run in close to shore to find shelter and "that in the thirty-foot-plus waves, he struck bottom and holed the ship." Observations of the wreck showed that the ship was anchored, her engines and electrical system shut off, and her lifeboats launched. Seeing that sinking was inevitable, most or all of the crew (but not the captain) had attempted to abandon ship.

Garry thinks perhaps the *Price* met her end when she came about trying to help the *Regina,* got caught in a trough and capsized. Huge piles of coal a few miles south of the *Regina* off Lexington are probably the *Price*'s cargo. The *Price* then floated upside down almost to Port Huron before sinking.

Today Garry spends most of his spare time searching for other shipwrecks or taking recreational divers out to known ones. The *Regina* is a favorite. When she was first found, a salvage company recovered numerous items, including horseshoes and many bottles of champagne and Scotch. (Tasters found that "the champagne still had bubbles when we opened it up," though it tasted "a lot like cork." But the Scotch, they said, was "smooth.") Divers can still see a few Scotch bottles lying around, along with barbed wire, spoons, pulleys, brass name plates, freshwater tanks, heavy ropes, and other relics. All must remain, protected in the Sanilac Shores Bottomland Preserve.

I joined Garry one day when he was taking two divers to the *Regina* in his twenty-six-foot cruiser, the *Huron Explorer.* Ron Bumgartner, from Richmond, Virginia, and Craig Bouckaert, a police officer from Bay City, Michigan, had been diving together for five years. They were now on a two-week diving vacation on Lake Huron. The day before they had made dives on the *Checotah* and *Col. A. B. Williams,* two wooden sailing vessels that lie farther north, and a night dive to the *Sport,* farther south near Lexington. "That night dive was great," Ron said. "We saw lots of perch and bass," besides enjoying their exploration of the well-preserved steel tug, built in 1873 and sunk in December 1920. The next day they were going to go to Tobermory, Ontario's diving mecca.

We eased through small southeasterly waves up to a blue and white plastic bottle marking the wreck, three and a half miles offshore between Port Sanilac and Lexington. Three other divers, in a boat from Port Huron, were already tied up to the other float. Ron and Craig went down while Garry stayed above to watch for freighters, as we were anchored in the middle of the upbound shipping lane. Garry recalled some unsettling experiences with freighters while anchored at wrecks. "I think some of them just want to show who's boss on the lakes," he said. "One ship was coming right at me. I radioed the captain to change course. He said, 'You move.' I said I had divers down and couldn't move. I told him I was a police sergeant and could get him arrested. He said, 'I'll change course.' " Another ship passed "within spitting distance," much closer than the 200 feet minimum the laws allow. "I wrote to the company, sending them a ticket. They paid the fine but didn't apologize. I've noticed, though, that ships from that company always stay farther away now."

As two ships approached us, one behind the other, Garry said, "If you can see the side of a ship you know it will miss you, but if you can't, it's headed straight for you." I was relieved to see a little bit of the sides of these two ships. The 698-foot *Buckeye* churned by at several hundred yards, but the 806-foot *Charles M. Beeghly* passed at only 200 feet.

When Ron came up at the end of his first dive, he said, "That ship vibrated my whole body. I felt like I was in a mixmaster." Seventy-seven feet below, he and Craig had explored part of the upside down, zebra-mussel-encrusted hull of the *Regina* and entered the cargo area through a fifty-six-foot gap in her port side. Ron's video camera hadn't functioned, though, and he looked annoyed now. He found that a setting was wrong, adjusted it, and on the second dive, an hour later, got good footage. He was especially happy with his sequence of the anchor chain, which he had followed out from the starboard side of the bow until it disappeared under the sand, in a northeast direction, the direction the wind was coming from that fatal day in 1913.

As the divers rested on deck above, the 1,013-foot *Paul R. Tregurtha* passed us, its eight-level superstructure rising above a square stern. "What a great wreck that would make," Garry said. "Look at all those portholes we could penetrate. Maybe we should torpedo it."

In these days of radar, global positioning systems, and advanced communications, as well as stronger ship construction, it's not likely that a ship like the *Paul R. Tregurtha* will go down in a storm. But it's not impossible. And it is sure that fierce November storms will pound Lake Huron again, perhaps one as terrible as the Great Storm of 1913.

CHAPTER **18**

# BIRDS AT CHRISTMAS

For several years I had planned it: joining the Christmas bird counts on Manitoulin Island. Christmas bird counts, in which groups of people count birds for one day within a fifteen-mile-diameter circle during a prescribed period bracketing Christmas, are conducted all over North America and many parts of Latin America. They are one of my favorite activities, ranking right up there with the other joys of Christmas. It seemed a book about Lake Huron wouldn't be complete without Christmas bird counts, which would give a good picture of winter bird populations around the lake. And what could be more Christmasy than Manitoulin Island, with snow draping the dense conifers and the likelihood of winter finches seeking their cones.

As it turned out, I was not disappointed. The previous winter had been warmer and less snowy than usual. This one corrected the balance. As I drove westward across Sanilac County the morning of December 10, the bank thermometer in Carsonville registered seven degrees and one in Sandusky six degrees. A radio report forecast a low of zero to minus three for Detroit that night. We had about three inches of snow on the ground. Farther north, at Oscoda, I pulled into a parking lot by the mouth of the Au Sable River and promptly got stuck in foot-deep snow. With low four-wheel drive on my Isuzu Trooper, I soon got out, unlike some people in a sedan who couldn't budge even with their four-wheel capability. At Alpena, Thunder Bay was frozen. A man in a store where I bought heavy socks for the days ahead said they had already had forty inches of snow this winter.

This was nothing, however, compared with what lay ahead. The snow under the birches and conifers along the shore seemed to grow deeper as I progressed northward. Crossing the Mackinac Bridge, the Trooper was buffeted with powerful northwest gusts. I kept a tight grip on the steering wheel as I looked down at the icy water far below. Soon snow began to fall. Near Sault Ste. Marie blowing snow nearly obliterated I-75, and cars lay stuck in snowbanks off the sides.

Entering the city, with snow still falling, I drove along roads almost like tunnels, with snow piled so high that at intersections I couldn't see what was coming. I asked a man if they had storms like this very often in Sault Ste. Marie. "About once every hundred years," he replied. Five feet of snow had fallen over the weekend.

Eastward, along the shore of the North Channel, the snow depth was less, but still impressive. Bruce Mines had over three feet on the ground. I was relieved to find the roads clear, however, and enjoyed the final miles driving over the La Cloche Mountains, down then onto flat limestone country, across the bridge at Little Current to Manitoulin Island, and at last walking into the warmth of Gordon's Lodge at Gore Bay. I called Terry Land, who informed me that the snow depth there was one and a half feet and they already had had twenty below (Fahrenheit). A real winter, I thought, happily.

The next morning I drove out Janet Head. The sailboats from Toronto and Miami and Ottawa and Gore Bay were all parked together up on their cradles. Through the window of the Gore Bay Fish Hatchery, the blond woman who tended the chinook salmon eggs could be seen at her work. Hoar frost sparkled on all the trees, preserved by air temperatures still not far above the early morning seven below. Though the inner part of Gore Bay was frozen, the outer part remained open. A few goldeneye ducks and herring gulls sought food out there, as did a large dark bird that through binoculars resolved itself into an adult bald eagle. It flew slowly and regally along the edge of the ice, looking for a dead fish or infirm duck, then disappeared up over the East Bluff.

My first real order of business was to go see Doreen Bailey. I had a Christmas present for her—one that would link three birdwatchers. Early in December I had visited Myles Willard at a craft show at Sandusky, in my county. Myles now makes his living—or tries to make it—selling his outdoor photographs at these shows from spring to early winter. I had wanted to see him at work and find out how his year had gone.

"I think I'll break even this year," he said, "which is better than losing money, like last year." With a good stock of prints and adequate optical equipment, his main expense now was travel to shows. Today he had a large number of excellent photographs on his exhibit stands, but people weren't buying. Mostly they were going for Christmas decorations, dolls, and other items of the season. Perched on his high stool, Myles looked a bit forlorn. "I've only cleared $15 today," he said. That spurred me to do a little Christmas shopping. I came up with a harlequin duck, photographed at the Au Sable River mouth, and a magnificent great gray owl, its yellow eyes blazing at the viewer out of dark gray feathers. I thought Doreen Bailey would like this latter photo of a bird of the north that occasionally invades Manitoulin Island when winter food becomes scarce in the great boreal forests of northwest Canada.

Doreen did indeed like it. I asked her how her bird list was going. "I've got 224," she said. "I'd like to make 225, but there's not much else I can get this time of year. One is a great gray owl." The next day a friend phoned her. "There's a great gray owl sitting in our maple tree out front," she said. No amount of her chronic gout would have stopped Doreen from racing over there, and this great gray, the first of a tremendous invasion on Manitoulin Island that winter, became Doreen's 1995 species number 225. Myles appreciated this story when I told him.

Now it was time to think seriously about the bird counts. This was Thursday and the counts were to take place on Saturday and Sunday. It was necessary to find out where the birds were, especially the rarer ones, so we could locate them on count day. Chris Bell, organizer of the counts, had come two days early for this reason, and together we cruised the roads of Manitoulin, seeing what was where.

Chris, then around fifty, is a mining engineer with the International Nickel Company (INCO) in Sudbury. He grew up in England, near London, but right after university, in 1968, came to Sudbury to work for INCO. "I'd been a birder since I was fourteen," he said. "I discovered Manitoulin the first summer I was here. It had farmland and a Great Lakes shoreline. There seemed to be more birds than at Sudbury," which is inland, in rugged, forested Canadian Shield country. "I bought an old farmhouse and 100 acres at Green Bay, on Manitoulin, in 1971, spent a lot of weekends there, summer and winter. Another birder, John Nicholson, had also arrived at Sudbury from England in 1968. We started the Gore Bay count that year, just the two of us. Around 1973 we started the Mindemoya count." They got other Sudbury birders interested and gradually the counts grew. "In the early years there weren't many local people involved, but now we have some keen local people who have recruited a lot of feeder-watchers as well."

Our search that Thursday showed Chris and me three things: Some of the winter finches, like pine grosbeaks and redpolls, as well as Bohemian waxwings, had come down in good numbers; waterbirds would be scarce, because all inland lakes and most north-side bays had frozen; and walking would be difficult—after new snowstorms, there was two feet of snow on the ground. We didn't find any of the rarer birds reported earlier but hoped they would show up on count day at the bird feeders and other places where they had been seen. We didn't find Doreen's great gray owl, either, but it had in any case been outside the count circles.

Chris had mentioned a few misadventures his counters had experienced in earlier years, such as a man's falling through ice at a beaver dam, and he warned me about the roadside ditches, which are invisible when snow covered. Thursday evening, as I was driving along the Janet Head road looking for waterbirds, I forgot Chris's advice and let my car drift to the right, where it sank sideways into deep snow covering a ditch. An hour later a truck from McQuarrie Chevrolet pulled me out, but only after a great deal of effort. Don't do this on count day, I cautioned myself.

I tried to approach the two counts impartially. As I always do, I would try to find as many birds as possible within my allotted sector. But I had to lean a bit toward the "Manitoulin" (Gore Bay) count, because of my association with Terry Land and Doreen Bailey. Strong competitors, they always hoped Gore Bay would get more species than Mindemoya. One year Doreen had even put out dead suckers at Indian Point to keep bald eagles around.

Chris Bell and the members of the Sudbury Ornithological Society who come down for the counts profess neutrality. But usually some of them go home after the Mindemoya count, leaving Gore Bay the next day at a numerical disadvantage. The few Mindemoya natives who participate have not moved on to help Gore Bay. "Usually Mindemoya beats Gore Bay," Chris said. "It's got more water areas, including the south shore habitat. And the spring-fed Hare's Creek is not in the other count. It probably has better farmland, too." Laughingly he called it the banana belt. The preceding year, with a relatively mild winter, Mindemoya had found a record fifty-eight species, with 4,669 individual birds, and Gore Bay fifty species, with 4,794 individuals. This year Gore Bay would need some luck to get back in the winning column.

Early on December 16, four of us drove to Providence Bay to begin coverage of our sector of the Mindemoya count. Steve Thorpe, a math teacher at the Manitoulin high school, had brought his thirteen-year-old son Derrick and Ron Zondervan, a biology teacher at the high school. As one who was writing about Lake Huron, I thought it was only appropriate to join this party, whose assignment was to walk the south shore from Providence Bay to Timber Bay and then inland. The water on exposed parts of the island's south side remains open, although the bays there gradually freeze. Today we found Providence Bay nearly all open and in it 100 gulls, including a great black-backed gull and a beautiful pale glaucous gull. A few goldeneyes and common mergansers, as expected, were diving there. Unexpected was a tundra swan, whose massive whiteness caught our eye as it flew around the bay, acting uncertain about the wisdom of being so far north of its fellows, most of whom were now settled for the winter on the central Atlantic Coast. It was, as it turned out, a new species for either Manitoulin Island Christmas bird count.

We now faced the difficult task of walking through two-foot snow to Timber Bay, three miles distant. The shoreline was treeless for fifty to 100 yards back to the spruce-fir forest bordering it, but the limestone rocks underneath the snow were uneven and ice-covered. When your boots sank deep enough, they slipped on the ice. I had some borrowed snowshoes in my car, but Steve, a native of the area, thought walking the shore would be easier without them. So we floundered on.

Fortunately, the day was clear and the temperature in the twenties. The wind at first hit us from the open southwest but later shifted around to the north, where it was felt less because of the forest screen. Where the snow-covered rocks met the water, ice dunes had built up, here and there roughened with jagged slabs of lake-piled ice. The lake waves slapped up against this white barrier, imperceptibly building it higher. Derrick felt an irresistible attraction to these mounds of ice, and Steve, visualizing his son falling into the frigid water, kept calling him back.

The water beyond the ice was our focal point, as the dark forest edge gave us nothing but an occasional raven. Offshore, a few goldeneyes and herring gulls flew by, and once a bufflehead, but there was nothing of special interest until we began seeing small groups of black and white oldsquaws far out, getting up, flying a short distance, then flopping back down on the water in their distinctive oldsquaw way. These would turn out to be the count's only oldsquaws that day.

After a mile of hard, slow trudging, we decided to turn back. It would take us a long time to reach Timber Bay and the trail out through the forest from there would be difficult to find in the deep snow. We worked the inland roads instead, finding a gray jay and northern shrike among

Some oldsquaws winter in the Great Lakes. We found a few on the Mindemoya Christmas bird count. (Credit: Myles Willard)

other, more common birds. Wanting to play North Woodsman, I tried my snowshoes on a woodland trail and discovered that even these sank uncomfortably deep into the snow. Hard walking or not, though, it was an invigorating, happy day.

The evening gathering, where everyone digs into the (usually) potluck supper and reports their findings, is half the fun of a Christmas bird count. What rarities were found, what agonizing misses, what adventures of the day? This roundup took place at the Mindemoya Curling Club, under supervision of the Mindemoya Nature Club. Chris Bell had skied part of the Manitou River shore, but found no waterbirds on the open parts of this small stream. Red-haired Heather Baines, an ear, nose, and throat specialist from Sudbury, had brought her two dogs along as usual. Even the husky had found it hard going following her as she herringboned laboriously up hills and skied down. The corgi, less than half as high as the snow level, had had to stay in Heather's truck during these patrols through likely bird habitat. Doreen Bailey, generously joining this rival count, had seen the day's only bald eagle at Providence Bay. While there, she too saw the tundra swan, giving her 226 species for the year on Manitoulin and easily winning her running competition with Chris Bell, who ended with 206.

As Chris went through the list of possible species, we called out our numbers group by group. There were twenty-six of us, organized into nine parties. Around forty more had counted birds at their feeders and phoned in the results. Charlie Whitelaw reported a meadowlark. Cheers. "Bohemian waxwing?" Silence. Inexplicable miss. When we had gone through house sparrow, at the end of the list, Chris toted up the species. "Looks like forty-five, forty-six, or forty-seven," he said, "depending on whether I count that ring-billed gull [questionable identification] and what that 'flicker-like' bird was that a feeder watcher reported." It was about the number he had expected, given the small amount of open water.

I spent that night at Chris Bell's old farmhouse near the east end of the island. You could easily guess his interest in birds when you walked in. Bird paintings and posters adorned the walls, bird sculptures stood on stands. Five of us, including Heather Baines, all looking ruddy from the cold and tired from the day's exertions, had a Scotch or two, told a few stories of the day, and went to bed. Heather and her two dogs had their own room. The dogs, perhaps as tired as we were, didn't make a peep.

The next day dawned clear but cold—eight degrees. Thirteen people in seven parties fanned out from a meeting at Terry Land's law office to work their territories for the Gore Bay count, and fifty-nine people watched their bird feeders. I was assigned to the western sector—mostly farms and woods, with frozen shoreline at Lake Wolsey and Bayfield Sound. In my Trooper were Charlie Whitelaw, a retired high school teacher from Sudbury, and Steve Hall, a local farmer. Steve grew up on Manitoulin, cut pulp and did other jobs, then worked thirty years for INCO in Sudbury. He came back when he retired from INCO and now runs his small farm, where he has twenty-five cows, chickens, a garden, and some pasture. He traps, too, in the winter—fox, coyote, mink, fisher, muskrat, beaver, otter, raccoon. "I always enjoyed nature," he said, "and when I retired I got even more interested." He knew where to find rare orchids, and what kinds of reptiles and amphibians lived in various wetlands. As we drove the gravel roads, through field and forest, he told us about the people who owned the land, and what birds he had seen there in times past.

Our day began auspiciously. Sitting on a corral across the road from the Gore Bay airport, a pure white, adult male snowy owl stared at us as we approached. Charlie wanted to photograph it out the car window, but when we came close enough the owl flew, vanishing mysteriously as its whiteness blended with the whiteness of the snow. Soon after that we saw fifteen sharp-tailed grouse high in a birch tree eating buds. With its many wide shrubby fields, Manitoulin is home to a strong population of sharp-tails. They are hard to see on the ground in summer but easier in winter when up in bare trees eating buds.

After that, the birding slowed down. It seemed there was almost nothing in the countryside, although what we did see was interesting, like a flock of pine grosbeaks eating conifer seeds, or Bohemian waxwings feeding on crabapples—birds I don't see around my home town of Washington, D.C. It's like birding on the ocean, I thought. The birds are few and far between, but what you see seems special. Only around homes with bird feeders did we see an assortment of birds—the inevitable chickadees and blue jays, sometimes white-breasted nuthatches, evening grosbeaks, or snow buntings, once a couple of grackles, lingering north. We saw no hawks—not even a rough-leg, which had been common the winter before. With snow this deep, making it hard to find mice, most of them had moved farther south. I made an ill-advised turn down a once-plowed road to look for a hawk owl Steve had seen in November. Only low four-wheel drive got me out, and no hawk owl.

I wondered how the other parties were faring. Later I learned about Terry Land's and Dan Crawford's day. Their territory, around Gore Bay, included the only open water in the count circle, and they had scanned it carefully. Dan, a retired forester from Sudbury, snowshoed out along the shore of Janet Head to examine the few leads remaining in the ice. He saw two common loons flying—"south I hope." A red-necked grebe took off from one patch of open water but crashed onto the ice, apparently too weak for sustained flight. There were few ducks. "Terry and I virtually saw outer Gore Bay and the North Channel freeze over today," Dan said. The wind might open the ice a time or two in the days to come, but soon it would all be frozen solid until spring. Soon snowmobiles would be making the crossing, following lines of discarded Christmas trees placed on the ice. The Janet Head lighthouse remained on to guide snowmobilers at night.

From stories like Dan's and my party's experience, I was thinking we'd all had a poor day, species-wise. But the dinner at Terry and Judy Land's house cheered me up. Entirely on their own, the Lands had prepared a sumptuous dinner for us all, one of the most elegant Christmas count dinners I had ever experienced. The two Land girls came around with hors d'oeuvres, including shrimp, and a main course of lemon chicken and lasagna was graced with red and white wine. The dinner was a great success, even if the count turned out to be disappointing.

I asked Chris Bell how his day had gone. "Well, OK," he said, "except that I lost a boot. It got wedged in a crack in the limestone and I couldn't pull it out because of the steel toe and sole. I had to walk back to the car in my stocking foot and put on a running shoe for the rest of the day."

After dinner, Chris started the tally. Nobody had had a spectacular day, and waterbirds, as expected, were few, but one by one the species rolled in. Les Bailey, Doreen's husband, had walked a ridge and scared up a great horned owl. Somebody found a red-tailed hawk—always scarce on Manitoulin, especially in winter. The feeder watchers had phoned in some good birds—rusty blackbird, rufous-sided towhee, brown thrasher, white-crowned sparrow, and others. At the end, Chris said, we had forty-eight species, and maybe two more, including a possible goshawk that he would check out the next day. With our much smaller number of troops, we had beaten Mindemoya. Terry and Doreen glowed. (Final tabulation: Mindemoya—forty-eight species, 3,087 individuals; Gore Bay—fifty-one species, 2,881 individuals.)

I don't mean to slight the scientific value of Christmas bird counts with this emphasis on the sporting element. They are a great deal of fun, but the ultimate purpose is to gather information. When all counts are considered together, they show the winter ranges of individual species, and over the years they indicate population trends, which then can be confirmed and causes investigated by more rigorous scientific studies. During the days of DDT use, for instance, the decline of certain raptors was clearly reflected in Christmas bird counts.

When I got back to the cottage, I called a couple of friends to see how their lakeside counts had gone, and later examined the published reports of many around Lake Huron. Myles Willard said the count at Port Austin, at the top of the Thumb, had been fun as usual but they had a small species total—around forty-three. Saginaw Bay was frozen out to the Port Austin lighthouse, which stands well offshore, but there was open water on the east side of the Thumb. Waterbirds had been scarce, but they found a few good land birds, such as Bohemian waxwing, short-eared owl, and two meadowlarks. It was apparently a big year for northern shrikes—they counted about twenty-five. The small band of ten people had gathered for dinner at the cabin of count leader Monica Essenmacher and enjoyed not just the dinner and camaraderie but also the after-dark antics of a flying squirrel at Monica's bird feeder.

Farther south, at Kettle Point on the Canadian side, Dennis Rupert said they had had a very good count, with many record-high totals for individual species. Some forty participants had found seventy-three species, including their first wild turkey. Although waterbirds were scarce, and it was hard to see them with rough water and a wall of ice twenty feet high, they had tundra swan and mute swan. Most of the gulls, including a rare Thayer's, had left the lake and gone to the St. Clair River before the count. Inland, they saw a lot of shrikes and hawks, a golden eagle, and some 500 Bohemian waxwings. I asked Dennis about the local Indian situation, since a band had taken over the Army camp property here in a land dispute. "We had no problem at Kettle Point itself," he said. "The Natives there don't mind us birdwatching. But we stayed out of the Army camp—just viewed it from outside."

The National Audubon Society publishes the Christmas bird counts, and for the 1995–96 count period, there were fifteen published counts from locations around the shores of Lake Huron, with a total of 308 observers in the field. To get a lakewide picture of waterbird populations I recorded the total for each waterbird species, plus the bald eagle, which is a fish-eater. They are listed below in descending order of abundance.

| | |
|---|---|
| herring gull | 7,974 |
| common merganser | 3,391 |
| Canada goose | 3,369 |
| mallard | 2,967 |
| common goldeneye | 2,837 |
| canvasback | 2,580 |
| redhead | 2,253 |
| ring-billed gull | 777 |
| American black duck | 335 |
| red-breasted merganser | 238 |
| bufflehead | 150 |
| great black-backed gull | 137 |
| oldsquaw | 122 |
| red-necked grebe | 76 |
| glaucous gull | 28 |
| common loon | 24 |
| unidentified scaup species | 22 |
| bald eagle | 20 |

| | |
|---|---|
| trumpeter swan | 17 |
| hooded merganser | 16 |
| mute swan | 14 |
| greater scaup | 13 |
| horned grebe | 10 |
| tundra swan | 10 |
| lesser scaup | 9 |
| white-winged scoter | 9 |
| unidentified scoter species | 8 |
| double-crested cormorant | 7 |
| great blue heron | 7 |
| wood duck | 5 |
| American wigeon | 4 |
| Iceland gull | 4 |
| harlequin duck | 4 |
| surf scoter | 3 |
| ring-necked duck | 2 |
| northern pintail | 2 |
| pied-billed grebe | 1 |
| gadwall | 1 |
| Barrow's goldeneye | 1 |
| American coot | 1 |
| snow goose | 1 |
| red-throated loon | 1 |
| Bonaparte's gull | 1 |
| mallard × black duck hybrid | 1 |
| hooded × common merganser hybrid | 1 |

Some of these birds were seen on open water or fields near but inland from Lake Huron, but the list should give a general picture of the relative abundance of various species around the lake at Christmas time—early winter. If such counts were made in late winter, say early February, the number of species and numbers of individuals would undoubtedly be less. Lingering migrants like ring-billed gulls and red-breasted mergansers, for instance, would probably dwindle to just a few, and some species, like double-crested cormorant and red-throated loon, would probably disappear altogether as more open water froze and food supplies shrank.

Of the top seven species, four were found on fourteen or fifteen counts, the Canada goose on six, and the canvasback and redhead on just one—Port Huron—where many of these ducks congregate on the

St. Clair River. As you might expect, the majority of ducks and gulls were found in the southern half of the lake, where conditions are less severe (and bird-counters more numerous). Port Huron, for instance, had 10,315 waterfowl (ducks and geese) of seventeen species and 1,121 gulls of five species; whereas Sault Ste. Marie, even with thirty-nine observers, had just 870 waterfowl of seven species and no gulls whatsoever.

Whether he or she sees few birds or many, however, the Christmas bird counter takes joy from the contribution to knowledge and from the exhilaration of being afield with friends at this special time of year.

CHAPTER **19**

# Closing Up

The journey back from Manitoulin, after the bird counts, was a sort of farewell to the lake, a closing of my Huron year. I probably would not see the lake in its colder months for some time to come.

Before leaving the island, however, I dropped in on some fishermen to see how they were ending the year. For most commercial fishermen on Lake Huron, winter is a down time—a pause and preparation for the season to come. But not Mike Meeker, fish farmer. When I arrived at his house among the firs on Lake Wolsey, he had just loaded 3,000 pounds of rainbow trout into a Coldwater Company truck. "From the end of November to April I harvest heavily," he said. "The fish aren't growing and the price is best then. So I sell a lot of them."

Down at the dock, with the five net cages on each side, his helpers were breaking ice that had formed over some of the cages in spite of the bubblers. To do this work, one man stood in a canoe that rested on the ice, swinging a mallet. The surface had to be ice-free so nets could be lowered to scoop up the fish. Mike and his men would be breaking ice and loading fish most of the winter days to come.

Out back of Murray Hore's house the *Charlie H* sat high and dry on a wheeled carrier at the edge of Bayfield Sound. I found Murray on the second floor of his net shed cutting mesh from a net strung taut the length of the forty-foot room. "I got this net from the Ministry of Natural Resources," he said, "but I have to cut the twine off and put my own on. Their mesh is too small—not legal for me. They use it for fisheries assessment."

"How did your year go?" I asked. "The best yet for whitefish," he replied, "and the perch were up a little from last year. I fished until November 17 but only went out about a dozen times after September because I was filling my quota and there were so many fish on the market." Now he would work on the nets and repair his boat. "I may finish the work in two months if I work hard. I don't take many days off."

The Purvises, operating on a bigger scale, told a similar story. "We've had a good year," said Irene. "We'll be finishing next week. We filled our quota so we rented quotas from somebody else so we could keep fishing this long." After they quit, they'll repair gear and work with their auditors. By the end of January they'll be done. In February they will go once again to Mexico for a month. They need it. With an operation this big and complicated, it can be harder work in the office than it is on the boats.

Passing Sudbury, I thought about Chris Bell and his birding friends, who would soon conduct another Christmas bird count here. To them, Manitoulin must seem like a tropical paradise compared with Sudbury, where scrubby trees cover the nearby hills, once bare from smelter fumes, and you have to go several miles to get into older forest. Besides that, nearly all the water is frozen, usually sending ducks and gulls farther south by Christmas count time.

South of Sudbury, a moose silhouette on a highway sign warns that your irresistible force may meet with an immovable object if you don't watch out. It also adds a little North Woods aura to your trip. Today, though, with dark spruce and fir rising above the deep snow, I didn't have to be reminded I was in the north. At a restaurant near Parry Sound, on the eastern shore of Georgian Bay, the snow lay three feet deep outside the window. "We got hit hard last week," the waitress said.

On my car radio, the announcer said the Parry Sound Rockets split two hockey games over the weekend—a matter of special interest in this hometown of Bobby Orr, where I suppose ice hockey fever runs even higher than it does in most Canadian towns.

At the Wye Marsh Wildlife Centre, I stopped to find out how the trumpeter swans were doing. Bob Whittam, the executive director, said that two pairs had bred in captivity this year, another pair nested out in the marsh, and still another at a beaver pond twenty miles to the east. "The latter pair migrated with two cygnets to Burlington [on Lake Ontario] this winter but one appears to be sick—perhaps from lead shot ingested at Wye Marsh. Lead shot has now been banned in Canada and we hope it will soon sink far enough into the sediments to be out of reach of feeding swans. Our other free-ranging swans have not migrated yet. We have bubblers at some ponds and supplemental feed, but we want the swans to migrate in winter—it's the natural thing to do." Watchers in Ontario would be on the lookout for Wye Marsh's trumpeters with their yellow wing tags, trying to reestablish a free-living population moving with the seasons as their ancestors had.

At Collingwood a ridge known as Blue Mountain runs perpendicular to the shore, catching snow on its flanks that in turn attracts skiers. One year my wife and I had come here after Christmas to play in the snow but found only rain. Today, however, as I drove past, Blue Mountain was appropriately white.

Even whiter was Owen Sound, which had caught the full force of the weekend snowstorm (one that fortunately had missed us bird-counters on Manitoulin). Steve Gile, in his office at the Lake Huron Management Unit, was working on the data from lake trout assessment sites in southern Georgian Bay. "So far the lake trout rehabilitation is falling short of the rehab criteria," he said. It would be a few months before he could do any field work, and probably not much then, but he looked forward to going on the Tobermory Christmas bird count the next day—another form of hunting pursued by some fish biologists.

Southward down the lakeshore, the snow gradually lessened, until at Sarnia most of the ground was bare. Stopping at the parking lot at Point Edward, I faced into a strong north wind. A 100-foot-wide band of white broken ice was moving alongshore into the river, as was another on the Michigan side. Out here on the lake, gulls and one lone merganser were all that remained from the fall aggregation of birds, though many were in the river. The Canadian ice-breaker *Samuel Risley* came out of the river headed north, perhaps to help us Americans get late-moving ships in and out of Saginaw Bay, or perhaps to assist the last boats coming through the St. Marys River. The *Kristy-Lyn II,* a gillnetter out of Chatham, Ontario, came down the lake into the river.

Later I saw the *Kristy-Lyn* tied up at the Purdy dock. She was unloading fish that the Purdy people would sell for the boat's owner. Today—whitefish, some lake trout and perch, Milford Purdy told me. "We had a problem with brown slime on the trap nets in spring, and green slime on them in summer," he said. "Nobody knows what caused the green slime—first time we've had that. Then in the fall and winter we had a problem with zebra mussels attaching to the nets—first time for that too. Still it was a good year. We'll probably reach our whitefish quota, though we didn't quite finish our pickerel quota. The trap nets are all up as of last week—we were starting to get needle ice on them." Like other commercial fishermen on the lake, Purdy Fisheries people would be repairing gear this winter, but unlike most of them they would be repairing gear the rest of the year as well, since their operation is year-round. It looked like this winter might be harder than usual, but when the ice and weather allowed, they would go out.

Driving up the Michigan shore, I found snow reappearing on the ground, until at the cottage it was again three inches deep, as when I had started out. Nice, I thought, to maintain the Christmasy look. The Blue Water Inn advertised the next Detroit Lions football game, now a post-season playoff.

Up on Saginaw Bay, when I called him, Forrest Williams was busy with the account books, building repairs, and gear of the Bay Port Fish Company. He echoed the comments of other commercial fishermen. "It's been a pretty good year," he said. "We quit before Thanksgiving—about November 17. It was December 11 last year, when the ice came later. Spring was cold—not too great for fishing, but there's been a strong demand. It was a good perch year. We'll hope for a cold winter. For some reason it makes better fishing the next year. Before you know it, it'll be March, and we'll be out there again."

Myles Willard, like most of the fishermen, had switched to indoor work, figuring out his income tax returns, labeling slides, planning the next year. Dennis Schommer went on with his painting and indoor home decorating. I, however, after getting the heat up in the cottage, kept my attention on the scene outdoors. Before my trip north, the weather had turned wintry. I would hear Canada geese overhead, flying through light snowfall to the fields inland or to the lake for the night. On the morning of December 7, the harbor had been frozen and gulls huddled on its ice like lumps of snow. One of Gene Knight's barges had been dredging there, cracking through the ice, trying to finish the job before the ice got too thick. Now on December 20 I took a last walk down to the harbor:

"7:45–8:30 A.M. 21 degrees, NW wind. Tracks of rabbit, red squirrel, and fox in the crusted snow at the cottage. Low little ice cliffs along shore, beyond that a band of flat, packed ice, then ice dunes with 'volcanoes' and 'sea arches' about a hundred yards out, waves splashing up on these dunes, heaving broken ice beyond that. I make it across the 2-inch ice on Liens Creek, but I hear cracks under me. Only one house on the way to the harbor looks occupied. It has a tall peaked front with big windows looking out from a two-story living room and, inside, a two-story Christmas

Last walk to the harbor.

tree, all lit up—cheerful on this chilly morning with grey skies and snow flurries. A lone juvenile herring gull, dark against the white ice, flies up and down the shore. The outer side of the north breakwall is sheathed in ice, and a ridge of ice leans outward on top of the wall. Inside the harbor, two female mergansers fish in the open water at the entrance. A flock of snow buntings, very like snowflakes against the grey sky, lands on the crusty beach, gets up, alights somewhere else. A shrike lands on the breakwall, perhaps stalking the snow buntings. After I'm home, a hundred

251

Canada geese fly over, honking loudly, perhaps headed inland in search of corn. Bits of blue appear between the clouds."

Now the long-distance boats are making their final runs through the Soo Locks or the Welland Canal. Not much else will stir on Lake Huron, besides a few ducks and gulls. Within its waters, life again has slowed down, trying to conserve energy through the long winter. Soon Mike Hanson will appear at the harbor, ready once again to capture hungry brown trout through the ice.

I pack my bags, let the fire in the wood stove die out, and say goodbye to the cottage. Then I say goodbye to Lake Huron—to its frequent beauty, its occasional horror, and its broad, always sustaining waters.

# APPENDIX I
# COMMON AND SCIENTIFIC NAMES OF PLANTS

This list includes all plants mentioned in the text. Most scientific names follow those used in Morton and Venn, *The Flora of Manitoulin Island,* 1984. The few others follow Fernald, *Gray's Manual of Botany,* 8th ed., 1950.

| | |
|---|---|
| Algae, blue-green | *Anabaena, Oscillatoria,* etc. |
| Apple | *Malus domestica* |
| Arborvitae | *Thuja occidentalis* |
| Ash | *Fraxinus* spp. |
| Aspen | *Populus tremuloides,* |
| | *P. grandidentata* |
| | |
| Basswood | *Tilia americana* |
| Beachgrass | *Ammophila breviligulata* |
| Bearberry | *Arctostaphylos uva-ursi* |
| Beech | *Fagus grandifolia* |
| Birch, paper | *Betula papyrifera* |
| Birch, yellow | *B. lutea* |
| Bluestem, big | *Andropogon gerardii* |
| Bluestem, little | *A. scoparius* |
| Bog-bean | *Menyanthes trifoliata* |
| Bog-rosemary | *Andromeda glaucophylla* |
| Bouncing-bet | *Saponaria officinalis* |
| Bulrush | *Scirpus* spp. |

| | |
|---|---|
| Bulrush, hard-stemmed | *S. acutus* |
| Bulrush, three-square | *S. americanus* |
| Butterwort | *Pinguicula vulgaris* |
| | |
| (no common name) | *Carex scirpoidea* |
| (no common name) | *Carex viridula* |
| Cattail | *Typhus latifolia,* |
| | *T. angustifolia* |
| Cedar, red | *Juniperus virginiana* |
| Cedar, white | *Thuja occidentalis* |
| Cherry | *Prunus* spp. |
| Cherry, black | *P. serotina* |
| Cherry, sand | *P. pumila* |
| Chickweed, field mouse-ear | *Cerastium arvense* |
| Chokecherry | *Prunus virginiana* |
| Cinquefoil, shrubby | *Potentilla fruticosa* |
| Columbine, wild | *Aquilegia canadensis* |
| Coral-root, striped | *Corallorhiza maculata* |
| Cordgrass | *Spartina pectinata* |
| Cranberry | *Vaccinium* spp. |
| | |
| Diatom | *Cyclotella, Melosira,* etc. |
| Dogwood, red-osier | *Cornus stolonifera* |
| Dropseed, northern | *Sporobolus heterolepis* |
| | |
| Fern, holly | *Polystichum lonchitis* |
| Fern, polypody | *Polypodium virginianum* |
| Fir, balsam | *Abies balsamea* |
| | |
| Gale, sweet | *Myrica gale* |
| Gold, Manitoulin | *Hymenoxis acaulis* |
| Goldenrod | *Solidago* spp. |
| Goldenrod, Houghton's | *Solidago houghtonii* |
| Grape, riverbank | *Vitis riparia* |
| Grass, sand reed | *Calamovilfa longifolia* |
| | |
| Hairgrass, tufted | *Deschampsia cespitosa* |
| Hawkweed, yellow | *Hieracium piloselloides* |
| Helleborine | *Epipactis helleborine* |
| Hemlock | *Tsuga canadensis* |

| | |
|---|---|
| Indian-plantain | *Cacalia tuberosa* |
| Iris, dwarf lake | *Iris lacustris* |
| | |
| Juniper, creeping | *Juniperus horizontalis* |
| Juniper, ground | *J. communis* |
| | |
| Lady's slipper, showy | *Cypripedium reginae* |
| Leather-leaf | *Chamaedaphne calyculata* |
| Lichens, crustose | *Xanthoria, Parmelia* |
| Lilac | *Syringa vulgaris* |
| | |
| Maple, red | *Acer rubrum* |
| Maple, sugar | *A. saccharum* |
| Moss, reindeer | *Cladonia rangiferina* |
| Moss, sphagnum | *Sphagnum* spp. |
| | |
| Nettle, stinging | *Urtica dioica* |
| Ninebark | *Physocarpus opulifolius* |
| | |
| Oak, black | *Quercus velutina* |
| Oak, dwarf chinquapin | *Q. prinoides* |
| Oak, red | *Q. rubra* |
| Oak, white | *Q. alba* |
| Orchid, Alaska | *Piperia unalascensis* |
| Orchid, calypso | *Calypso bulbosa* |
| Orchid, green | *Platanthera hyperborea* |
| Orchid, prairie white-fringed | *Habenaria leucophaea* |
| Orchid, round-leaved | *Platanthera orbiculata* |
| Orchid, white bog | *P. dilatata* |
| | |
| Paintbrush, Indian | *Castilleja coccinea* |
| Phragmites (Common Reed) | *Phragmites australis* |
| Pine, jack | *Pinus banksiana* |
| Pine, red | *P. resinosa* |
| Pine, white | *P. strobus* |
| Pink, grass | *Calopogon tuberosus* |
| Pitcher-plant | *Sarracenia purpurea* |
| Pogonia, rose | *Pogonia ophioglossoides* |
| Poplar, balsam | *Populus balsamifera* |
| Primrose, bird's-eye | *Primula mistassinica* |

255

| | |
|---|---|
| Puccoon, yellow | *Lithospermum caroliniense* |
| Pussytoes | *Antennaria neodioica* |
| | |
| Rush, baltic | *Juncus balticus* |
| Rush, twig | *Cladium mariscoides* |
| | |
| Shield-fern, marginal | *Dryopteris marginalis* |
| Silverweed | *Potentilla anserina* |
| Solomon's seal, starry false | *Smilacina stellata* |
| Spikerush | *Eleocharis compressa* |
| Spleenwort, green | *Asplenium viride* |
| Spleenwort, maidenhair | *A. trichomanes* |
| Spruce, black | *Picea mariana* |
| Spruce, white | *P. glauca* |
| St. John's-wort, Kalm's | *Hypericum kalmianum* |
| Sumac | *Rhus* spp. |
| Sundew, linear-leaved | *Drosera linearis* |
| Sweet-clover, white | *Melilotus alba* |
| | |
| Tamarack | *Larix laricina* |
| Thistle, Hill's | *Cirsium hillii* |
| Thistle, Pitcher's | *C. pitcheri* |
| Tulip-tree | *Liriodendron tulipifera* |
| Twayblade, heart-leaved | *Listera cordata* |
| | |
| Violet, shore (bog) | *Viola nephrophylla* |
| | |
| Wall-rue | *Asplenium ruta-muraria* |
| Water-lily, white | *Nymphaea odorata* |
| Wheatgrass, Great Lakes | *Agropyron psammophilum* |
| Willow | *Salix* spp. |
| Willow, hoary | *S. candida* |
| Willow, sand dune (Broad heartleaf willow) | *S. cordata* |
| Windflower, red (Cut-leaved anemone) | *Anemone multifida* |
| Wormwood | *Artemisia* spp. |
| Wormwood, field | *A. campestris* |
| | |
| Yarrow | *Achillea millefolium* |

# APPENDIX 2
## FISHES OF LAKE HURON

This list is taken from *Fish Community Objectives for Lake Huron,* written by the Lake Huron Committee, 1993, under the aegis of the Great Lakes Fishery Commission. (P)—planned introduction; (A)—accidental introduction; (E)—extinct.

Petromyzontidae
    Northern brook lamprey        *Icthyomyzon fossor*
    Silver lamprey        *I. unicuspis*
    American brook lamprey        *Lampetra appendix*
    (A) Sea lamprey        *Petromyzon marinus*

Acipenseridae
    Lake sturgeon        *Acipenser fulvescens*

Lepisosteidae
    Spotted gar        *Lepisosteus oculatus*
    Longnose gar        *L. osseus*

Amiidae
    Bowfin        *Amia calva*

Clupeidae
    (A) Alewife        *Alosa pseudoharengus*
    (A) Gizzard shad        *Dorosoma cepedianum*

Salmonidae (Salmoninae)
    (A) Pink salmon               *Oncorhynchus gorbuscha*
    (P) Coho salmon               *O. kisutch*
    (P) Chinook salmon           *O. tshawytscha*
    (P) Kokanee salmon          *O. nerka*
    (P) Rainbow trout            *O. mykiss*
    (P) Atlantic salmon           *Salmo salar*
    (P) Brown trout              *S. trutta*
    Brook trout                 *Salvelinus fontinalis*
    Lake trout                  *S. namaycush*

Salmonidae (Coregoninae)
    Lake whitefish              *Coregonus clupeaformis*
    Lake herring (cisco)        *C. artedii*
    (E) Longjaw cisco           *C. alpenae*
    Bloater                    *C. hoyi*
    (E) Deepwater cisco        *C. johannae*
    Kiyi                      *C. kiyi*
    (E) Blackfin cisco           *C. nigripinnis*
    Shortnose cisco             *C. reighardi*
    (E) Shortjaw cisco          *C. zenithicus*
    Round whitefish            *Prosopium cylindraceum*

Salmonidae (Thymallinae)
    (E) Arctic grayling          *Thymallus arcticus*

Osmeridae
    (A) Rainbow smelt          *Osmerus mordax*

Hiodontidae
    Mooneye                   *Hiodon tergisus*

Umbridae
    Central mudminnow        *Umbra limi*

Esocidae
    Northern pike               *Esox lucius*
    Muskellunge               *E. masquinongy*

Cyprinidae

| | |
|---|---|
| Northern redbelly dace | *Phoxinue eos* |
| Finescale dace | *P. neogaeus* |
| Lake chub | *Couesius plumbeus* |
| (A) Grass carp | *Ctenopharyngodon idella* |
| (A) Carp | *Cyprinus carpio* |
| (A) Goldfish | *Carassius auratus* |
| Brassy minnow | *Hybognathus hankinsoni* |
| Hornyhead chub | *Nocomis biguttatus* |
| Golden shiner | *Notemigonus crysoleucas* |
| Emerald shiner | *Notropis atherinoides* |
| Common shiner | *N. cornutus* |
| Blackchin shiner | *N. heterodon* |
| Blacknose shiner | *N. heterolepis* |
| Spottail shiner | *N. hudsonius* |
| Rosyface shiner | *N. rubellus* |
| Spotfin shiner | *N. spilopterus* |
| Sand shiner | *N. stramineus* |
| Mimic shiner | *N. volucellus* |
| Bluntnose minnow | *Pimephales notatus* |
| Fathead minnow | *P. promelas* |
| Longnose dace | *Rhinichthys cataractae* |
| Creek chub | *Semotilus atromaculatus* |
| Pearl dace | *S. margarita* |

Catostomidae

| | |
|---|---|
| Quillback | *Carpiodes cyprinus* |
| Longnose sucker | *Catostomus catostomus* |
| White sucker | *C. commersoni* |
| (A) Bigmouth buffalo | *Ictiobus cyprinellus* |
| Silver redhorse | *Moxostoma anisurum* |
| Shorthead redhorse | *M. macrolepidotum* |

Ictaluridae

| | |
|---|---|
| Yellow bullhead | *Ictalurus natalis* |
| Brown bullhead | *I. nebulosus* |
| Channel catfish | *I. punctatus* |
| Tadpole madtom | *Noturus gyrinus* |

Anguillidae

| | |
|---|---|
| American eel | *Anguilla rostrata* |

Cyprinodontidae
    Banded killifish                *Fundulus diaphanus*

Gadidae
    Burbot                      *Lota lota*

Atherinidae
    Brook silverside            *Labidesthes sicculus*

Gasterosteidae
    Brook stickleback          *Culaea inconstans*
    (A) Threespine stickleback   *Gasterosteus aculeatus*
    Ninespine stickleback      *Pungitius pungitius*

Percopsidae
    Trout-perch               *Percopsis omiscomaycus*

Percicthyidae
    (A) White perch           *Morone americana*
    White bass                *M. chrysops*

Centrarchidae
    Rock bass                *Amblophites rupestris*
    Pumpkinseed            *Lepomis gibbosus*
    Bluegill                  *L. macrochirus*
    Longear sunfish           *L. megalotis*
    Smallmouth bass          *Micropterus dolmieui*
    Largemouth bass          *M. salmoides*
    White crappie            *Pomoxis annularis*
    Black crappie            *P. nigromaculatus*

Percidae
    Yellow perch            *Perca flavescens*
    Sauger                  *Stizostedion canadense*
    Walleye                 *S. vitreum*
    Iowa darter             *Etheostoma exile*
    Johnny darter           *E. nigrum*
    Logperch               *Percina caprodes*
    Channel darter           *P. copelandi*
    Blackside darter         *P. maculata*

Sciaenidae
    Freshwater drum (sheepshead)      *Aplodinotus grunniens*

Cottidae
    Mottled sculpin      *Cottus bairdi*
    Slimy sculpin      *C. cognatus*
    Spoonhead sculpin      *C. ricei*
    Deepwater sculpin      *Myoxocephalus thomponi*

# Principal Published Sources

I found the following publications especially useful in writing my story of Lake Huron. They range from technical to popular. Generally, the title suggests where the publication falls along this continuum.

Ashworth, William. *The Late, Great Lakes.* Detroit: Wayne State University Press, 1987.

Bellrose, Frank. *Ducks, Geese, and Swans of North America.* Harrisburg, Penn.: Stackpole, 1976.

Berst, A. H., and G. R. Spangler. *Lake Huron: The Ecology of the Fish Community and Man's Effects on It.* Technical Report No. 21, Great Lakes Fishery Commission, Ann Arbor, Michigan, 1973. A concise, authoritative summary.

Brewer, Richard, Gail A. McPeek, and Raymond J. Adams, Jr., eds. *The Atlas of Breeding Birds of Michigan.* East Lansing: Michigan State University Press, 1991.

Cadman, Michael D., Paul F. J. Eagles, and Frederick M. Helleiner, eds. *Atlas of the Breeding Birds of Ontario.* Federation of Ontario Naturalists and the Long Point Bird Observatory. Waterloo, Ontario: University of Waterloo Press, 1987.

Cleland, Charles E. *Rites of Conquest: The History and Culture of Michigan's Native Americans.* Ann Arbor: University of Michigan Press, 1992.

Environment Canada, Atmospheric Environment Service. *Great Lakes Climatological Atlas.* 1986.

Fox, William Sherwood. *The Bruce Beckons: The Story of Lake Huron's Great Peninsula.* 2d rev. ed. Toronto: University of Toronto Press, 1962.

Gile, S. R. and L. C. Mohr. *Status and Outlook for the Major Commercial Fish Species of Lake Huron, 1995.* Lake Huron Management Unit, Report 1–95. Ontario Ministry of Natural Resources, 1995.

*The Great Lakes: An Environmental Atlas and Resource Book.* Jointly produced by Environment Canada, U.S. Environmental Protection Agency, Brock University, and Northwestern University, 1987.

Henry, Alexander. *Travels and Adventures in Canada and the Indian Territories.* 1809. Reprinted by Mackinaw Island State Park Commission, Michigan, 1971, 1978.

Hoagman, Walter J. *Great Lakes Coastal Plants.* Michigan Department of Natural Resources, 1994.

Hubbs, Carl L., and Karl F. Lagler. *Fishes of the Great Lakes Region.* Ann Arbor: University of Michigan Press, 1958.

Jameson, Anna. *Winter Studies and Summer Rambles in Canada.* New York: Wiley and Putnam, 1839.

Kurta, Allen. *Mammals of the Great Lakes Region.* Toronto: Fitzhenry & Whiteside, 1995.

Lake Huron Management Unit. Annual Reports, 1993 and 1994. Ontario Ministry of Natural Resources, 1994, 1995.

Landon, Fred. *Lake Huron.* New York: Bobbs-Merrill, 1944. A history.

LeLievre, Roger, ed. *Know Your Ships: Guide to Boatwatching on the Great Lakes and St. Lawrence Seaway.* Sault Ste. Marie, Mich.: Marine Publishing Co., 1996. Published annually.

Marshall, Ernest W. *Air Photo Interpretation of Great Lakes Ice Features.* Ann Arbor: Great Lakes Research Division, Institute of Science and Technology, University of Michigan, 1966.

Mershon, William B. *Recollections of My Fifty Years Hunting and Fishing.* Boston: The Stratford Co., 1923.

*Michigan Natural Resources,* Great Lakes Special Issue (Lansing: Michigan Department of Natural Resources) 55, no. 3 (May–June 1986).

Morton, J. K., and Joan M. Venn. *The Flora of Manitoulin Island.* 2d rev. ed. Waterloo, Ontario: Department of Biology, University of Waterloo, 1984.

———. *The Flora of the Tobermory Islands.* Waterloo, Ontario: Department of Biology, University of Waterloo, 1987.

Munawar, M., T. Edsall, and J. Leach, eds. *The Lake Huron Ecosystem: Ecology, Fisheries, and Management.* Amsterdam, The Netherlands: SPB Academic Publishing, 1995. Technical, expensive, and full of information, from limnology and plankton to fishes, birds, Saginaw Bay, toxic sediment, and exotic (alien) species.

National Research Council of the United States and the Royal Society of Canada. *The Great Lakes Water Quality Agreement: An Evolving Instrument for Ecosystem Management.* Washington, D.C.: National Academy Press, 1985.

Nicholson, John C. *The Birds of Manitoulin Island and Adjacent Islands within Manitoulin District.* Sudbury, Ontario, 1981.

Parker, Jack. *Shipwrecks of Lake Huron . . . The Great Sweetwater Sea.* Au Train, Mich.: Avery Color Studios, 1986.

Pearen, Shelley J. *Exploring Manitoulin.* Toronto: University of Toronto Press, 1992.

Raymond, Oliver. *Shingle Shavers and Berry Pickers.* Privately published, 1976. A history of Port Sanilac.

Schoolcraft, Henry. *Narrative of Travels from Detroit Northwest through the Great Chain of American Lakes. 1821.* New York: Arno Press, 1970.

Smith, Bradley F., and Jeremy W. Kilar. *Tobico Marsh: A Story of The Land and The People.* Bay City, Mich.: Jennison Nature Center, 1987.

Stayer, Pat and Jim. *Shipwrecks of Sanilac.* Lexington, Mich.: Out of the Blue Publications, 1995.

Theberge, John B., ed. *Legacy: The Natural History of Ontario.* Sponsors: Ontario Heritage Foundation and Federation of Ontario Naturalists. Toronto: McClelland & Stewart, 1989.

*The Waters of Lake Huron and Lake Superior, Vol. II (Part B), Lake Huron, Georgian Bay, and the North Channel.* Report to the International Joint Commission by the Upper Lakes Reference Group. Windsor, Ontario, 1977.

Weeks, Ron J. *Birds and Bird Finding in the Saginaw Bay Area.* Chippewa Nature Center and Midland Nature Club, Michigan, 1995.

*Life after the Line,* by Josie Kearns, 1990

*Michigan Lumbertowns: Lumbermen and Laborers in Saginaw, Bay City, and Muskegon, 1870–1905,* by Jeremy W. Kilar, 1990

*Detroit Kids Catalog: The Hometown Tourist* by Ellyce Field, 1990

*Waiting for the News,* by Leo Litwak, 1990 (reprint)

*Detroit Perspectives,* edited by Wilma Wood Henrickson, 1991

*Life on the Great Lakes: A Wheelsman's Story,* by Fred W. Dutton, edited by William Donohue Ellis, 1991

*Copper Country Journal: The Diary of Schoolmaster Henry Hobart, 1863–1864,* by Henry Hobart, edited by Philip P. Mason, 1991

*John Jacob Astor: Business and Finance in the Early Republic,* by John Denis Haeger, 1991

*Survival and Regeneration: Detroit's American Indian Community,* by Edmund J. Danziger, Jr., 1991

*Steamboats and Sailors of the Great Lakes,* by Mark L. Thompson, 1991

*Cobb Would Have Caught It: The Golden Age of Baseball in Detroit,* by Richard Bak, 1991

*Michigan in Literature,* by Clarence Andrews, 1992

*Under the Influence of Water: Poems, Essays, and Stories,* by Michael Delp, 1992

*The Country Kitchen,* by Della T. Lutes, 1992 (reprint)

*The Making of a Mining District: Keweenaw Native Copper 1500–1870,* by David J. Krause, 1992

*Kids Catalog of Michigan Adventures,* by Ellyce Field, 1993

*Henry's Lieutenants,* by Ford R. Bryan, 1993

*Historic Highway Bridges of Michigan,* by Charles K. Hyde, 1993

*Lake Erie and Lake St. Clair Handbook,* by Stanley J. Bolsenga and Charles E. Herndendorf, 1993

*Queen of the Lakes,* by Mark Thompson, 1994

*Iron Fleet: The Great Lakes in World War II,* by George J. Joachim, 1994

*Turkey Stearnes and the Detroit Stars: The Negro Leagues in Detroit, 1919–1933,* by Richard Bak, 1994

*Pontiac and the Indian Uprising,* by Howard H. Peckham, 1994 (reprint)

*Charting the Inland Seas: A History of the U.S. Lake Survey,* by Arthur M. Woodford, 1994 (reprint)

*Ojibwa Narratives of Charles and Charlotte Kawbawgam and Jacques LePique, 1893–1895. Recorded with Notes by Homer H. Kidder,* edited by Arthur P. Bourgeois, 1994, co-published with the Marquette County Historical Society

*Strangers and Sojourners: A History of Michigan's Keweenaw Peninsula,* by Arthur W. Thurner, 1994

*Win Some, Lose Some: G. Mennen Williams and the New Democrats,* by Helen Washburn Berthelot, 1995

*Sarkis,* by Gordon and Elizabeth Orear, 1995

*The Northern Lights: Lighthouses of the Upper Great Lakes,* by Charles K. Hyde, 1995 (reprint)

*Kids Catalog of Michigan Adventures,* second edition, by Ellyce Field, 1995

*Rumrunning and the Roaring Twenties: Prohibition on the Michigan-Ontario Waterway,* by Philip P. Mason, 1995

*In the Wilderness with the Red Indians,* by E. R. Baierlein, translated by Anita Z. Boldt, edited by Harold W. Moll, 1996

*Elmwood Endures: History of a Detroit Cemetery,* by Michael Franck, 1996

*Master of Precision: Henry M. Leland,* by Mrs. Wilfred C. Leland with Minnie Dubbs Millbrook, 1996 (reprint)

*Haul-Out: New and Selected Poems,* by Stephen Tudor, 1996

*Kids Catalog of Michigan Adventures,* third edition, by Ellyce Field, 1997

*Beyond the Model T: The Other Ventures of Henry Ford,* revised edition, by Ford R. Bryan, 1997

*Young Henry Ford: A Picture History of the First Forty Years,* by Sidney Olson, 1997 (reprint)

*The Coast of Nowhere: Meditations on Rivers, Lakes and Streams,* by Michael Delp, 1997

*From Saginaw Valley to Tin Pan Alley: Saginaw's Contribution to American Popular Music, 1890–1955,* by R. Grant Smith, 1998

*The Long Winter Ends,* by Newton G. Thomas, 1998 (reprint)

*Bridging the River of Hatred: The Pioneering Efforts of Detroit Police Commissioner George Edwards, 1962–1963,* by Mary M. Stolberg, 1998

*Toast of the Town: The Life and Times of Sunnie Wilson,* by Sunnie Wilson with John Cohassey, 1998

*These Men Have Seen Hard Service: The First Michigan Sharpshooters in the Civil War,* by Raymond J. Herek, 1998

*A Place for Summer: One Hundred Years at Michigan and Trumbull,* by Richard Bak, 1998

*Early Midwestern Travel Narratives: An Annotated Bibliography, 1634–1850,* by Robert R. Hubach, 1998 (reprint)

*All-American Anarchist: Joseph A. Labadie and the Labor Movement,* by Carlotta R. Anderson, 1998

*Michigan in the Novel, 1816–1996: An Annotated Bibliography,* by Robert Beasecker, 1998

*"Time by Moments Steals Away": The 1848 Journal of Ruth Douglass,* by Robert L. Root, Jr., 1998

*The Detroit Tigers: A Pictorial Celebration of the Greatest Players and Moments in Tigers' History,* updated edition, by William M. Anderson, 1999

*Letter from Washington, 1863–1865, by Lois Bryan Adams,* edited and with an introduction by Evelyn Leasher, 1999

*Father Abraham's Children: Michigan Episodes in the Civil War,* by Frank B. Woodford, 1999 (reprint)

*A Sailor's Logbook: A Season aboard Great Lakes Freighters,* by Mark L. Thompson, 1999

*Wonderful Power: The Story of Ancient Copper Working in the Lake Superior Basin,* by Susan R. Martin, 1999

*Huron: The Seasons of a Great Lake,* by Napier Shelton, 1999